Classics in Psychoanalysis
Monograph No. 1

Psychoanalytic Supervision

A Method of Clinical Teaching

Classics in Psychoanalysis
Monograph No. 1

Psychoanalytic Supervision

A Method of Clinical Teaching

JOAN FLEMING, M.D.

THERESE F. BENEDEK, M.D.

INTERNATIONAL UNIVERSITIES PRESS, INC.
New York • New York

Library of Congress Cataloging in Publication Data

Fleming, Joan, 1904-
    Psychoanalytic supervision.

    (Classics in psychoanalysis; monograph no. 1)
    Reprint. Originally published: New York: Grune & Stratton, c1966.
    Bibliography: p.
    Includes index.
    1. Psychoanalysis—Study and teaching—Supervision.
I. Benedek, Therese, 1892-   .   II. Title.   III. Series.
DNLM: 1. Organization and administration.   2. Learning.
3. Psychoanalysis—Education.   W1 CL122D no. 1 / WM 19.5
F597p
RC502.F55   1983   616.89'17'07   83-22763
ISBN 0-8236-5041-3
ISSN 0735-0341

Manufactured in the United States of America

Contents

Examples in Text

* Name of case refers to the student's code name in association with the number of his case.

† S.S. refers to the sequential number of the supervisory session.

Preface

A volume that is out of print but constantly and continuously read, referred to, and discussed sixteen years after its publication is worthy of being designated a classic. In this fiftieth anniversary year of the Chicago Institute for Psychoanalysis, three new monograph series have been launched. The Fleming-Benedek volume will be the first in the *Classics of Psychoanalysis* series of our Institute.

The work by Joan Fleming and Therese Benedek merited its classic status because it carefully and in detail delineated the problems in learning and teaching psychoanalysis. These problems have never before nor since been presented to the professional public in such an *in extenso* fashion. In addition, the monograph presents many clinical examples, from all three phases of the psychoanalytic process, that illustrate the learning requirements of the student and how they may be met by the teacher-supervisor.

In clarifying the teaching-learning situation the authors systematically examine the psychoanalytic process and in so doing make a valuable contribution to understanding the nature of (1) dynamic diagnosis, (2) the psychoanalytic situation, (3) the psychoanalytic process itself, (4) the therapeutic regression, (5) interpretation, (6) the many aspects of transference and resistance, and (7) conflict resolution.

In short, the authors of this work have contributed to psychoanalytic pedagogy and have written an authoritative statement on the technique and the theory of technique in psychoanalysis that is still of great merit. The volume by Fleming and Benedek is of value to psychoanalytic educators all over the world and to all teachers "of every clinical science," especially the psychological sciences where individual psychotherapy is the main patient-therapist interaction.

The authors have carried on the long standing tradition of innovative research in psychoanalysis leading to productive clinical application and teaching which characterizes the Chicago Institute for Psychoanalysis. Their work has stimulated their colleagues and students to continue discussion and examination of the problems in supervision. Currently, the Institute's training and supervising analysts are discussing these problems of supervision in continuing meetings. In such a setting the monograph continues to supply fruitful ideas.

In light of the needs of psychoanalytic educators that are met by this monograph, the Chicago Institute for Psychoanalysis and International Universities Press, Inc. have undertaken to publish this book once again. It will fulfill a continuing requirement of teachers and supply to their students an understanding, of the psychoanalytic process and its components, that will enrich their learning.

The editors and publisher are grateful to the families of Joan Fleming, M.D. and Therese Benedek, M.D. for their kindness and generosity in permitting the re-publication of this valuable volume.

George H. Pollock, M.D., Ph.D.
Henry Seidenberg, M.D.

September, 1982

Introduction

THIS BOOK IS DEVOTED TO AN EXPLORATION OF THE PROBLEMS EN-
countered in the clinical teaching of psychoanalysis. This may seem to be
a limited subject but, nevertheless, it concerns the challenging problems
which face educators in every clinical field—for example, how to apply
theoretical knowledge to the treatment of patients and how to teach the
art of therapeutic communication. These problems, inherent in the teaching of every clinical science, have received singularly little attention, except
in social work.* Recently, more interest in the subject has developed in
medicine and other disciplines where special skills of therapeutic interaction are necessary. However, most of the attention seems to be directed
toward problems of teaching professional attitudes and procedures rather
than the processes of communication which are fundamental both to doing
therapy and to learning it.

In psychoanalysis, as in other fields, the clinical phase of a student's
training is a culmination of learning acquired in other educational situations. Each situation contributes a different kind of experience which
forms a link in the sequence of progression from the acquisition of knowledge necessary for understanding clinical phenomena to the practical on-
the-job situation where the student learns by treating a patient on his own.
It is the final stage of this sequence that interests us the most, the stage
in which the student and teacher work toward integrating theory with complex diagnostic and therapeutic skills.

Educators in such clinical fields as medicine, social work, counseling,
and teaching have devised various on-the-job situations where basic attitudes and skills can be practiced under the guidance of a "clinical"
teacher. Although of great interest, a comparison of the supervisory
process in the various disciplines is beyond the scope of this book. We
also have to omit the comparison of supervision with the apprentice-
master craftsman relationship. These two teaching-learning situations have
often been represented as analogous, but to explore their differences and
similarities would take us too far into a discussion of learning theory. We
prefer to concentrate here on the phenomena of the supervisory process
as they can be observed in the teaching of psychoanalysts. We offer this
study as a demonstration of an investigation of clinical teaching, and must

---

* The bibliography for social work on this subject is long and cannot be reviewed
here, but we would like to mention an exhaustive study by Towle entitled *The
Learner in Education for the Professions.*[92]

1

leave to readers from other disciplines the task of identifying the application to their own fields.

The psychoanalytic supervisory process is especially well suited to an intensive study of clinical on-the-job learning, since what needs to be learned is also the foundation of the teaching relationship. The skills which lead to successful teaching are essentially the same which the student needs to develop in himself for therapeutic work with his patient. Basic aspects of the relationship between therapist and patient are common to the relationship between student and supervisor. Both are built on rapport, understanding, objectivity and judgment. The supervisor, like the analyst in the therapeutic process, is the instrument of the teaching-learning process and simultaneously the observer of it. The objectives of teacher and learner are, of course, influenced by individual differences in aptitude, personality traits, levels of theoretical knowledge and experience. These variables play a vital role in the success of the learning experience.

Nevertheless, in spite of the many elements in common between the therapeutic and teaching situations, we found it possible in studying the psychoanalytic supervisory process to distinguish between the variables pertinent to the three participants (patient, student and teacher), to identify teaching objectives and learning difficulties, and to differentiate teaching techniques from the therapeutic techniques whose development was the aim of the learning experience. Problems inherent to supervisory teaching stem from the highly personal and individualized nature of the communication between therapist and patient and between student and teacher. They also contribute to the difficulty in studying the process. On the other hand, all of these factors emphasize the importance of learning more about supervision in order to develop a body of concepts and principles for making the supervisory teaching process more effective for good learning.

For many reasons the didactic problems of supervision, although they loomed on the horizon from the beginning, have never been subjected to systematic investigation. Indeed, resistance against a systematic investigation of supervisory teaching has been expressed as concern that "structuring" the method might interfere with the free operation of the preconscious intuitive processes so important for the supervisor's understanding of the student and his patient. Moreover, "methodical" teaching in supervision has been seen as an interference with the development of the "free-floating attention" which is a primary learning objective for the student of psychoanalysis. We feel that these concerns have some validity, especially as long as the function and activities of the supervising analyst are not formulated more clearly.

A psychoanalytic supervisor often finds himself confused by his overlapping functions as teacher of the student-analyst and as supervising therapist of the patient. His professional identity is that of a therapist who in his capacity as supervisor has some responsibility for the welfare of the patient whom his student is treating, but as a supervisor he is not the primary therapist. As a teacher his aim is to help the young analyst learn how to conduct an analysis. This requires that he shift from his accustomed position of therapist to one which may feel strange and awkward and demands entirely different kinds of differential diagnoses (educational problems) and techniques (pedagogic).

The problem of this double function confronts every clinical teacher, but in many clinical fields, such as internal medicine, personality factors are less involved in the conduct of the treatment. This fact creates less confusion from overlapping roles. There is no sense of dilemma, since it is easier for the teacher to maintain his professional identity as therapist of the patient. In psychoanalysis, however, many circumstances in the teaching situation compound the feeling of confusion. The psychoanalytic supervisor does not usually have any direct contact with the patient since the information on which he bases his diagnostic thinking and his opinions about treatment come through the observing powers of the student. In addition, personality factors in both student and teacher are deeply involved in the conduct of therapy and of learning. Factors outside of the awareness of each party influence the interactions of each and blur the boundaries relevant to therapeutic or pedagogic roles. Analytic techniques for dealing with personality problems may be indicated but cannot be carried out in the teaching situation. Thus, the double function which faces all clinical teachers becomes a dilemma for psychoanalytic supervisors. Lewin and Ross[69] have described it as "syncretistic" or unsolvable. In our experience, unsolvable as the dilemma may seem to be, each supervisor is forced to find some way out. Frequently, he chooses to limit his role to one position, to the exclusion of the other. He may stress the instructional aspect of teaching and confine himself to giving information, either suggestions about the dynamics of the patient or prescriptions for correcting the mistakes of the student. Or he may be so patient-oriented that he feels himself to be the analyst of the patient, relegating the student to the role of middleman; he gives information, but only in terms of how he would respond to the patient. A third type of role-limited supervisor keeps his focus on the student-analyst's blind spots or countertransference and proceeds to "analyze" them. In this solution, the supervisor maintains his identity as a therapist but confuses therapeutic with teaching objectives.

Each aspect of the dilemma has given rise to persisting controversy among psychoanalytic educators and has often prevented free discussion of pedagogical problems. Since it is widely recognized that therapeutic and learning experiences have much in common, it seemed to us the answer could be found not in a strict separation of the functions of teacher and therapist, but in learning more about the educational process in supervision and is discovering what skills derived from his experience as an analyst enable a supervisor to be more effective in teaching.

We assumed that to explore these problems it would be necessary to become more specific about what we expect student-analysts to learn and about how we try to teach them, that to define these two dimensions better we would have to have data that would document what happens in a supervisory session and that could be examined by more than one person. We assumed that only when supervisors can talk about what they want to teach and how to teach it will they be able to evaluate a student's performance objectively and, reciprocally, their own as teachers. With these ideas in mind, we proceeded to study electrical recordings of supervision done by ourselves in the hope that such a study would increase our own efficiency and that making our experience available to others would stimulate their thinking about the supervisory teaching process.

This monograph contains the report of our investigation. It is not intended as a handbook on supervision or on the technique of psychoanalysis, although much of the content naturally has to do with both teaching and therapy. Our emphasis is on the study of the supervisory process as it could be observed in our material. We are aware of the incompleteness of the study which, by the nature of psychoanalysis and the techniques of inquiry, can never be complete. We know that we undertook a "reasearch" in which no variable can be repeated, yet we feel that the empirical exploration of the phenomena studied here will take us beyond a reliance on the pedagogy of imitation and identification as the only teaching methods available to us.

The examples used in this monograph are offered as samples of what two supervisors did with two students at different stages of professional development. Just as no student presents the same level of competence and the same variety of learning problems as any other student, so no two supervisors are alike in their attitude toward the teaching-learning situation, their methods of teaching, or their evaluations of student or teacher performance. There is no one way to teach and no "best way" to supervise. We hope the illustrations selected from the voluminous material studied will be viewed in the total context of the inevitably wide range of variability of phenomena inherent in the material. Our aim is to bring such data under systematic scrutiny, not only of ourselves but of other teachers of psychoanalysis whose backgrounds and experiences may be different. Their objective evaluation of this material and this method of studying it can contribute much to our knowledge about psychoanalytic education and its objectives, techniques and problems.

In the beginning of our study we were reassuringly surprised at the ease with which we, as readers of the transcripts, could slip into empathic communication with all of the parties involved. This experience was consistently repeated with each rereading of the material. It reinforced our appreciation of the experiential nature of the analytic and supervisory processes and the role of preconscious perceptiveness in teaching as well as learning, and it supported us through the vicissitudes of studying the data and preparing it for publication. Experiencing over and over again the stimulating freshness of the recorded reports of analysis and supervision, we came to the opinion that this feedback from the investigative effort was one of its most valuable findings. This fact raised intriguing questions pointing toward the field of learning theory and pedagogy on a more general level. Obvious self-interest did not seem enough to explain this recurrently persisting phenomenon. The quality of this personal experience encouraged us to hope that, by presenting the transcript data in a form limited mainly by discretion for the patient, we could convey the vitality of the supervisory process which could be empathically "tasted" by the reader. We earnestly hope that this venture will stimulate the undertaking of similar studies by other investigators.

We wish to express our gratitude to all those who assisted us in making this project possible. The financial cost of such a research is considerable in collecting the data and preparing it for study. We wish to thank the American Fund for Psychiatry for generously supporting a pilot project on recorded supervision; the Chicago Institute for Psychoanalysis and its Director, Dr. Gerhart Piers, not only for expense money but also for immeasurable moral support; the Foundations Fund for Research in Psychiatry for the generous grant which permitted the completion of the study by providing freedom from distracting responsibilities. We are indebted to the *Psychoanalytic Quarterly* for permission to reprint parts of a preliminary report on this project.

Many persons from the past contributed to the resources of experience and knowledge with which we came to this work—our teachers, our patients and the many students who have been instrumental in our own development. We are especially grateful to the students G and H, now graduate analysts, who generously agreed to cooperate as principal subjects in the study and permitted the publication of their transcript data. Our thanks go also to the other students whose supervision provided us with pertinent examples.

No book could be completed without the devotion of secretaries who faithfully produced the many revisions of manuscript in readable form: Miss Maibelle Mohrherr, Mrs. Harold Gordon and Miss Mary Ann Kehoe.

Our special appreciation goes to our colleagues who read the manuscript and provided valuable suggestions for improving it: Dr. Charlotte Babcock, Miss Kate Rosenthal and Dr. Henry Von Witzleben. To many others from whom we have learned in the exchange of ideas and experiences, we express our thanks.

— I —

A Historical Review of Supervision
in Psychoanalysis

PSYCHOANALYTIC SUPERVISION HAS BEEN A FORMAL PART OF THE EDU-
cation of an analyst since it was "invented" by Eitingon[25] in the early
1920's at the Berlin Institute. A good deal of thought was given to the
subject in Europe in the 1920's and 1930's. According to Lewin and
Ross, no one has raised any "official question of its usefulness except
regarding numerical requirements."[69, p. 236] This preoccupation with quantitative standards, however, seems to have bypassed the formulation of an
educational philosophy underlying these more procedural regulations. The
survey of educational practices in the United States undertaken by the
American Psychoanalytic Association in 1954 restimulated thinking on
this subject and opened many channels for discussion of various aspects
of learning objectives in psychoanalysis and the learning experiences which
aim to achieve them. Systematic study of these educational matters, however, still remains to be achieved.

Supervision as a teaching method has had a slow evolution for many
reasons. Probably the most important retarding factor is the experiential
nature of the psychoanalytic process. Because so much of what happens
in a psychoanalysis occurs on unconscious-preconscious levels, principles
have been difficult to formulate. The immediacy of the clinical process
has been too pressing for both analyst and teacher. This fact has tended
to limit any study of the process to the individual case under scrutiny and
therefore to prevent formulation of general principles, regarding either the
therapeutic or the teaching process.

The slow conception and birth of an educational philosophy is not surprising when one considers how close we still are to the origins of psychoanalysis. Excitement in discovery has claimed the energy of student and
teacher, both of whom were immersed in learning the new discipline, not
yet a unified field of knowledge. The fragmentary nature of the records
pertaining to teaching goals and methods is disappointing but understandable when we take these special factors into account. Formal training did
not exist as it does today, and yet the pioneer analysts learned much from
little teaching.

Freud, in his *History of the Psychoanalytic Movement*, set the beginning of psychoanalytic training at the year 1902. In that year his "splendid isolation," his lonely but "glorious heroic age" was interrupted. He wrote: "From the year 1902 onwards, a number of young doctors gathered round me with the express intention of learning, practicing and spreading the knowledge of psychoanalysis. . . . Regular meetings took place on certain evenings in my house, discussions were held according to certain rules. . . . On the whole I could tell myself that (the group) was hardly inferior in wealth and variety of talents to the staff of any clinical teacher one can think of."[43]

In 1936, Eitingon[25] described the ways of learning psychoanalysis in those early times: "We devoted intensive study to the psychoanalytic writings then available. What we did not dig out of books we hammered out in discussion; highly animated and exceedingly fruitful discussions they were; they were the germs out of which our present seminars developed." Indeed, for almost two decades, until 1920, the learning of theory was unsystematized and left to the zeal of the individual student. Kovacs[60] described the emphasis on absorbing what Freud had discovered when she wrote: "Freud supposed that in stating the theory of analysis he was putting into the hands of all who grasped his principles the key to their unconscious." Freud seemed to look upon the struggles of his own "self-analysis"[38] as primarily a task of his research, and he did not advise his disciples that a self-analysis was an important part of their learning until 1910 when he addressed the second International Psychoanalytic Congress in Nuremberg.[40] By 1912[41] he was more emphatic that a physician should begin his analytic training by being analyzed himself. Nevertheless, an analysis was not accepted as indispensable until later.

Even then, the full significance of self-knowledge for psychoanalytic training was only slowly appreciated (see Chapter II). In 1918, at the fifth International Psychoanalytic Congress in Budapest, Nunberg[25] proposed that every student of analysis should have a thorough therapeutic experience with the method applied to himself. This proposal was accepted as a desideratum which could not be achieved at the time, but it remained a vital goal. With the establishment of psychoanalytic institutes in Berlin (1920) and Vienna (1921) "training analysis" became part of the training program. By 1922, the seventh International Psychoanalytic Congress in Berlin agreed that "only those persons should be authorized to practice psychoanalysis who, as well as taking theoretical courses of training, had submitted to training analysis conducted by an analyst approved by the Society at that time."[60] Eitingon in 1936 stated, "Most of us thought that Nunberg's demand could never be realized. And yet in these seven years (1918-1925) instructional analysis became a matter of course." He continued his report of further developments: "Since then, we in Berlin in-

augurated what we called . . . 'An Introduction to Psychoanalytic Therapy.'
By this we meant a course of practical training not limited to any definite
period for those who completed their training analysis and were beginning
to practice analysis themselves. In other words, we inaugurated 'Kontroll
analysis.' "[25] A growing tendency toward more organized training and
away from private apprenticeship was evidenced at the ninth Congress
(1925). This Congress established the International Training Commission
and defined three phases for the training program: the training analysis,
the theoretical curriculum, and the supervised analysis. Each branch society was to set up an educational committee which was to be responsible
to the I.T.C. for ensuring high standards in the training of future psychoanalysts. In the Homburg Congress the leading motif seemed to be:
"Psychoanalytic training ought no longer to be left to the private initiative
of the individual."[23]

Gradually changes have taken place in the selection of candidates as
well as in the sequences of training. From the beginning of organized
training the qualifications of candidates to be trained have been implicitly
correlated with success in the training and supervised analyses. Just what
these qualifications were and just how their presence or absence correlated
with success or failure in being analyzed or in doing analysis has not yet
been objectively accomplished, although more systematic study of these
matters is receiving wider interest and attention, especially by the Committee on Psychoanalytic Education of the American Psychoanalytic
Association.

In the early stages of psychoanalytic education, applicants were few.
They were, so to speak, self-selected;[81] their interest and dedication qualified them. Those who belonged to the Wednesday evening discussion
group in Freud's home were selected by him. As the "psychoanalytic
movement" spread and eager study groups formed in many countries, an
interview with the leading psychoanalyst in an area sufficed for acceptance
of the applicant. The "selector" was an "experienced" analyst. It was
assumed that because of his *Menschen-Kenntnis*, his experience in inter-
viewing and his dedication to psychoanalysis, he could discern whether the
applicant's motivations and his psychological aptitude would enable him
to devote himself successfully to the profession.

One should not forget that in many instances the relationship between
selector and applicant began as a therapeutic one. If a patient appeared
talented and devoted, he was accepted as a student of analysis, after a
shorter or longer period of psychoanalytic therapy, and was invited to participate in the discussions of the local psychoanalytic group. Patients were
referred to him for treatment. Thus in many instances the personal experience of psychoanalysis came before application and acceptance, even
before "training analysis" was inaugurated. In these instances, the selector-

analyst had the opportunity to assess his patient's aptitude for free association, for self-observation and communication with his unconscious. He
was able to evaluate his intelligence, his cultural sophistication and his
integrity in interpersonal relationships. The disadvantage of this selection
method lay in the countertransference of the analyst which sometimes
manifested itself in overoptimism about the therapeutic effectiveness of
psychoanalysis. Thus many who began as patients became psychoanalysts
after an incomplete therapeutic experience.

One of us (T. B.) belongs to the generation of students of analysis before
psychoanalytic institutes were established. Since her experience coincides
with many of the points just stated and also covers the early period of
training at the Berlin Institute (1920-1923), her introduction to psychoanalysis and some of her memories seem pertinent to record as an example
of the methods of psychoanalytic training at that time.

Enough information about the new science had reached Budapest to
arouse the curiosity of a small club of girls in the gymnasium which I at-
tended. This group, wishing to learn about things not taught in school,
invited Eugene Harnik in 1910 to talk to us about psychoanalysis. I was
deeply impressed and decided to study medicine and become a psychoanalyst. As a medical student I audited Ferenczi's popular lectures. In
those lectures, the necessity of being psychoanalyzed came through to me.
After the first World War, when I asked Ferenczi for an interview, the
course was clear to both of us.

Short as my analysis was (five months), it was a meaningful experience,
which carried with it the conviction of knowing something that was unknown and unknowable before. It was the specific experience of one's self
against something else that was also oneself, from which new awareness and
new knowledge emerged. Also experienced were the simple requisites for
the analytic process: listening, observing, and interpreting. In other words,
the basic experience of analysis was the same when analysis was short. In
those days, such short analyses constituted the prepararation for psychoanalyzing.

The analytic relationship was highly personalized and the analyst of the
student was often the first to send him a patient and to recommend him to
the local society. In this way, before institutes existed, a student began to
participate in groups and to learn theory as well as clinical analysis in discussions with more experienced colleagues. In my own case, since I lived
in Leipsig, circumstances were slightly different and my first case was a self-
referral. He probably had read more psychoanalysis than I had at that time.
This case was unsupervised—very different from the procedure today. My
second case, referred by a local physician, was very puzzling and I sought
help from Eitingon, whom I saw irregularly sometimes in Berlin and sometimes in Leipsig in his parents' home. He did not charge me for these
consultations nor did Abraham, my other supervisor—another evidence of
the informality of the times.

Such consultations were a part of the training program at the newly established Berlin Institute but were far from being clearly formulated as a method of teaching. Little is on record about this easygoing relationship between experienced analysts and the novices. I remember presenting the patients' problems much as students do today, but perhaps I talked about my feelings of insecurity in handling them. Individual teaching styles were different then as now. How vividly I recall Eitingon's verbally sparse but emotionally expressive instruction—a go-ahead reassurance with a nod of his head, or the clarification of an issue just by a question. Abraham, on the other hand, carefully and methodically explained his suggested interpretations.

As we trace the development of psychoanalytic education, it is interesting to note the informality which characterized the relationship between teacher and student. Dedication on the part of each to the task of learning the still embryonic body of psychoanalytic theory and technique probably accounts for much of this atmosphere which did not seem troubled by the syncretic dilemmas of today.

Not only in the early "apprenticeship" period, but even after the establishment of psychoanalytic institutes, it was a great promotion for the student to be sent a patient by his own or another analyst. The referring analyst usually became the consultant for the case. The student's eagerness to learn was highly stimulated by the gratification of this relationship between himself and his teacher. The infrequency and irregularity of the consultations enhanced his ambition, and his willingness to learn was stimulated by the expectation that his tenure as a student would be short. Thus the interpersonal relationship between teacher and pupil held much immediate gratification for the student. One learned, by identification with a highly libidinized object, ideas and techniques which were emotionally invested not only with the wish for professional competence and recognition, but also with the excitement of continuing the discoveries which had begun with one's own analysis. Indeed, the known and formulated psychoanalytic knowledge constituted merely a foretaste of what was to come.

The attitude of the student toward supervision did not change immediately after supervision became institutionalized. When the beginning of supervised analytic work depended not only on the recommendation of the training analyst but also on approval by an Education Committee, the training analyst's opinion still carried much weight. Later, when the training analysis changed into a long or therapeutic analysis, the beginning of supervised analysis served several purposes. It gave enhanced impetus to the slowly moving personal analysis by permitting the student to develop professionally, and the experience of psychoanalyzing and discussing a patient with an experienced analyst enlivened the personal analysis of the student by opening new avenues for working through his own problems in analysis. Even today such motivations for beginning supervised analysis are often topics for discussion by education committees. However, regardless of how "institutionalized" psychoanalytic education may have become, the education of each psychoanalyst remains a highly personalized procedure.

The therapeutic aim of the personal analytic experience enunciated by Freud in 1910 became more widely accepted by 1925 but dissatisfactions with the effectiveness of a "didactic analysis" for professional training began to appear. Eitingon[23] stated what he considered to be the difference between a therapeutic and a training analysis: "The point in which instructional analysis or didactic analysis differs from therapeutic analysis (I must ask for your indulgence if I am obliged to emphasize trivialities) is *not in having a special technique but, as we say in Berlin, in having an additional aim, that supersedes or goes hand in hand with the therapeutic aim.*" (Italics ours.) He did not spell out further what this additional aim was, but he emphasized the necessity of adding a supervisory experience. In that convention *Kontroll-Analyse* or supervised analysis as an indispensable phase of psychoanalytic training was unequivocally accepted.

In 1924, Ferenczi and Rank published a small volume, *Die Entwicklungsziele der Psychoanalyse* with the subtitle, *Wechselbeziehung von Theorie und Praxis.*[30] In this book they stressed that training analysis must be deeper and more thorough than a therapeutic analysis. They argued that psychoanalysis is essentially an experience involving both the patient and the analyst and is therefore an onerous emotional task for the analyst, for which he has to be prepared through his training analysis. They apparently did not believe that training analysis alone can adequately prepare the student for practice; hence they recommended that *Kontroll-Analyse* serve as a continuation of the training analysis. According to these authors, *Kontroll-Analyse* should have the task of dealing with the unresolved complexes of the candidate as they emerge during his work with his patient.

Eitingon, proposing supervised analysis as a part of the training program, conceived of it differently. He emphasized that "the instructional analysis is but one experience which leaves the student helpless, if confronted with a patient, when he comes straight from his so-called complete analysis."[23, p. 132] He described some of the characteristic inadequacies and learning problems of the beginner and maintained that it was necessary to teach the technique of psychoanalysis through another method because "there is a great danger that the mistakes and the lack of skill of his first independent work will, either directly or by their overcompensation for them, develop into constitutional defects."[23, p. 133] Eitingon was certain that the supervising analyst could soon detect such mistakes in the beginner, even if he had not known the candidate through working with him as his training analyst. He emphasized the principal that "the beginner ought to see more than one individual analyst at work."[23, p. 134] Ferenczi, on the other hand, felt that Eitingon's separation of the supervised analytic work from the training analysis would only divide psychoanalytic training into separate entities instead of providing the candidate with an opportunity for continuous development through various methods of teaching.

The discussion about supervised analysis continued among those training analysts who represented their branch societies in the I.T.C. Three of those representatives presented papers at the next Congress of the International Psychoanalytic Association in Innsbruck (1927). Sandor Rado spoke on "The Construction of the Psychoanalytic Curriculum"; Hanns Sachs, "On Training Analysis"; and Helene Deutsch, "On Supervised Analysis."[24] We know about these papers only from Eitingon's report to the Association because they were never published or abstracted. For whatever reasons, the discussions remained behind the closed doors of the I.T.C., not available to the growing group of training analysts. The young training analysts at the time were left to their own devices, hardly troubled by the problems of pedagogy.

The aim of the I.T.C. was to establish an international training organization with unified standards for every branch society all over the world, at the same time allowing freedom for necessary local variations. This aim, however, came into conflict with the conviction that psychoanalysis, if its basic tenets were accepted, would develop naturally from the individual's accumulated experience. Teaching itself was considered secondary. There was a general aversion toward organized, postgraduate teaching.* The high standards, so important to the founders of the psychoanalytic training organization, had to be formulated cautiously as minimal standards, emphasizing freedom of learning more than its methods and goals. The problems created by these conflicting philosophies overshadowed and delayed work on such special problems as the methodology of teaching by supervision.

Supervision, however, continued in all the psychoanalytic institutes and training centers, and more analysts assumed responsibility for teaching. When a psychoanalyst accumulated experience (five years was considered adequate), he was appointed a training analyst by the Education Commit-

---

* This was not a special attitude of psychoanalysis. The traditional European emphasis on "freedom of learning" was carried to the ultimate regarding postgraduate learning. This tradition might have accounted for many of the covert struggles within the psychoanalytic training organization. An indication of this is Eitingon's reference to his report to the I.T.C. in 1927. When speaking about regulations for admission of candidates for psychoanalytic training, he stated, "Some friends in London found it very difficult and apparently incompatible with the Anglo Saxon idea of liberty to subject a graduate, possibly one who held a medical degree, to a further examination as to his personal qualifications."[24]

tee of his society; he also became a supervisor. Being an enthusiastic clinician of psychoanalysis, the supervisor felt that he fulfilled his task if he conveyed to the student his understanding of the case, not only in terms of diagnosis, genetic and dynamic formulations, but also the details of the evolving transference. Looking back with a critical eye, one might say that the supervisor tended to take over the case. He demonstrated more or less skillfully how *he* would deal with the material presented and he seemed to expect his student to learn by imitation.

This was the early concept of supervision. Since the supervisor was a clinician, his attention was naturally focused on the treatment of the patient and on his student only as an intermediary. Regardless of the pedagogic philosophy of supervision in this atmosphere of "psychoanalysis a trois," the supervisor in his role as clinician could easily recognize the blind spots of the student. As the analytic process evolved, the supervisor could see the influence of the student-analyst's "unresolved complexes" upon the analytic process, and by pointing out to the student the intrapsychic origin of his mistakes the supervisor could help him to carry on his self-analysis. Supervision, as it was practiced in the decade after 1925, depended on the student's positive transference to his teacher, on his devotion to psychoanalysis and obligation to his patients, to motivate his learning.

Balint critically termed this kind of teaching "superego training."[5] Glover also expressed concern about the "great investment" in psychoanalytic training which, by establishing positive identifications, may limit the development of the potential creativity by lasting fixation to a teacher and his theories.[50]

The method of supervision, however, remained undefined, and the subject of the supervisor as teacher was little discussed. The publication on the "Hungarian System" by Kovacs initiated an ardent controversy carried on in the Four Countries Conference.* The first Conference, held in Vienna in 1935, devoted its business meeting to the problem of "Training Analysis and Control Analysis."[35] Imre Herman presented the views of the Hungarian Society. Anna Freud read Helene Deutsch's paper on the principles and practices of the Vienna Society which, by that time, firmly supported Eitingon's conviction that "there is more to supervision than analyzing the countertransference." In the same meeting, Alice Balint, for the first time, described psychoanalysis as an interactional process and discussed problems arising from the fact that the analyst is not simply a screen. As stated in the synopsis of her paper, she said, "The character of the analyst is an integral factor in the analytic situation and with the best will

---

* These were conferences in which psychoanalysts of Central Europe—Austria, Hungary, Czechoslovakia and Italy—met for presentation of papers and discussions of problems.

in the world it cannot be eliminated."[4] The other papers read were not published, but from the report it would seem that the difference of opinion had sharpened the thinking on the philosophy of education.

The discussion on supervision was continued in the Second Four Countries Conference in May 1937 in Budapest. The subject of the Special Meeting was "Methods and Technique of Control Analysis." Edward Bibring of Vienna and Karl Landauer of Amsterdam were the main speakers. Bibring presented an outline of the purposes of supervision, stressing the didactic goals and evaluative aspects of the supervisor's work. He was the first* to formulate the concept that the supervisor not only instructs the student but is also in a position to evaluate his ability to grasp problems, make decisions about dealing with them and apply what he learned to new situations. Implicit in this formulation are the objectives of supervisory teaching as he saw them. At the same time he warned against a "hypertrophy" of teaching, while also pointing out the disadvantages of "analyzing the candidate in the control situation."[12]

Landauer dealt with "Difficulties in Controlling an Analysis," grouping them according to the objective and subjective nature of their motivation. He hints at difficulties which the supervisors must have had. Perhaps some resistance against a more rigorous teaching appeared in the candidates. Otherwise, one cannot understand such advice as, "The candidate's hostility must be allayed by self-sacrifice on the part of the control-analyst," and other similar comments.[66]

The discussion of the papers did not deal with such details, but turned directly to the control question: Is the primary goal of "control analysis" to give instruction in the art of analysis, or is its main objective simply the analysis of a candidate's practical analytic work? In other words, is the aim of supervision the "control" of an analysis or the "analysis" of the candidate being supervised? Clearly, as the extreme positions were stated, both parties aimed at arriving at workable compromises and at friendly solutions of their conflicts. The Hungarian School agreed, as a matter of principle, that the training and control analysis should not be conducted by the same individual. The Berlin-Viennese School conceded that the practical supervised work should begin while the candidate was still in analysis. To differentiate matters clearly, two new terms were coined: (1) *Kontroll-Analyse* and (2) *Analysen-Kontrolle*.† The former meant the analysis of

---

* The paper which Helene Deutsch read at the Innsbruck Congress in 1927 reveals that she may have been the first to call attention to the evaluative function of supervision.[30]

† The word "control" has a stricter, more limiting connotation to English-speaking people than it has for Germans. Indeed, the dictionary (Muret-Saunders, *Encyclopedisches Worterbuch*) translates the German word *Kontrolle* as *supervision* in the first place and *checking* in the second.

the candidate being supervised; the latter meant the Kontroll—that is, the supervision of the analysis conducted by the candidate.[60]

A continuation of fruitful study and discussion concerning problems and methods of supervision was interrupted by world events. The expansion of Hitler's Germany compelled a number of experienced psychoanalysts to leave Europe. Many of them migrated to the United States before the Second World War began and were welcomed in the growing American institutes as valuable reinforcements to the small corps of training and supervising analysts.

In the United States the war did not retard the development of psycho-analytic training. Rather, the social situation accelerated its progress in several ways. In the first place, the influx of trained analysts from Europe who already were qualified teachers left American institutes with adequate faculties even when a large number of training analysts joined the armed services. Many of the Europeans followed the Americans into the medical corps, increasing the number of psychiatrists who offered a new point of view in diagnosis and treatment. In the second place, the opportunity for psychoanalysts to work with war casualties stimulated intense interest in many young psychiatrists and doctors just out of medical school who had had little, if any, contact with the illuminating theories and techniques of psychoanalysis. This interest produced a rapid increase in the number of applications for training and a dilemma for psychoanalytic training facilities. Satisfaction in the popular demand created a temptation to accept applicants without careful screening; but since training facilities were not adequate to accommodate a larger number of students without shortening and diluting the training experiences, the problem became focused in the late forties on how to maintain high standards with an increasing number of students.

To decide this, a national conference on education was called in 1946.[48] One group of teachers and institutes wanted to meet the demand by relaxing the requirements, reducing the customary five or six weekly analytic hours and also the frequency of supervisory sessions. The majority maintained that the unity of psychoanalysis as a discipline could best be safeguarded by strict adherence to the classical technique of training analysis and by high standards of classroom and supervisory teaching. This position was justified by the increasing responsibilities of the profession, not only to its students but to other disciplines as well. As psychoanalysis was "coming of age," its reciprocal communication with other branches of medicine and with the social sciences had expanded. In such an atmosphere of highly desirable scientific exchange, only well-trained psychoanalysts could maintain the identity of their science and at the same time broaden its scope for research and further development. On the other hand, the focus of the controversy remained on the level of quantitative regulations, and formulation of the educational goals on which quantitative standards should be based was unfortunately postponed. The elaboration of an educational philosophy begun in Europe prior to 1939 was forced into the background by the preoccupation with numbers. The accommodating changes in procedure seemed to be based more on rationalizations than on sound, carefully thought-out educational principles.

Gradually, however, a more professional attitude toward the education of new generations of analysts began to take shape. Edward Bibring, who was on the European frontier in 1936 and 1937, played a significant role in this development in America. He formulated the early definitions of an institute and a training center in terms of the number of training analysts necessary for an adequate faculty. He spoke against training being carried out by an individual, isolated geographically from his professional colleagues, and thereby tending to reestablish the private apprenticeship system.

Still expressed mainly in quantitative terms, the standards set during the forties and early fifties by the Board on Professional Standards of the American Psychoanalytic Association[75] reflected the educational philosophy that a thorough-going experience of being analyzed was a basic prerequisite for clinical training, and that learning from more than one supervisor was important for widening the student's range of clinical experience. In calling these quantitative standards "minimal," the Association recognized the advisability of some flexibility in meeting individual needs of students but indicated that five analytic sessions per week "constitutes an optimal condition for the continuity of analysis." A minimum number of supervisory sessions was specified: 200 in 1950[75] and 150 in 1957.[76]

In 1957 the revised minimal standards clearly stated didactic goals for supervision as follows: "The student's readiness to begin supervised psychoanalytic work with patients is determined by the educational committee of the approved institution at which he is training. The aims of the supervision are: (1) to instruct the student in the use of the psychoanalytic methods; (2) to aid him in the acquisition of therapeutic skill based upon an understanding of the analytic material; (3) to observe his work and determine how fully his personal analysis has achieved its aim; (4) to determine his maturity and stability over an extended period of time." The generality of these aims is apparent but the attempt at formulation of objectives and standards is notable.

After a long lull in the literature on supervision, Blitzsten and Fleming in their paper "What Is a Supervisory Analysis?" focused attention again on problems of supervision.[14] They attempted to meet the problem of unresolved conflicts in the student-analyst in terms of an educational diagnosis of a learning problem. Even the title of their paper revived the old conflict of *Kontrol-Analyse* in contrast to *Analysen-Kontrolle*. The authors advocated that the supervisor assume some responsibility for dealing with countertransference problems. They felt it might become necessary, under certain circumstances, for the supervisor and training analyst to confer and even to collaborate with each other in order to meet the educational needs of the student. The cool reception afforded this proposition reflected the intensity of the dilemma which the psychoanalyst faces when confronted with the double role of therapist and teacher. Following this paper in 1953, a series of publications dealing with the problem of countertransference in supervised analysis appeared.*

The Program Committee of the American Psychoanalytic Association arranged a panel discussion on problems of supervision for the midwinter meeting of 1955 under the title, "The Technique of Supervised Analysis."[58] In spite of the inaccuracy of the title, the focus of the discussion had returned to objectives of teaching by supervision. The subject matter of that discussion singled out the teaching of psychoanalytic technique as "the most important task of supervision." Many psychoanalytic teachers, however, still recoiled from a statement made in this discussion by Windholz: "The supervisor clarifies for the student the value, meaning and effect of different technical devices."[58] The panel considered this to be a task of supervision, but it was concerned lest formalizing the analytic process in teachable propositions would freeze the experience of psychoanalysis. Even in a later panel discussion in 1959, Annie Reich warned that "the systematization of our knowledge may interfere with the student's intuition."[27]

Probably because of this aversion to teaching devices, the first panel turned to the administrative aspects of supervision, such as (1) criteria for determining the readiness of a student to begin supervised analysis, (2) the selection of the first case, (3) evaluation of progress, and (4) an attempt at classification of learning problems. Lively discussion led to a restatement of the old question of whether supervision should be patient-centered only or should help the student gain insight into his own problems as they arise in relation to his case. This obstinate problem with its "either/or" proposition has returned again and again. In the second panel[85] it was stated in the following way: (1) To what extent is the supervisory process a means of acquiring experience in psychoanalytic technique, recognizing transference and analyzing the defenses on the part of the beginner? (2) To what extent does it involve recognition and the resolution of the candidate's personal problems?

---

* A Critical Digest of the Literature on Psychoanalytic Supervision by De Bell[19] presents an excellent summary of the issues as they have been expressed before 1950 and through 1960. Our review in this chapter is oriented to a particular point of view and is not intended to cover the literature as completely as De Bell did. We have attempted to draw a rough map indicating the journey which the development of an educational philosophy of psychoanalysis has followed up to now. For an organized critique of various individual opinions and attitudes we refer the reader to De Bell.

This second panel discussion was conceived as a continuation of the first, but with a sharpened focus upon the function of supervision in relation to countertransference. Hall illustrated various aspects of the theory of countertransference by clinical material, leading to the conclusion that the personal analysis of the candidate and his supervised analytic work with patients should overlap in time sufficiently to give the candidate an opportunity to analyze his blind spots and countertransference in his continuing analysis.[58] In contrast, Reich, who participated in both panels, presented a different opinion in the second and emphasized that the technique of "analysis must be learned," that many difficulties are simply due to lack of knowledge and experience and not every reaction, positive or negative, is countertransference.[85] In the discussion it was agreed that the main task of supervision is to teach, not to analyze the candidate or to "deal with countertransference." In spite of this agreement, it was recognized that the problem could not be avoided. Confronting the student with his countertransferences was accepted as part of supervisory technique, but warnings were voiced regarding the tact and care with which the confrontation should be made.

Ekstein and Wallerstein, in their book *The Teaching and Learning of Psychotherapy*,[29] brought a fresh viewpoint to psychoanalytic supervision, although they deal mainly with the teaching of dynamic psychiatry to psychiatric residents. The authors illustrate with samples of teaching material that the various "modes" of psychotherapeutic supervision can be integrated if the supervisor applies didactic principles consistently. With this aim they emphasize the significance of an "educational diagnosis" that differentiates the nature of the student's learning problems.

The subject matter of the next panel was "Teaching of Psychoanalytic Technique."[27] It continued the 1955 and 1956 panel discussions in agreeing that technique should be taught in supervision. At the outset, discussion was limited to *what should* and *what can* be taught, explicitly. However, in remarks from the floor, Frosch related the task of supervision to that of analysis in a specific way. He stated that as the student in his personal analysis has learned how to differentiate his experiencing and observing ego, in supervision he should learn how to utilize both his experiencing and observing ego in the analysis of his patient. Thus he brought into focus the fact that with our present knowledge of the psychoanalytic process, especially from the point of view of ego psychology, we can define objectives for supervisory teaching in terms of the dynamics of the therapeutic experience. In continuing the same subject, Bibring emphasized the significance of training analysis as prerequisite for supervisory learning: "There has to be appropriate soil, an aptitude, the right endowment, a freedom achieved in one's personal analysis, so that there can be teaching and learning."[27]

Indeed, in each of these panel discussions, in attempting to formulate a general goal of supervision several remarks were made which indicated that supervision is, in a deeper sense of teaching, an extension of the experience of the training analysis. This concept had been explicitly developed by Isakower in a presentation to the Curriculum Committee of the New York Psychoanalytic Institute in November 1957.[56] Recognizing the personality of the analyst as the tool of the analytic process, he saw the task of supervision as the "clarification of this instrument."

Such a task is an interminable process, as Freud recognized,[47] since in his professional work the analyst is required to be continually aware of psychological processes in himself as well as in his patient. Kramer[61] describes explicitly the way in which the analytic process, begun in the training analysis, can be continued by conscious effort at self-analysis. Both Kramer's and Isakower's concepts enable us to take a fresh look at psychoanalytic education as an integrated experience in which the training analysis initiates and supervision continues the development of the student's personality as an instrument of his professional work.

— II —

The Experiential Nature of
Psychoanalytic Learning

THE NATURE OF PSYCHOANALYTIC WORK REQUIRES KNOWLEDGE AND skills which probe the world of psychological experience—a world not knowable through the usual sensory pathways, a world of processes which influence behavior and well-being without the subject's awareness of what is motivating him. Freud discovered that when a person became aware of previously unconscious motivations, he could change his behavior so as to be no longer at the mercy of the forces which created his symptoms. This discovery is the assumption basic to psychoanalytic therapy. To learn how to enter this intimate inner world, to discover what was unknown and to make it knowable is the goal of psychoanalytic treatment. To learn how to help another person achieve this kind of self-knowledge and mastery is the objective of a student-analyst, an objective that can be accomplished only by learning experiences of a special nature. For such learning traditional instruction is inadequate, since the means of exploring and influencing the inner world of psychological experience cannot be achieved by reading a book, hearing a lecture or observing someone else do it. Cognitive processes are essential but play a role secondary to learning by experience during the greater part of the development of a psychoanalyst.[31]

Intuitively we understand what is meant by experiential learning: to know by testing it.* For purposes of clarifying the educational process, however, we shall attempt to identify the significant experience a student-analyst goes through to attain his goal. We shall also attempt to distinguish the elements of learning-by-experiencing from learning-by-cognizing, and to identify the part played by each in the education of an analyst.

Although it goes without saying that a student of psychoanalysis should possess the aptitudes necessary for the job, it is not a simple matter to

---

* Oxford English Dictionary—from the Latin: experiri, meaning to try, to put to the test. Several illustrative quotations have bearing on our thesis regarding experience as a source of knowledge and a means of learning. 1736, Butler—Anal. I. ii. 35: It is not so much a Deduction of Reason as a matter of Experience. 1826, Disraeli—Viv. Gray, v.i., Experience is the child of thought. 1874, Carpenter, Ment. Phys. I, ii. 58, The experiential acquirement of knowledge.

define these aptitudes. Several authors have emphasized psychological sensitivity, a capacity for empathic understanding and tactful responsiveness[32, 33] as being related to the special tasks of psychoanalysis. Discussion of these and other selection criteria, however, is beyond the scope of this study, since our main concern is with the best way to develop a student-analyst's aptitudes into freely accessible, useful tools for his professional work.

The psychoanalytic training program at present is divided into three phases, each of which makes a special contribution to the total learning experience of the student and each of which emphasizes a different aspect of his professional development. In sequence the training analysis comes first, imbricated with a period of theoretical instruction and clinical demonstrations which overlap with the culminating phase of analyzing patients under supervision. Although the structure of the system could evolve only through trial and error without a formulated rationale for the total program until Eitingon's proposals in 1925,[23] history reveals that the educational philosophy behind this training system has been "experiential" from the beginning.

Development of the training system has paralleled in many ways the development of psychoanalysis as a clinical science. The empirical observations made by Freud in collaboration with Breuer[15] led to discovery of a method which could reach below the surface and was found useful not only for observing behavior not previously observable, but also for discovering its motivations. Freud's earliest observations became foundation stones in the theoretical structure which gradually evolved; yet this structure might never have been built if Freud had not had the fortitude to "experiment" by testing out his new method of observation on himself. His letters of those early days[38] reveal more authentically than his studies in hysteria the "origins of psychoanalysis" in the depths of his own experiences.

In Letter 130 written on November 3, 1900,[38, p. 312] he describes a period of incubation and preconscious working through of resistances he could feel but whose origins he did not know. His tactics correspond to the "regression in the service of the ego" which Kris[62] holds equally significant for analytic and creative work in general—an activity of mind in which synthesis and integration proceed subliminally before illumination of the problem by conscious recognition. Freud says, "I adopted the expedient of renouncing working by conscious thought, so as to grope my way further into the riddles only by blind touch. Since I started this I have been doing my work, perhaps more skillfully than before, but I do not really know what I am doing." This shift in working occurred in a period of frustration following a realization that "all the hypotheses that until then had seemed plausible" had to be thought through further. In this example of Freud's observation of his own reaction and behavior, we see again his record of experiencing a process which calls forth discovery of hidden meanings in manifest behavior. His urge to find the master keys of concepts and theories by experiencing this hitherto unexplored world met the resistances with which he became so well acquainted and later conceptualized with such benefit to psychology and analytic therapy.

Freud's genius expressed itself in his ability to observe and to objectify his own emotional responses. His driving curiosity and his reactions to self-observations became the material for his "self-analysis." By means of introspection and interpretation of his own dreams he arrived at insights on which far-reaching conceptualizations could be based. With this introspective beginning, he was able to empathize with similar phenomena in others, and from these observations he gradually developed a psychological theory and a method for investigation of human behavior that has revolutionized the study of man.

Since his own learning was so firmly rooted in the examination of his own experience, it is not surprising that from the earliest days of the student meetings at Freud's house, the experiential nature of the learning necessary for becoming an analyst was recognized. It was accepted that the student should try the method on himself, "analyzing" his dreams, slips of the tongue, and emotional reactions to the new ideas and the discussions about them. Such personal experiences convinced his students that behavior was unconsciously determined, that some process of censorship existed, and that emotions could interfere with objective thinking. They kept at it spurred by the pleasure of discovery and by their attempts to anchor the fleeting phenomena of experience in the cognitive framework of concepts and theory.

The complexities of analyzing patients soon confronted the early analysts, as they had Freud, with the phenomena of "blind spots"[87] or "countertransferences."[40] They realized that experiencing the method through "self-analysis" was not enough. They went through all of the vicissitudes Freud described in his letters to Fliess before 1900 and began to understand how often something of which they were not aware crept into their communication with patients. Thus, these first analysts learned that to associate freely was not easy in the face of ever-present resistances and, consequently, that a deeper examination of their own inner life was necessary. In 1910 Freud emphasized the therapeutic aims of self-analysis. He said: "We have become aware of the 'countertransference' which arises in him [the analyst] as a result of the patient's influence on his unconscious feelings, and we are *almost* [italics ours] inclined to insist that he shall recognize this countertransference in himself and overcome it. Since analysts have begun to exchange observations with each other we have noticed no psychoanalyst goes further than his own complexes and internal resistances permit; and we consequently require that he shall begin his activity with a self-analysis and continually carry it deeper while he is making his observations on his patients. Anyone who fails to produce results in a self-analysis of this kind may at once give up any idea of being able to treat patients by analysis."[40, p. 145] This statement is still a long way from the concept of a training analysis as we think of it today. Freud's tentative insistence on a therapeutic aim seems related to his experience of internal resistances in himself and to his experience with public opposition to psychoanalytic theories which many persons, including some early analysts, found intolerable because of what tended to be stimulated within themselves.[43]

Freud had learned by experience what the struggle with resistances involves and that outside assistance can help,[38, Letter 75, p. 229] but there was no one to help him as he helped others. The use of a therapeutic relationship as an aid in the self-analytic process was advocated in 1912[41] when he said, "I count it one of the many merits of the Zurich School of Analysis that they have laid increasing emphasis on this requirement and have embodied it in a demand that everyone who wishes to carry out analysis of other people shall first himself undergo an analysis by someone with expert knowledge."[43, p. 116] Thus the principle fundamental for psychoanalytic education gradually took shape, the principle that a personal analysis is a prerequisite, a *sine qua non* for professional learning.* The therapeutic aim, strongly enunciated by Nunberg in 1918, became established as a standard practice by the International Training Commission in 1925,[23] about 30 years after Freud's first entrance into this unexplored territory.

How knowledge is derived from the noncognitive experience of analysis was described by Freud in his attempts to communicate to Fliess his excitement in discovery and the ideas so generated. He said in Letter 72, dated October 27, 1897,[38, p. 226] "I am now experiencing myself all the things which as a third party I have witnessed going on in my patients."† In Letter 74, dated November 5, 1897,[38, p. 228] there is recognition of the absence of conscious cognitive work: "At the moment I can neither read nor think. I am sufficiently absorbed in observation. My self-analysis is stagnating again, or rather it trickles on without my understanding its progress." In this statement he alludes to a shadowy awareness of which he was only partially conscious. In *Remembering, Repeating, and Working Through*,[42a] Freud comments on the remark many patients make when something forgotten is being recalled: "As a matter of fact I've always *known* it; only I've never *thought* of it." (Italics ours.)

---

* The terms applied to this experience with analysis, such as "didactic," "preparatory," "preliminary," "training," etc. are matters we cannot discuss here. The choice of term is often influenced by extraneous issues. We will use the term "training analysis" most frequently, since this is the commonly accepted one.

† Why did Freud call himself a "third party"? Perhaps because he saw in the patient two persons as protagonists.

Letter 75, dated November 14, 1897,[38, p. 230] describes the birth of a new piece of knowledge: "Truth to tell, it was not entirely new; it had repeatedly shown and then withdrawn itself again; but this time it remained and saw the light of day. In a strange way I am aware of these events sometime in advance." His language suggests something that moves in and out of conscious awareness, something only partially visible before it becomes clearly so—something that is experienced as actively working inside of himself but whose cognitive connections are only slowly established and cannot be *known* before the preconscious process of creating a new gestalt has taken place. Thus the process of experiential learning by introspection and interpretation in self-analytic work was put into communicable form by Freud[38, Letter 67, p. 213]: "the chief patient I am busy with."

This primary stage in the education of an analyst could be described as an *in*-the-job learning experience compared to the *on*-the-job learning provided in supervision. Immersed in the analytic process, the student learns something of the analytic method of investigation by applying it to himself. From his experience as a patient he learns what it means to make an effort to associate freely, to speak out loud against the various resistances aroused by inner conflicts and anxieties. As he works in his training analysis to understand his own developmental experiences, he reexperiences them in relation to his analyst. Through the many levels of that recapitulation he learns to understand his own life history and himself as an active and passive agent in it. What he experiences as a patient introduces him to the tools of analytic work: introspection, empathy and interpretation.

Introspection takes precedence in the training analysis, but the task of a patient in the psychoanalytic process involves more than looking into oneself by oneself alone. It includes communicating to someone else what has been "seen" by introspection. The patient's success in putting his introspected experience into words, saying it out loud in the presence of another person, expands the field available for awareness and cognition. As a patient the student-analyst realizes that psychoanalysis includes interpersonal communication based on an alliance with another person who also does introspective work.

The second tool, empathic understanding, which develops out of vicarious introspection by the analyst[59] as a supplementary instrument for the patient's self-observation becomes a part of the student-analyst's experience. In this beginning phase of training it is usually not integrated cognitively, but through firsthand experience the student learns that an analyst can hear meanings not recognizable to a patient and can empathically translate his understanding into an interpretation which enlarges a patient's area of awareness.

The experience of being understood empathically by his training analyst is fundamental for the development of the student's own capacity for empathy. He learns to listen not only to his analyst's interpretations but to himself as well, to interpret his manifest behavior in terms of its latent aims and its genetic roots, and to observe his own experience with empathic understanding for the childhood selves he once was. Empathy with those parts of himself that belong to the past, that he has outgrown, dislikes, or even rejects is an essential ingredient for self-understanding; it opens the way for the understanding of others. By way of experiencing himself against something else that is also himself, new awareness, new knowledge and new professional skills emerge for the student-analyst. He discovers from direct intimate experience what it means "to make the unconscious conscious"[44] and to build ego where id used to be.[46]

The concept of the analyst's personality as an instrument of the analysis is not a new one. It was clearly recognized by Freud when in 1912[41] he described how "blind spots" in the analyst interfere with his use of himself as an instrument of therapy. But the earliest aims of the training analysis, to demonstrate the analytic method (didactic) and to relieve neurotic conflicts (therapeutic), have been expanded by the professional aim to develop the specific functions of the analyst's mental apparatus that are "instrumental" in the analytic process. This addition to the goals of the training analysis is possible because of advances of psychoanalytic psychology which afford increasing insight into the structure of the personality with concomitant insight into the interpersonal dynamics of the therapeutic process. Thus with new knowledge gained from clinical work the educational objective of the training analysis can be formulated in terms of providing an experience which develops the ego functions of introspection, empathy and interpretation that are essential for work as an analyst.

Regardless of how thorough-going a training analysis may be, it is just a beginning of an interminable process of self-analysis. This aspect of the training analysis, which has its personally protective as well as its professional value, has not been given its due emphasis in discussions of the first phase of training. An analyst may be confronted by any of his patients in any period of his professional life with one or another vulnerable area in his own personality. Healthy defensive systems and character traits are never completely immune to pressures which may be generated by work with patients, and changes caused by aging, fatigue, illness or other external events may increase the analyst's vulnerability to the challenge of a patient's demands. In self-defense, his resistance to these demands may bring about technical mistakes which are generally called countertransferences (see Chapter VI). Or these challenges may stir up symptomatic responses which could disturb the analyst's balance between health and illness. Protection against these hazards of the profession is provided primarily by the training analysis and continued in the development of his self-analytic function during supervision.

One might say that although past and present experience plays a part in all learning, the student in the first phase of psychoanalytic training makes his own experiencing a primary object of study. In the analytic "experiment" he is the subject as well as the observer of the nature, language, and mechanisms of the unconscious, and his discoveries in this situation constitute basic learning about the psychoanalytic method and its tools—introspection, understanding, and interpreting.

After the experience of analysis from the position of patient has laid the groundwork,* the second phase of the training program refines the instrument still further. The chief objective of the second phase is concerned with learning to articulate the behavioral data of an analysis with explanatory concepts and theories. This task has been described by Bruner as "going beyond the information given."[16] He defines this as a cognitive operation which seeks the coding system that establishes the relationships between the information given and the concepts which permit generalizing from one case or a prediction of probabilities. Such a cognitive operation enables the student to make sense out of an otherwise overwhelming mass of particulate phenomena which often seem to be unrelated to each other or to any "known" frame of reference. The patient's individual personal experiences are brought into the analyst's field of cognitive scrutiny where he can find equivalences in more general terms. In this way he correlates an analytic event with his learned concepts of dynamics, economics and the genetics of behavior, and he so deepens his understanding of the dimensions of a specific phenomenon. Concepts and theories provide the student with a store of new information which gives explanatory power to the knowledge acquired by experience.

Two lines of experience, developing two kinds of knowing—empathic and cognitive—are continuously active in the process of analytic interaction. These two lines are essential for the analyst's work toward a diagnostic understanding of his patient. In the second phase of his education, the ability to experience introspectively and empathically that began in the training analysis is continued and organized into cognitive structures. One might describe these two tasks, whether in the analytic situation or in the learning situation, as making first an "experiential fit" and second a "cognitive fit." They have many operations in common. Both use synthetic, integrative and introspective functions of the ego; both are inferential and interpretive in their aims; both deal with meanings "beyond the information given"; both start from a specific behavioral event whether in the past or present and attempt to enlarge the scope of understanding and knowing.

---

* To discuss the criteria for progression from training analysis to theoretical and clinical learning experiences is beyond the scope of our present study. Their formulation, however, is essential to the total educational process. In practice, the personal analysis may continue all through or beyond the other phases.

Empathic understanding, however, leads to a different kind of knowing than the explanatory coding which the cognitive process involves. The message from the patient, whose latent as well as manifest meanings are "heard" with the analytic ear, is often responded to without any cognitive mediating step. The patient and the analyst can and do interact intuitively and "unknowingly," often with very beneficial results. The "experiential fit" facilitated by empathy enables the analyst to identify the communication behind the patient's words and translate it into words not yet available to the patient. This cognitive step in the process of interpretation provides explanatory answers to the questions *why* and *how*, sometimes to be communicated to the patient and sometimes not. Making a "cognitive fit" builds a bridge between otherwise incongruous and contradictory behaviors and renders them understandable. An analyst moves back and forth across this bridge as he reconstructs the life story of the interactions of innate and environmental forces on his patient.

In the stage of active learning, traveling back and forth between these two kinds of knowing is more conscious and explicit than it becomes later. To know what one knows and how one knows it becomes part of the process of learning,[7] and to be able to express this level of insight in words becomes a significant (albeit often ideal) part of the interaction between teacher and student. The pedagogic task is to provide the situations and experiences which facilitate this learning.

One source of material for building this bridge between direct experiencing of unconscious forces and organizing the experience into more general frames of reference is the student's personal analysis. Subjected to secondary processes of thinking and to correlation with a theoretical system, the student's experience in being an analytic patient can be objectified and given more meaning when cognitive understanding of that experience becomes a goal of learning. On the other hand, concepts and theories take on added significance when compared and contrasted with a student's personal experience. This level of insight is not an explicit aim during the personal analysis, although it may happen with a rare analysand and in rare moments as described by Kris[63] when he speaks of the ego observing its own functioning. For a student of psychoanalysis, however, this kind of understanding should become a learning goal. When it is accomplished, a dimension is added to his professional work ego.

This new level of self-knowledge may take shape preconsciously either late in the training analysis or after it is terminated; it may become conscious and explicit without active incentive supplied by classroom teachers or in clinical situations. A sudden recall of an event in his own analysis may occur to a student while he is listening to a lecture and illuminate with new meaning both the analytic event and the ideas being presented by the lecturer. A step in the cognitive organization of experience has taken place;

the synthesizing function of the ego has "gone beyond the information" to a new level of integration; and knowledge has been created from experience.

Such a moment of learning gives intimations of the active preconscious metabolizing of stored experience with the inflow of new information which is the core of a creative process. Learning at this level can be compared with the therapeutic experience of working through,[57] in which defenses against change are gradually eroded, permitting shifts of energies, modifications of structure and development of more mature modes of experiencing. How to utilize the creativity of the preconscious[10, 64, 83] and build the cognitive structures that will make it more effective for the practice of analysis is the pedagogic problem at this stage of a student-analyst's development. The bridge between what happened in his analysis and a cognitive understanding of it can be facilitated by teaching which directs the student's attention to a scrutiny of that experience as a source of valuable information about technique and the analytic process. Many training analysts will disagree with this point of view, raising the objection that the emphasis on cognitive learning in the classroom encourages intellectualizing resistances which interfere with the affective experience essential for a good analysis. Such an outcome may occur, especially if the student is still in analysis. On the other hand, that outcome becomes material for interpretation and can be treated as such.

The crucial question is the teacher's method of approach to this kind of learning experience. In terms of timing, it seems to belong to courses on the theory of technique and can be introduced by the teacher's raising the question, "What did you learn about technique from your training analysis and how did you learn it?" The answers will be varied and the class discussion can be used as an exercise in on-the-spot self-observation. Such an exercise touches upon part of an analyst's job: a constant need to tolerate self-examination and to learn from it—vividly experienced in the training analysis and reinforced in classroom and supervision.

Strangely enough, many students are startled at being confronted with this question, which seems never to have occurred to them consciously. Moreover, they respond as if the objective examination of their own experience were a forbidden activity, a transgression of the role of "patient" in analysis. This is understandable in view of the fact that many students overcome resistance to "being a patient" only after great effort, but the resistance to observing that experience is also something that needs to be overcome. What the student experiences as a patient must be related to the process of experiencing and to the process of change. The factors that modify both the experiences of childhood and the childhood mode of experiencing must be identified and organized into schemata of concepts and cognitive structures that construct a framework of theory relevant to the work of psychoanalyzing.

This kind of classroom activity does not involve "analyzing" the student by expecting free-associations or by making interpretations. It consists more appropriately of a confrontation with an attitude of self-inquiry and the value of generalizing from one's own experience. Such an exercise in a classroom situation goes only a short distance on the road toward the skill in self-analysis that belongs to a competent analyst, but it takes the first steps in a direction that continues in clinical conferences and supervision. Moreover, Freud provides an excellent model for identification in this phase of cognitive learning. His own experiences in self-analysis as well as with his patients were his chief source of data for theory-building. Motivated by scientific curiosity and a search for truth, he freed himself from his transference identifications with Fliess[17] and subjected his generalizations to continuous revisions in the light of new knowledge.

It is well recognized that identification is a vital factor at all levels of learning, but its mechanisms and processes are not clearly understood. Since identification takes place unconsciously, we see only the effects rather than the process itself. We can, however, recognize the source and often the motivational determinants of behavior as it reflects the shadows of persons and events belonging to childhood development. The psychoanalytic method of reconstruction facilitates discovery and recall of the developmental experiences influential in the formation of psychic structure. Moreover, through recapitulation in the transference, a patient's childhood identifications can become conscious and the phenomena of identifying with the analyst can be observed. As these identifications are examined with all of their positive and negative carry-overs, the building of regulatory systems and modifications of ego functions can be traced.

Identification, however, is not confined to childhood, but plays a part in learning experiences throughout life. It is a powerful force in every teacher-student relationship at all levels of education and in other life situations as well. It is important for the student of psychoanalysis to learn not only about his childhood identifications, but also how he uses his analyst and his other teachers as a source of supply for incentives, knowledge and objects for imitative learning. When he achieves this degree of self-insight, he will be able to differentiate his primitive transference identifications from present-day models, and his motives for learning by identification can be more consciously integrated with his professional aims.

However, since the process of identification is such a powerful and pervasive force and, since it operates unconsciously, it becomes a problem in psychoanalytic education for teachers as well as students. Many authors have recognized it as a factor in countertransference problems seen in training analysts and supervisors. Balint,[5] Glover,[50] Benedek[9] and Szasz,[90] to mention only a few, have called attention to the tendency of analytic teachers to permit and even subtly to encourage their training candidates to establish identifications with their own points of view and techniques. Whether or not this results in perpetuation of infantile patterns of behavior depends upon the immaturity of the candidate which may be manifested in uncritical imitation of the behavior of the individual identified with or in intense resistance to a differing point of view. Anxieties and defensiveness at the root of such patterns are difficult to deal with except in the analytic situation; yet the dangers of their persistence, described by Balint[5] as stultifying to the individual student and to psychoanalysis as a science, present clear-cut problems for psychoanalytic educators.

Educators are confronted with a particularly difficult but interesting challenge since the problem stems from forces basic to psychoanalysis and related to its value systems as a developmental and clinical science. The aim of psychoanalysis—to increase the field of conscious knowledge and consequently to provide freedom for more reality-oriented choices—is at stake, but is threatened by the very forces which have positive as well as negative value for growth and learning.[54] There is no simple solution to this problem, since it is so closely related to the question of insight into resistances in both analytic teacher and student—a question which has plagued analysts from the days when Freud struggled with his own conflicts and when he recognized that an analyst can learn only as far as his complexes permit.[40]

There are many variables which influence the factor of identification in the learning of psychoanalysis. Only two will be mentioned here. One factor is the stage of resolution of the transference neurosis at the time the student begins his theoretical and clinical work. The other factor is the relative skill of the classroom teacher and supervisor in helping the student overcome resistances stemming from transference reactions.

In the classroom, displacement of transference identifications and various forms of defense offer resistances to learning rooted in dependency conflicts and ambivalences. If these inevitable conflicts and their corresponding anxieties have not been worked through in the training analysis, progression to the next phase of training will not result in optimal learning. In a recent article Langer et al.[67] describe this problem as they saw it in a seminar on the theory of technique. This paper is of interest because it is the only one of which we are aware that discusses classroom learning experiences. Lewin and Ross[69] discuss "school problems" but describe them in general terms applied mainly to supervision. Langer's paper is interesting because it describes an effort to encourage an attitude of unprejudiced objectivity toward differing points of view, a basic attitude for an analyst and for a learner in any field.

The principal problem for the classroom teacher lies in his ability to differentiate the various phenomena of identification in terms of their facilitation of learning or their obstruction of it. This diagnostic task is especially difficult in a classroom situation because of the individualized aspects of the problem and the number of persons likely to be involved simultaneously. The techniques relevant for an analytic situation do not apply, yet the mechanisms of identification which operate ubiquitously demand that the classroom teacher of psychoanalysis understand both the positive and negative aspects of the role of identification in learning and that he develop techniques for using the process constructively. The same consideration holds true for the supervisory situation and the supervisor, as will be discussed later.

In the theoretical phase of training, the clinical conference provides a variation on the classroom situation which is comparable to the laboratory in other sciences. Here the correlation of theory and practice is closer to the work of analyzing and the student has an opportunity to practice, in the sense of rehearsing—to exercise his diagnostic understanding and his interpretive technique. In the classroom he learns the cognitive language of psychoanalysis, while in the clinical conference he identifies the behavioral cues which he can then categorize as anxiety, resistance, defenses, transference, etc. He follows vicariously the technical maneuvers of the analyst, assesses their therapeutic effectiveness, and makes trial interpretations of his own. This "laboratory" experience has a stimulating effect on the student's self-observation and correlation of his own experiences, past and immediate, with that of the patient being presented or with that of the student-analyst whose work is under scrutiny. How far each individual goes in investigating his personal reactions in a clinical conference situation cannot be made explicit. Each student must follow his own path in this direction. It is to be hoped, however, that he possesses the attitude and the ability to let his preconscious processing come into consciousness. Many of his responses to the immediate situation will remain on a preconscious level to become available for insightful closures as he achieves an integration of learning from all of these different kinds of experiences.

In the third phase of the training program, the phase of on-the-job practice of analysis under supervision, learning by doing continues the experiential testing out, which has been emphasized as the basic component of learning to become an analyst. In the supervisory situation the student tries out his "analytic instrument" in vivo. With his psychic processes clarified and refined in his training analysis, exercised and strengthened by theoretical learning tasks, the student enters the final step in the sequence of training experiences. He is called upon to carry forward what he has learned in other situations to performance as an analyst with a patient, a level of learning that presents its own hierarchy of objectives and teaching techniques.

A third line of experience comes into prominence as the student enters the clinical phase of his education. This line involves learning how to translate intuitive and cognitive understanding back into "experiential" language for communication to the patient. Such a task requires an integration of empathic (affective), cognitive, and executive (decision-making) functions into the act of "making an interpretation." The various principles to be followed in arriving at technical decisions about what, when, and how to communicate with a patient will be discussed later.

The two kinds of learning, experiential and cognitive, continue to confront both student and supervisor. Learning in supervision combines experiential testing of the tools of introspection, empathy, and tactful interpretation with recognition and coding of "what works" and "what does not work." Making a "cognitive fit" in clinical learning includes increasing awareness of why "this works" and "that does not." In other words, a good learning experience in supervision goes beyond following rules of thumb or imitation of what someone else did or might have done in similar circumstances. It increases the student-analyst's awareness of himself in the interaction with his patient. In the supervisory situation, the student travels back and forth across the bridge between his knowledge of how it should be done and what he actually did. There is a constant oscillation between experiencing and observing that experience, between empathy, introspection and insightful choices for technical action, and between analyzing his patient and himself in an effort to correct his mistakes and develop creative skill in his professional work.

Both student and supervisor become involved in "instrumental" learning—how to use what has been learned and how to make the instrument work. "The concept of the 'analytic instrument' recommends itself," according to Isakower, "primarily on the grounds of its heuristic value, as a point of reference for clarification of the psychic processes which constitute the foundation of the specific analytic activity."[56] These processes that make the instrument work operate unconsciously but can be observed through their effects and can be studied retrospectively. This retrospective view of the analytic instrument in operation is a major focus of attention in supervision. The training analysis begins to assemble the tools for functioning as an analyst; the clinical phase of training puts these tools to work and develops their instrumental use; and the process of self-analysis initiated in the training analysis is continued in supervision.

In *Analysis Terminable and Interminable*[47] Freud referred to the importance of an analyst's capacity to analyze himself: "We hope and believe that the stimuli received in the learner's own analysis will not cease to act upon him when that analysis ends, *that the processes of ego transformation will go on of their own accord and that all further experiences will be made use of in a newly acquired way.** This does indeed happen and in so far as it happens, it qualifies the learner who has been analyzed to become an analyst." Kramer, in her beautifully elaborated, significant paper describing observations on the continuation of the analytic process in herself,[61] explains what she means by the analytic process going on of its own accord.

---

* Translated from the German by Maria Kramer and quoted in her paper.[61]

Because of the automaticity of the process and the spontaneity of resulting insights, she coined the term, "auto-analysis," and defined it as an independent ego function existing only in those persons who have been analyzed.

To define this process of intrapsychic activity and structural change as an ego function is an interesting question which would take us beyond the scope of this book. The total process is, of course, a complex operation employing various ego functions, each contributing to the total result. Since we are interested in how these ego resources can be developed for professional work, we find it more useful for our purposes to concentrate on the separate learning experiences that will help a student-analyst acquire the ability to use these "processes of ego transformation . . . in a newly acquired way."

The chief obstacles to overcome are the inevitable resistances. Kramer paints a vivid picture of these resistances. Freud does also in Letter 71[38, p. 221]: "My self-analysis is the most important thing I have in hand, and promises to be of the greatest value to me, when it is finished. When I was in the very midst of it, it suddenly broke down for three days, and I had the feeling of inner binding about which my patients complain so much. . . ." In the next letter, twelve days later,[38, p. 225] he writes, "Business is hopelessly bad, . . . so I am living only for my 'inner work.' It gets hold of me and hauls me through the past in rapid association of ideas; and my mood changes like the landscape seen by a traveler from the train. . . ." Later, in the same letter (p. 226), he reemphasizes the strength of the forces opposing insight when he recognizes, "Resistance has thus become an objectively tangible thing for me. . . ."

Both Freud and Kramer stress the frequent sense of failure in active attempts to follow a line of associations against resistance. Insights cannot be forced either in a formal analytic situation or in self-analysis. Every analyst learns to assess the strength of a patient's resistance at a given moment, and when his probing interpretations fail, he waits or focuses on a smaller, more peripheral area that shows signs of weakness. Insight, whether it comes in formal analysis or self-analysis, is achieved slowly by a gradual integration of many pieces of working through akin to the process of creativity.[10]

Active efforts may not bring insight with conviction[82] at the conclusion of a given period of "activity," yet a deliberate effort to use the tools of analysis on oneself opens channels of inner communication and a flow of associations, preconsciously "processed"[64] until a gestalt can be integrated. When this gestalt meets ego-syntonic requirements, it acquires a cathexis strong enough to break through barriers to consciousness, and it then appears to have been achieved spontaneously. The sense of spontaneity, however, is illusory since it does not happen without effort. An energy drain often accompanies this integrative "work" of the ego.

Knowledge about how resistance feels, and the recognition that it can be overcome are parts of the insight resulting from analysis, although the preconscious operations remain outside conscious control. This experiential knowledge is reinforced by the cognitive appreciation of concepts about conflicts, defenses and symptom formation. The ego operates "auto-analytically" within a field of forces given cohesion by the insights previously achieved in formal analysis, and theoretical knowledge provides a frame of reference for organizing the dissonant, fleeting signals of psychic activity not usually in the foreground of consciousness.

These self-analytic processes undoubtedly proceed more automatically and with less active effort in an experienced analyst. For a student whose attitude of self-scrutiny is not yet disciplined by practice, some assistance is required during the period of initiation into the work of analyzing. A natural tendency is to feel that with the shift from patient to analyst he need no longer listen to himself but only to the person on the couch. The difficult task of associating freely is now for someone else to do—or so it may seem to the student. He may tell himself with a sense of truimph, "Now *I* will make the interpretations." Although this description is exaggerated and students are now told from the beginning of training that analysis is a never-ending process for an analyst, conviction that this is so has to be learned from experience. It is in this area of practicing self-analysis that a supervisor serves as a catalyst for these processes.

In this chapter we have emphasized the role of experiencing unconscious-preconscious, as well as conscious, knowledge in learning psychoanalysis. We have described different kinds of experiences which contribute to the development of a professional work-ego. In learning the clinical science of psychoanalysis the problem does not seem to come under either the first or the second "family of learning theories."[55] Both the stimulus-response association theories and the cognitive-field theories seem to apply. The most successful learning of psychoanalysis results from a cognitive integration of associative patterns into general principles which are then applied to practice, tested for success, and modified into new forms of technical behavior. The essential step in this clinical learning, however it is achieved, lies in the development of the learner as an instrument not only to accomplish learning but also to measure it. To be able to objectify the process and to evaluate degrees of success marks the independent learner who can teach himself and who is invested in maintaining an attitude of inquiry directed toward discovery about his patients, himself and his field.

In summary, we reiterate our thesis: To make self-analytic functions readily available equipment for working as an analyst is the basic and continuing goal of psychoanalytic training. Each phase of the training program contributes in special ways to this overall goal, and each psychoanalytic teacher can enhance his effectiveness if he orients the content and method of his teaching in this direction.

— III —

Method for Study of Supervision: Our Project

SINCE WE ASSUMED THAT A STUDY OF THE EDUCATIONAL PROCESS OF supervision would increase our effectiveness as teachers, it became necessary to decide how best to proceed with such a study. How could we find answers to such questions as the following: What happens in a supervisory situation? What is taught and how is it taught? How does a supervisor contribute to the development of a student's personality as an instrument in a psychoanalytic treatment process? What kinds of learning difficulties appear in the work of a beginner compared to an advanced student? Do they change in response to supervisory teaching? How do different teachers deal with similar learning problems?

In any study of supervision, the problem of data collecting is primary and formidable. Attempts have been made to approach this problem from various angles and with different purposes. The usual administrative reports on student progress reflect this evaluative purpose but contain little information on the supervisory process itself. A number of supervisors make notes regarding the sessions but use them only as a basis for administrative reports. Others have audited supervisory hours for the purpose of teaching younger supervisors how to supervise.[69] These audited hours are then followed by conferences between supervisors. Electrical recordings of supervisory hours have been used for the same purpose by both analytic and psychotherapy supervisors.[91] Video tapes are also becoming a possible resource. Recordings of supervision have been played back to the supervisee, followed by discussion of the demonstrated learning problem.[8] Transcripts have been used for the same purpose with some economy of time.

Electrical recordings of analytic hours have been studied by supervisor and student together, and Kubie[65] has written of the advantages of using recordings in this way in order to bring the supervisor into more accurate contact with what actually happens in analytic interactions. He argues that the student distorts much of the data in his selective and condensed reporting, and that the supervisor cannot teach well if he does not know accurately and completely what actually occurred in the analysis. There is much to be said in favor of Kubie's argument, especially when the objective is study of the therapeutic process. Details of interactions can be studied and comparisons made between the supervisor's and the student's understanding of the dynamics. However, it seems to us that exercise of the associative and interpretive functions involved in selecting what to report to a supervisor is an important part of the student's learning experience and should not be bypassed. These functions play an essential role in an analyst's diagnostic and instrumental activity in the analytic process and they can be developed by his gradual awareness of the factors in himself that interfere with their free operation. These factors are revealed in the student's pattern of reporting and become an objective for supervisory teaching. If the data of the therapeutic process are transmitted to the supervisor by electrical recording, an opportunity for teaching fundamental objectives is missed.

On the assumption that interaction with the supervisor is an essential factor for clinical learning, one of us (J.F.) in 1954 began a pilot study of the events and process of supervision. Supervisory hours of psychoanalytic students were recorded on Gray Audograph discs. The material of each hour covered from 4 to 8 analytic hours plus any discussion that took place between the student-analyst and the supervisor. Each student was invited to cooperate in the project, with the understanding that the machine could be turned off whenever he wished. This occurred only very rarely; students usually became accustomed to the microphone, and the mechanics of recording did not seem to interfere with the usual procedure of summarizing a segment of the analysis. The supervisor list·ned to the student's report and made notes on the disc filing envelope. This step was considered of special value because the supervisor's silent thought processes contributed to the completeness of the data. These notations included items that indicated the dynamics of the patient, the flow of the analytic interaction, and the supervisor's associations to the material, which were sometimes discussed with the student and sometimes not. A special effort was made to note reactions by the student-analyst which indicated a learning problem. Transcripts of the recorded supervisory sessions were studied in conjunction with the notes on the filing envelopes. This procedure was based on the assumption that retrospective examination of the material would lead to a clearer understanding of the types of learning and teaching problems which a supervisor encounters. It was hoped that answers might be found to some of the questions repeatedly troubling psychoanalytic teachers.

The material of this early pilot study has not been a part of our present investigation, although the early observations were valuable as an orienting framework. Some preliminary statements from the pilot study were reported to the Chicago Training Analysts Seminar in October of 1956 but nothing has been published because of insufficient time to study the data.

The recordings and transcripts have been used, however, as a source of clinical illustrations of various aspects of the phenomena of the psychoanalytic process. These illustrations have proved of value for classroom teaching of psychoanalytic technique. Some of the students involved have benefited from study of the transcripts in obtaining a perspective on a long period of the analysis and as an aid in formulating various special problems which the particular case material demonstrated. In this respect, the material of the pilot study has also been used in stimulating investigative interests in the students.[34]

With data on supervised analysis collected in this form, it is possible for other supervisors to listen to the records or read the transcripts. Critical study of these data by different supervisors would provide checks on the diagnosis of learning problems and the effectiveness of teaching methods. The recorded material could be studied at leisure with a detached, objective, investigative attitude free of the pressures of the immediate teaching situation. For various reasons, however, no such specific project was initiated until one other supervisor (T.B.) began to record her supervisory sessions for another investigative purpose.

It was by chance that we discovered we were supervising the same students. One of us had supervised an elementary case (i.e., the first or second) of two students, both of whose advanced cases (fourth) were being supervised by the other. Our shared interest in teaching stimulated us to undertake an intensive study of the recorded material. The principal goal in the beginning was to observe the supervision conducted by each of us in order to discover (1) if we could independently identify the learning problems, the correlated teaching problems, and teaching technique used in each instance; (2) evidence for progress in the student's competence as he moved from the beginning to the later stages of the analysis; (3) evidence of changes in competence as he progressed from the beginning to the advanced level of learning; (4) evidence that teaching by supervision had any effect on the changing competence.

Both student-analysts were males and good students approaching graduation at the time our project began in August 1960. Both had terminated their training analyses before the supervision was recorded on the beginning cases. They were completing the theoretical curriculum by the time the fourth case began. These facts eliminated certain variables, such as limited knowledge of theory and the stressful impact of personal analysis, at least as far as the fourth case was concerned. The analysis of each of the beginning cases had terminated when we began to study the transcripts. One student was in the second year of analysis with his fourth patient and one was about four months along. One student had a woman patient for his beginning case and a man for his fourth. The situation was reversed for the other student (Table 1).

Table 1

Code	No. of Case and Sex of Patient		No. of Psychoanalytic Hours	No. of Supervisory Hours	Initial Frequency of Supervision	Outcome of Therapy
GB	I	F	630	94	weekly (4 Psa. H.)	terminated
HB	II	M	597	92	weekly (4 Psa. H.)	interrupted
GF	IV	M	570	48	biweekly (8 Psa. H.)	terminated
HF	IV	F	1200+	100+	biweekly (8 Psa. H.)	terminated

Table 1 presents in summarized form these facts regarding coded references to analyst and supervisor, sex of patient (*P*), analytic and supervisory hours, frequency of initial supervision, and outcome of the analysis. Both advanced cases continued in supervision after graduation of the analysts.

Supervision took place once a week on the beginning cases and continued at this rate for approximately 1½ years before being reduced to once every two weeks for the rest of the analysis (2 to 2½ years). Supervision of the fourth cases began on the basis of once every two weeks. It continued at that rate with one student for reasons of other investigative interests in the patient, while with the other student supervision was reduced to once a month for the two years prior to completion of treatment. Each patient was seen four times a week.

It is clear that an enormous mass of material was available for study. Our first task concerned the method of deriving data from the raw material in the transcripts, since psychoanalytic material, however it is recorded, is not yet data but must be subjected to interpretations referable to the problem under investigation. The number of variables which influence the collection of psychoanalytic material complicates the process of making inferences from it. It is not easy to decide what constitutes primary and what secondary data, since a process of selective focusing is inherent in the interaction between analyst and patient as well as in the report of the analytic process to the supervisor. We have commented on this point in reference to Kubie's question about methods of data collecting. The transcripts provided the basic material and contained information on many topics which could be investigated. For example, observations could be made on analyzability of the patients, on factors related to "cure," on the theory of technique, on special forms of pathology, etc. However, we confined ourselves to observations and inferences about the teaching-learning process and, sometimes reluctantly, avoided becoming involved in these other areas.

In order to reduce the total material to reasonable size for a beginning, we decided to limit the initial study to the first recorded sessions of each case. Unfortunately these were not the first five supervisory hours, since on three cases recording of the supervision was not started with the first session. Each of us initially read five supervisory hours for each student on his elementary case and then proceeded to the comparable five hours on his advanced case. Notes made on the material of each supervisory session attempted to identify learning problems and the teacher's way of dealing with them. Since we were primarily interested in the educational process, we paid special attention to the communication between the student-analyst and the supervisor. This procedure was carried out by each of us independently for a total of 20 transcripts before we compared our observations.

When findings on each of the four cases were compared, the material divided itself into observations on the therapeutic process and on the teaching-learning process. The student reported on the therapeutic process, giving a picture of the patient and of the interaction between them. The teaching-learning material consisted of exchanges between the supervisor and the student-analyst. These exchanges constituted units of each session which gave data on the teaching process. From these data observations were made on what the supervisor considered to be the immediate teaching objectives, the learning needs, and his pedagogical techniques.

As we discussed our notes, we found ourselves describing the experience of reading the written material. We discovered that we had approached the material in similar fashion and had many similar reactions. These experiences should be mentioned because they belong to a statement of our procedure and also because the insights they generated contributed to other observations on the processes of interaction between communicating systems in the therapeutic and the teaching situations. First, we read descriptively, trying to establish a feeling for what was happening. This was not difficult since even the written word permitted an empathy with the experiences of the patient, analyst and supervisor to a degree which surprised us both. We found ourselves participating vicariously in the supervisory hour we were reading.

From our discussion of this mutual experience, we turned to the role of the supervisor. We observed that we read as a supervisor would listen to a student's report of analytic material and that we reacted as a supervisor would, empathizing first with what the patient was saying and trying to diagnose the meaning of his behavior on its multiple levels. In this activity we were oriented to the role of analyst of the patient, but simultaneously we were in empathic communication with the student-analyst; as we listened to our own associations to the patient's material, we also listened to what was going on in the analyst.

Studying our transcripts, it became obvious that investigation introduces a new factor to the usual supervisory situation. The two persons present are in empathic communication with each other and with an absent third person, the patient. An investigator is called upon to empathize with all three and with the total supervisory process. For this, he must maintain distance for objective observation. This should be taken for granted and may appear to be simple to accomplish, but we became increasingly aware of the effort required when faced with evaluating our own supervisory activity. We had before us the evidence of what we had said to the student-analyst. We listened to our responses to the analyst-patient transaction, remembering our own associative thinking at the time, and it was difficult to remain detached from that vividly recalled experience and to keep the aim of investigation in mind.

This experience took place early in the study and was salutary for each of us, since recognizing the problem permitted enough objectivity to continue the study. As far as we could tell, sensitivities about differences of interpretation of the same patient material or analyst-supervisor interaction were not aroused to any great extent. Defensiveness due to exposure of teaching techniques and mistakes which inevitably occur was present but produced minimal interference. Our investment in the investigation plus the vividness of the material combined to preserve the necessary atmosphere of collaboration. The decision to undertake such a project was truly "experimental" in the sense that we had to find out if we could work together with such personal material. We came to realize that the private and individualistic nature of such data did not need to stimulate the defensive competitiveness which has so often become an obstacle to psychoanalytic clinical research.

It was gratifying to discover in the preliminary phase of our investigation that we independently identified the same material as evidence of a learning difficulty in the student and a teaching problem for the supervisor. We were generally in agreement as to the dynamics and source of each problem, whether related to the therapy, the student's learning needs, or the teacher's technique. These findings will be illustrated and discussed in subsequent chapters.

As one would expect, the teaching techniques showed great variations. Each supervisor demonstrated an individual style in the interaction with the student-analyst, and we did not always agree about the way in which the therapeutic situation between the student-analyst and his patient had been interpreted. This is, of course, a perennial problem in any field concerned with interpretations of behavior and verbal communications. Multiple meanings are always involved and the factors determining which meaning is responded to are as multiple as the meanings. However, we kept in focus the goal of the project: to identify and understand the process of communication rather than to evaluate the content in microscopic fashion.

Anna Freud, in her discussion of the panel on the widening scope of indications for psychoanalysis,[36] referred to this point. She told about a seminar organized in Vienna to study the interpretive process as it unfolded in analytic case material. Although variables of experience, the theoretical background of the analysts, and the diagnosis of the patients were "constant," Miss Freud noted that consensus on interpretations was achieved only occasionally and then usually on early material. She stated an important fact for persons working in this field to recognize: "Even though the final results might be the same, the roads leading there were widely divergent."

Conceptualizing our observations became the next—and far more difficult—investigative task. Our psychoanalytic training tended to keep us focused on the individuality of an experience. This was adequate to describe the psychoanalytic treatment experience as a process of interactions with particular motivations, but we found ourselves at a loss when we tried to conceptualize the teaching-learning experience in terms of process. We turned to social science and received assistance from the work of Lennard and his collaborators, who reported a study of verbatim material from the psychotherapy of eight patients over a period of a few months.[68] These authors were interested in approaching their material from the framework of social-interaction theory and attempted to "dissect" the factors and processes observable in therapy. We found the problem-solving concepts of Bales[3] very useful as a frame of reference for ordering our data in more general statements as well as for breaking it up into episodes that could be studied singly and in relation to the total context.

One supervisory session covers several analytic hours, each of which has a unity of its own. Our problem in examining the data was to find a way of isolating episodes that had a beginning and an end, and tracing the theme that related one episode to another to produce the dynamic line of shifting tensions within one hour, between hours, and on a time curve throughout the analytic process. This focus for study referred most specifically to the therapeutic material as reported by the student-analyst. For the supervisory process we needed to define episodes in the teaching-learning interaction which represented a particular aspect of learning or teaching and which also could be followed through the cycles of changing tensions in relation to the student's progress in learning.

The application of concepts of system interaction and the process of shifting equilibria within and between the systems will be discussed in Chapter IV. Here we need only say that the systems in interaction in supervision could be defined and differing levels of tension could be identified in terms of the events which disturbed or restored an equilibrium. The steps in the cycles of change could be correlated with the technical activity of the student-analyst and/or the supervisor. This grouping of events in interaction made possible the isolation and differentiation of learning problems and their correlated teaching problems and techniques.

In Lennard's study, the recorded material was broken up into propositions, classified according to various kinds of information which they conveyed. They were then grouped according to expectations of the patient and of the therapist; they were then studied in sequence for their effect on the equilibrium in the patient-therapist system. Frequencies for various propositions were compared, noting changes and direction of changes over a period of time.

We had set ourselves to study far too great a mass of material for such an approach. Moreover, we were interested in the teaching-learning process, whereas Lennard was invested in the therapeutic process. Consequently, we used a larger unit of interaction and ordered the material into units of exchange between supervisor and analyst. Episodes were marked out which demonstrated a teaching-learning sequence with an identifiable focus on a particular learning problem, a particular learning objective, or some general question for discussion. These units of exchange could be grouped according to the supervisor's manifest teaching aim. They could also be examined for the state of system equilibrium which existed and for teaching techniques. In the course of supervisory work from the beginning of the analysis to the end, changes and the direction of change toward learning could be noted and assessed. We also had data on changes from elementary to advanced learning situations and could note the evidence for successful learning or the lack of it as the same student analyzed his fourth case compared with his first or second.

Thus far we have described the beginning of the project and our procedure for ordering the material. Reporting our findings confronted us with other difficulties. We felt it was important not only to present a summary of learning problems and other answers to our original questions but also to give the evidence on which we based our inferences. We wanted to preserve for the reader the flavor of the supervisory experience and the various aspects of the communication process which the transcripts provided. Since there is no one way to do supervision or to study it, we were interested in making documents available for scrutiny by others who might have a different point of view. It seemed that we could best explain the supervisory process as we see it by involving the reader in empathic participation with our raw material. This material, abundantly rich in examples of relevant phenomena, consisted of over 400 transcripts of supervisory sessions totaling about 7000 pages. Since it was clearly impossible to present all of this material, our first problem was the selection of segments which would represent our findings. We decided to present examples of each case at each level of experience. Each example is divided into teaching-learning exchanges as described above. Each exchange is accompanied by comments on the learning needs and teaching techniques which it illustrates; these comments represent summaries of our shared observations and inferences.

We present selected episodes from which comparisons could be made between the learning needs of the student in the beginning and later stages of an analysis and in an elementary or advanced stage of training. With this procedure for illustrating our findings, we necessarily sacrifice evidence for the continuity of the learning experience, but we have tried to compensate by summarizing the problem and progress of each student over the period of his training (Chapter VIII).

Publishing any clinical material raises the problem of confidentiality. In our situation, this involved not only the patient who needed protection against harmful exposure,* but also the student-analysts and the supervisors who had revealed various aspects of themselves which do not usually become part of permanent records. Anxiety about adverse reactions from professional colleagues in our own and related disciplines is an understandable concern of the professional participants in such a study. We realized, however, that since these intimate personal experiences were objects for scientific scrutiny, the anxiety had to be weighed against our investigative goals and decisions regarding public revelation made accordingly. Since we were convinced of the value of making our material accessible to systematic examination by nonparticipant observers, illustrations were chosen with due regard for personal anxiety about exposure. The cooperation of the student-analysts was enlisted toward this end with gratifying success. Copies of every transcript were made available to each student-analyst. Transcripts and episodes selected for publication were read by each student, who exercised veto power if he saw fit.

The following is an example of a transcript on an elementary case.

EXAMPLE I

HB (Case II), Supervisory Session 4 (First Recorded), Analytic Hours 13-16

This is the student's second psychoanalytic case in supervision. His interest in learning and his intellectual grasp of theoretical concepts as applied to the patient material, as well as his eagerness for participation in the supervisory process, were quite evident in the first three weekly supervisory sessions which were not recorded.

The patient is a very intelligent, unmarried, white male in his late twenties. He is a talented engineer with potential for a very successful career in his field. A man with extensive interests outside his profession and well-read in psychoanalysis, he shows a quick grasp of psychoanalytic

---

* The usual efforts to disguise a patient's identity were made in these cases.

concepts as well as their application in making intellectual formulations about himself, as if in competition with his analyst. The intensity of his drives, sexual as well as for mastery, requires strong control. However, his ego-superego integration is immature and his ego controls are not strong enough to protect him against "acting out" with women as a defense against homosexual conflicts and oedipal anger at his mother.

Exchange 1

A—The material today, four hours since last time, involves two dreams, and I don't know how to tell it.

S—Don't dictate; just tell the material as you always have.

A—All right. I'll get used to it. The two dreams: he is trying to find out from me whether I think an analysis is indicated for him, whether he has the strength.

S—Now, either we can work with the Audograph or if it interferes too much with your thinking, we can't. Don't summarize.

A—O.K. Last time—you know, I block a little bit, but I think I'll get over it. He came in last week with a feeling of accomplishment. He had a burst of self-discipline. He filed his application for the new job and had been almost beyond the time limit. He communicated with the Book Club that he hadn't been communicating with and that had caused him a lot of trouble with his parents. So he had the feeling that really he's doing something for himself. He then reports that he feels different in several ways because of the treatment. One, he feels more sexually aggressive.

Comments: This exchange reveals *A*'s tension about being recorded. There is a change in his manner of reporting. *S* recognizes the change and, already aware that it might disturb *A*, she advises him not to dictate and reassures him that the supervisory work is more important than the recording. It can be stopped if necessary. Evidence of some strain remains, but the tension in the *S*⇆*A* relationship is less and *A* continues reporting without too much difficulty.

Exchange 2

A—(Continued reporting about *P*'s sexual activity.) Then the next association brings us to a telegram from his father which says, "Call home at your convenience." He leaves his associations about his sexuality and talks about concern for his parents. Then he breaks his associations about his father's telegram and asks my advice about his plans for changing his job. But he does not give me a chance to answer; he says, "Apparently I am putting you in the position of my father which I always did—that is, never to really let him advise me because I always thought I knew better than my father." Then, in talking about the job, he found out, apparently—I don't know if it was in this hour or the next, whether it happened last week, it slipped my mind—he found out by the grapevine that there is a likelihood that he would not get the desired job this year, anyway. So he worried and then he says, "But after all, I have never been denied anything that I really wanted." [Without interruption, A continued to report the associations of the patient that refer to a repetitive dream that had been told and analyzed partially in previous sessions.] Now he added that whenever he was constipated in the past, if he wanted to get his bowels to move he would think of the repetitive dream in which he was being chased in a dark building and this would cause him to defecate.

S—Why, do you think?

A—Well, I don't see the evidence for it in the dream. "In a dark building" has something to do with sexuality, but I don't know exactly what.

S—Why should that cause the bowels to move?

A—It's my hunch that there's probably some fusion of the sexual function with the aggression.

S—No, I think this is farfetched, too theoretical. In fact, there is a tension. He even knows that this is the measure of his anxiety. I mean, one can be "too dynamic" about things and omit considering the simple physiological relation.

A—Yeah, that is right.

S—So, he knows that "when I am anxious enough my bowels move."

A—This man is scared.

S—The underlying homosexual meaning of the dream does not need to relate to the bowel movement directly; the bowel movement is the direct reaction to anxiety. The cause of anxiety is the homosexual conflict.

A—But I mean, what makes you see homosexuality in this dream of being chased in a dark building?

S—This is one of the typical homosexual anxieties: being attacked from behind. He talks about it, he dreams about it. You do not need to go into the unconscious motivations yet, but his associations started with anal material. Then hiding semen from his mother—the anxiety—bowel movement.

A—Yeah, yeah.

S—It seems you are surprised.

A—I am not surprised; I am just learning something. (He laughs.) I know all these things in little pieces but sometimes it is hard to put them together.

Comments: In this exchange, S orients A toward the technique of interpretation, indicating the necessity for understanding the material empathically—i.e., by vicarious introspection. The next step is to connect it with the cause of the anxiety. It is then up to A to decide whether this can be communicated to the patient or not. From A's responses to S, however, it seems that he integrated from this interchange more of what related to the dynamics of the patient than what was the other intention of S—namely, to indicate to A the step-by-step process of interpretation.

The word "us" in the second sentence of this Exchange is a significant characteristic of this analyst's participation in both the analytic and supervisory experiences. With this small word he bridges the distance between the $A \leftrightarrows P$ and the $A \leftrightarrows S$ systems, including himself in the former and bringing S in also—a good example of system sensitivity (see Chap. IV).

S might have questioned A about the transference manifestation in P's asking him for advice and comparing A with his father. She did not do so, however, since P was already using a defense of intellectualization, and to question A might have introduced too intellectual a note too early in this $S \leftrightarrows A$ relationship. She comes to it in the next exchange.

The teaching technique here shows how S proceeds to orient A to the ongoing dynamic process in P. She alerts A to associate to the communication from P as a story of P's experience in the here and now, and then to look for its possible motivation. (Compare with the interaction above when S chose not to focus on the transference meaning of P's associations.) A participates with S by asking questions and S answers not with explanations but with questions to stimulate A's associative functioning. A cannot answer the questions and for a moment is blocked. Then he reviews the material on which S's formulation was based. He reacts with surprise and pleasure, revealing the emotional impact of this bit of learning. Such step-by-step teaching occurs again in this same supervisory session dealing with material of the next exchange.

Exchange 3

A—Then, after talking about toilet training and so on, he comes at the end of the hour once again to wanting advice from me about his problem of the job. He implied the possibility that a change might also necessitate leaving town—that is, to interrupt the analysis.

S—Now, how did you handle this?

A—O.K. First of all, I say to him, "Do you really think that I am qualified to advise you in this particular aspect?" And he says, "No, I probably don't want you to advise me; if you did, I probably would not listen to you." So I said to him, "Well, what are you really asking me?" "Well, what I am really asking you is this: Do I really need analysis? Will it really help me? Is this really my chance to get what I want, which is to get help?" So I say to him, "This is hopefully what analysis will accomplish for you. I can't guarantee anything but I see every reason why this should be of some help to you." And he says, "Well, can I take it though?" So, remembering what you (S) told me last week—you know we were talking about how do you analyze a person whose defenses are very shaky—you told me in terms of interpreting a dream—last week the dream was about malignancy—you told me that the way you handled it is to let the patient know that you know how scared he is. So I did this, and my words were something like this, almost like I just said it. After he said, "Am I strong enough?" I said, "I realize how frightened you are of your feelings." And he said, "Remember that dream about malignancy?" I said, "You've been telling me over and over again that you have no physical complaints; obviously you don't have physical malignancy to worry about, and you once told me that you were malingering. You are dreaming of malignancy in terms of your feelings and your understanding of your problems. I understand that you would like to go away, on one hand, and on the other, you would like to stay and work it out." And I added, "Let's make it work out." And that's the way that hour ended.

S—Then you were prepared for this hour?

A—I was really prepared (laughing); it was right up my alley. Next time he comes in and starts the hour: "Should I go on with analysis . . .?"

S—He wants more reassurance.

A—He says he doesn't want my reassurance.

S—He wants more and more reassurance. Now we shall see why.

A—All right. He says. "First of all, I may be making a mistake changing my job, I don't know." Then he asks again, "Will analysis help?" Then he says that he really does not clearly see his problems but he knows they affect his life. The next association seems to be a break from this, but it is not; he tells me stories how he had close shaves in the past on bicycles and in automobiles. He would run his automobile as close as he could to parked automobiles to see how close he could get without accident. Then, after a while, he comes back to the theme that he is afraid I will reject him on the basis of not having enough problems for analysis—and then "I was very frightened yesterday when you told me that my problems are malignant." (A laughs.) So I said, "Now, wait a minute, I did not say anything about malignancy. You raised the issue of malignancy, and I told you that you are fearful of the malignancy of your problems." So we clarified the issue and then he told me a dream that he has kept for two days from telling me. [In order to conserve space we have omitted the verbatim account of the dream.] It was full of symbolic references to the primal scene: The climax seems to be "cows were waiting to be slaughtered by the machine." Finishing the dream, the patient went on spontaneously with his associations [these A summarized in his presentation, indicating the main topics]: (1) the problem of the job, his ambivalent attitude about it, and his envy of those who have the same kind of job; (2) he has to save mother from father, yet he is ambivalent toward mother; he worries about her health, yet plays with the idea of her death. He attempts to evaluate his problems himself.

S—What do you think about the meaning of this dream?

A—I made some marginalia when I was abstracting today. I was trying to read them now. I wrote too small.

S—Try to think about them; don't read them.

A—O.K. The first is that he is waiting and searching for the woman. Then the women who come on the scene are slaughtered. He is expressing his yearning for the woman and his sadistic impulse toward the woman.

S—I think that you had recognized earlier that this problem influences his decision about the job and/or causes his hesitation about it. The origin of the sadism might be related to father, but where we stand now—on the superficial level—the current job problem might stir up his sadistic impulses.

A—There is further material two to three hours later that confirms this, because he is talking about marriage and why he does not want to get married.

Comments: In this hour, *A* demonstrates his tact and sensitivity toward the patient. He deliberately uses what he learned from *S* in the previous session to reassure *P* and strengthen the therapeutic alliance. He makes a point of telling *S* how he handled a situation in which he was trying to keep the patient in analysis while at the same time avoiding involvement in the role of "advisor." He also reveals that remembering what he learned in the previous supervisory session was a great help. His integration and use of *S*'s explanations illustrate the developing learning alliance. Also, his inclusion of *S* in his field as he recalls the $A \leftrightarrows P$ interactions, is an indication of an ability to work simultaneously on multiple levels of relationship. This is an ability not always developed to this degree in the early stages of an analyst's career.

In this segment of the $A \leftrightarrows P$ interaction, *A* describes *P*'s conflict between the necessity for working out his problems and his wish to flee from the analysis. *A* demonstrates that he carefully followed the hesitations, oscillations and contradictions of *P*; that he perceived that the crescendo in *P*'s associations had the aim of convincing *A* about *P*'s need for treatment even if *P* still experienced ambivalent doubts.

S perceives in this presentation *A*'s satisfaction with his own diagnostic functioning. During his long presentation, *S* probably was able to convey to *A* her own satisfaction with him—although it was not verbalized.

In the last remarks of *A*, he demonstrates a grasp of the ongoing process of movement in the analysis. He presents evidence that he recognizes how associations verbalized in one hour reveal meanings more deeply buried at that moment but which come closer to the surface of consciousness after a period of time and further analytic work. (The material of these later hours has been omitted from this illustration.) *A*'s remarks here indicate an active synthesizing and interpreting function during a supervisory session. He has accomplished an important learning objective and is using his associative functions well in the service of his professional work (see Chap. V). In this session, *A* spontaneously offers his associations to *P*'s material. Often this activity must be stimulated by *S* with various teaching techniques.

SUMMARY

Placing this part of the first transcript of HB in this chapter, we attempt to illustrate our method of studying the material. Each exchange demonstrates the flow of *A*'s presentation and *S*'s response to it. Each unit reveals to the investigator a series of problems. Attention in this illustration has been focused on that aspect of the problem which was verbalized on the conscious level of communication between *S* and *A*; from this information the supervisor's teaching aims can be inferred: (1) *S* reassured *A* about the recording being secondary to the supervisory experience; (2) *S* oriented A about technique of interpretation; (3) A demonstrated his excellent communication with P and with S, establishing the "therapeutic alliance" with P and strengthening the "learning alliance" with S. Thus both systems seem to move in parallel equilibrium at this time.

In developing our concepts of the supervisory process, we tried to follow the lines of the immediate teaching-learning problems as they were presented by A. In this short analysis of this incipient $S \leftrightarrows A$ relationship, it is obvious that S stores preconscious perceptions of the student for elaboration when and if it will become necessary to use them. For example, S, noticing A's tension about the recording, became aware of his sensitivity to exposure; and considering the importance of that anxiety for the $S \leftrightarrows A$ relationship, she gave reassurance. She also registered the effect of her reassurance, the "recovery" of A. In the second exchange, S noticed A's response to "learning," his almost glowing satisfaction. In the third exchange, S was aware of A's pleasure in presenting his material as he did. Granting him his satisfaction and even participating in it, she considered the possibility of learning problems arising from that gratification.

The following summary of the activity in this supervisory session is a sample of our method of noting initial observations and inferences about student and teacher behavior:

1. Initial tension in A and in the $S \leftrightarrows A$ system is relieved by reassurance from S and by A's cooperative effort.

2. His reporting is clear, not notebound, although he gives quoted evidence for the dynamic shifts in P's associations and accompanies this by an account of his own introspection as well as his interactions with P.

3. His rapport and empathy for P are good. He follows the dynamic lines, demonstrates system sensitivity (see Chap. IV) and acts to maintain a therapeutic alliance.

4. A is less clearly aware of the manifest level of transference expectations in the $A \leftrightarrows P$ system. He has a tendency to intellectualize, as does the patient—a problem recognized by S.

5. The $S \leftrightarrows A$ relationship is good. A's motivation for learning is strong and he tries to integrate and to use what he learns from S.

6. Among many possibilities, S chooses to emphasize several teaching tasks:

   a. She warns A against permitting his theoretical knowledge to intrude into the analytic process.
   b. She teaches him about using his associative functions and introspective capacity.
   c. She concentrates on his observation of P's dynamics, and his awareness of the motivations for his responses to P.

– IV –

The Supervisory Situation and the
Supervisory Process

AS WE PROCEEDED WITH OUR STUDY OF THE VERBATIM MATERIAL OF supervisory sessions, our attention became concentrated on the processes of interaction between communicating systems in the teaching-learning relationship. This experience led us to examine in detail the structure of the supervisory situation and the factors which contribute to the effectiveness of the educational process. We were struck with the parallels between the analytic and the supervisory situations and found ourselves in agreement in many respects with Arlow,[2] who has described similarities and differences between them. In this chapter we will attempt to elaborate in some detail the structure of the supervisory situation as we see it, in relation to its goals and the activity of the supervisory process.

When we tried to follow the communications between analyst and patient and between student and teacher, what stood out in great clarity were the phenomena of process—that is, the sequential series of actions linked in a continuing pattern of shifting balances of tension moving toward a goal-directed change. Since such phenomena are inherent to the process of analysis, they are observed by every analyst, although for the most part conscious attention is more often focused on individual phenomena than on the reciprocating sequences that make up the whole movement. In our material, however, the sequential series could be identified. Moreover, as we observed the factors which facilitated or disturbed the balance of tensions, it became equally clear that both the facilitating and the disturbing factors made up the content of the communication between student and supervisor. The student's learning difficulties and mistakes with his patient were targets for corrective supervisory activity, but they were combined more frequently than was anticipated with teaching aimed at more positive learning goals. These observations enabled us to construct a diagram of the supervisory process of communication and the various activities it might include over the course of a supervisory experience (see Chart I). We have thought of this diagram as a model, not in the sense of ideal, but in the sense of representing general classes of events in supervision. It

50

attempts to convey the idea of movement toward long-range goals and the teaching activities of the supervisor (S) as he works with the student-analyst (A) to assist him in the analysis of his patient (P).

Before proceeding with further explanation and discussion of the different items in Chart I, we feel it will be helpful to review concepts of structure, system interaction and process, since we found them useful in describing supervisory events and in providing a framework for organizing our observations in more general terms. We stress them in this chapter because they offer a wide-angle view from which the total educational experience can be seen in breadth as well as in depth.

Concepts of interaction between systems in communication with each other and of processes which alter dynamic equilibria are not new to psychoanalysis. Indeed, they are a basic part of the professional learning of an analyst. Freud's thinking moved along this line in his early work on aphasia[37] and in the project[39] when he attempted to correlate mental activity with a theory of interrelated pathways in the central nervous system. Gradually, his ideas turned from an anatomical concept of structure implied in the term "system"* to the concept of structure as an organization of functions, the whole given cohesion by tensions of forces in various states of equilibrium.[11]† In other words, functions give structure to the systems operating in a field of tensions. These tensions activate processes of change that modify the structures and the behavioral reflections of psychic activity. These concepts have facilitated understanding of normal and pathological behavior and have contributed to the principles of technique which promote the psychoanalytic treatment process.

Process implies movement and change as differentiated from notions of a fixed, immobile state. The significance of this idea is given perspective by Whyte,[94] who relates the advances in philosophic and scientific thought in the nineteenth century to a shift from static to process concepts. Naming Darwin and Freud as the two persons who gave the greatest impetus to this advancement, he writes: "This great transformation found its best known expression in the development of evolutionary ideas but it coincided closely with the progressive recognition of unconscious mental processes. *By showing that organic species and individual minds are fundamentally modified by the processes in which they partake, these two thinkers carried on the transformation of thought which had already begun."* (Italics ours.)

---

* Among the many definitions of the concept "system" we found most appropriate to our purpose the following: "A system is two or more units related such that a change in the state of any one unit will be followed by a change in the state of that unit."[95, p. 402]

† For a more extensive review of these concepts see Beres D.: Structure and function in psychoanalysis. Int. J. Psychoanal. 46:53, 1965.

Ever since Freud published his recommendations for the beginning of a psychoanalytic treatment,[41] the psychoanalytic situation has been viewed as a structured interpersonal relationship which resembles an "experiment" in the degree to which its conditions and procedures are relatively constant. Stone's essay[89] on the psychoanalytic situation elaborated further on the dynamics of this special relationship and how the procedures (couch, frequency, rule of free association, etc.) set the stage for the action of the process. He emphasized how the structure of the situation provides a stable frame of reference within which the interactions between the personalities of the patient and the analyst mobilize intrapsychic processes in each that work toward therapeutic changes in the patient.

Some of the same principles and basic technical operations apply equally to the supervisory relationship. Overtly, the supervisory situation is a dyadic relationship between supervisor and student-analyst. However, since each member also functions in relation to a third person, the patient, we found it useful to think of the supervisory situation as a triadic system composed of subsystems in a complex process of communication with each other $(S \leftrightarrows A \leftrightarrows P)$. Each person in the triadic system is a member of a dyadic subsystem which, under certain circumstances, operates independently of the third component. For example, the therapeutic dyad of analyst and patient $(A \leftrightarrows P)$ forms the therapeutic system, whereas the teaching-learning dyad $(S \leftrightarrows A)$ constitutes a separate subsystem within the supervisory situation. In this subsystem, the analytic process between analyst and patient becomes the focus of supervisory teaching.

Within this total complex, there is a secondary set of subsystems: the intrapsychic systems of each member of the triadic constellation. The intrapsychic apparatus and its functioning in each of the three persons make up the basic units for the transactions of both the therapeutic and the learning processes. It is the psychic structure and functioning within the patient that the analyst works with for therapeutic purposes. The analyst's own mental apparatus becomes the instrument for this work and also for learning. For teaching, the supervisor uses his own intrapsychic equipment to promote both the therapeutic and the learning processes.

The structure of both the analytic and the supervisory situations is determined primarily by the goal which each participant expects to accomplish in their work together. These ultimate expectations, whether therapeutic or educational, orient the behavior of each member and guide their interactions through many vicissitudes. Expectations of giving and receiving therapeutic help initiate a bond of trust and confidence between analyst and patient without which analytic work cannot proceed. Freud[41] introduced the concept of *therapeutic alliance* to describe this relationship in the analytic situation. In supervision there exists the same necessity for acceptance of a mutually shared educational goal and the same need for confidence that the expectations of teacher and learner can be satisfied. The term *learning alliance* describes the essential characteristic of this relationship.

Motivation for health or learning, trust in the mutuality of goals, and confidence in the ability of the helper to help are the factors which the patient or the student bring to these respective relationships. When coupled with the motivation to help on the part of analyst and supervisor, an alliance is established and a state of rapport is manifest in each situation. Rapport, which is an expression of emotional resonance and intuitive understanding in a relationship, varies with the degree of ambivalence contributing to the tie. It has been called positive or negative, according to the amount of hostility involved. "Good" rapport or "bad" rapport is a result of gratification or frustration of various needs and fantasies originating in either party. These qualities of rapport are determined by the balance of need tensions operating between members of each system. This balance is easily disturbed by responses from one party that do not meet the expectations which motivate the other party at a given moment. When the tension resulting is too great in either subsystem, a strain is put upon the fundamental alliance and progress toward the mutually accepted goal is threatened.

Since the processes of interaction are also structured by goal-directed procedures and techniques in both therapeutic and learning situations, the balance in the systems, $A \leftrightarrows P$ or $S \leftrightarrows A$ must necessarily be intentionally disturbed from time to time. In fact, the essence of either the analytic or the supervisory process is the activity on the part of analyst or supervisor which regulates the disturbance of equilibrium in the system so that the variations in tension do not exceed the tolerance of any unit. It is the perceptiveness with which the causes of disturbance are diagnosed and the skill with which they are modulated that promotes the movement of analysis or learning.

As these observations on the structure of the analytic and supervisory situations took shape from examination of our transcripts, it became necessary to review separately the phenomena of the analytic process. These phenomena make up the reservoir of knowledge about the process and techniques of analysis which a student needs to comprehend and make his own if he is to move beyond the imitative or rule-of-thumb level of professional skill.

Teaching the student to regard psychoanalysis as a process is the most important and probably the most difficult of the supervisory tasks. Process needs to be differentiated from procedures and techniques, a distinction which Isakower has stressed.[56] In our study of recorded supervisory sessions, this teaching goal was a common denominator for all of the supervisory events. Though not always explicit, it could be demonstrated when looked for. Procedures and techniques also consumed much supervisory effort, partly because, being specific and definite, they are more easily taught.

More significantly, however, procedures and techniques are not only integral to the movement of the process of analysis, but learning about them is essential for understanding that movement. Hence, the abstract concept of process, even vaguely perceived by a student, serves as a background on which the clinical phenomena and the mutually facilitating relationship between the specific elements and the total process take shape and position, moving along a visible course. Like blips on a radar screen, specific phenomena so identified acquire more meaning when related to what they have come from and to what follows next. When these behavioral events are viewed in the perspective of their dynamic, economic, structural, genetic and adaptational dimensions and on the axis of change over time, they become units in a pattern of goal-directed process in which the analyst and the patient play instrumental roles.

Implicitly, if not explicitly, concepts of process and system interactions have become part of an experienced analyst's habitual way of thinking and acting. Such is not the case, however, for a student-analyst. Old habits tend to keep his observations on the surface or he is too easily satisfied with "typical" inferences and cliché responses. Supervision, however, provides the experience for building different ways of thinking and behaving as the student is taught to follow the process of an analysis which he is conducting. Specific procedures and techniques are part of this learning, but as the analysis goes on the student comes to recognize that procedures such as the couch, the frequency of sessions, the 50-minute hour, and even the rule of free association do not make an analysis; that *his* understanding is not the patient's; and that one interpretation does not result in insight.

As the student learns to follow the shifting tensions generated by the frustration or gratification of the patient's expectations, he learns to identify them as reflections of internal resistances, anxieties, conflicts, and transference phenomena. The statement is often heard, "He empathically understands the situation"—a statement which refers to a complex perception of many factors. Lennard and co-workers[68, p. 195] have applied the term "system sensitivity" to this quality of the analyst as "instrument" which intuitively registers the quality of rapport in the therapeutic alliance and the intensity of resistance, source of anxiety, frustration tolerance, and level of regression in the intrapsychic system of the patient. By way of his capacity to perceive the state of the total system (P, A, and $A \leftrightarrows P$), the analyst arrives at a diagnostic inference which influences his response to the patient.

We borrow again from Lennard the term "system responsiveness" to explain the task of the analyst to remain oriented to the therapeutic goal while he simultaneously takes into account the stresses in the system and responds appropriately. His system-responsiveness will enable him to regulate the timing and dosing of interpretations to facilitate the analytic process rather than to impede it. Analytic "tact" is a comparable term, although we feel that both "system sensitivity" and "system responsiveness" are terms more inclusive of the complicated dynamics of the situation and the process going on within it. Both sensitivity and responsiveness are essential factors in making a technical decision and in acting on it. Such a "system sensitive act"[68, p. 195] tends to keep the dynamic stability of the system on the optimal level for progress of the analytic process. The choice of content, the amount of information to be offered to the patient and the moment for exposure will reflect not only the analyst's understanding of the system but also his ability to adapt his responses to its needs. Sometimes it is best to permit the moment-to-moment disturbances of equilibrium to continue for the sake of ultimate movement of the process, but not beyond the tolerance of the patient to maintain a basic alliance for the long-term work. It is his appraisal of this tolerance which indicates adequate or inadequate system sensitivity in an analyst.

Adequate understanding and appropriate responsiveness do not always proceed hand in hand, however. Empathic awareness of the tensions in a moment of analysis, and even a correct understanding of their meaning, may not be accompanied by technical interventions adequate for the total process. Greenson[53] has termed this incongruity the pathology of empathy. He describes two types: inhibition of responsiveness in spite of good understanding (see Example 2); and loss of control of responsiveness, resulting in interventions uncalled for in relation to the analytic goal (see Examples 13 and 17).

Actually these are only two kinds of incompetent analytic behavior indicating difficulties which come under the broader term "countertransference." Internal resistances in the analyst which block his understanding in one way or another, leading to "blind spots" or other "flaws" in his analytic instrument, require supervisory teaching effort. It is this area in the teaching "process" that emphasizes the necessity for the student-analyst to pay close attention to his participation in the system $A \leftrightarrows P$ and to the operation of his instrument. Here the role of self-analysis in the smooth functioning of the analytic process comes under examination by student and supervisor. Sharpening his diagnostic perceptiveness directed toward the patient is only part of a student-analyst's learning (as we have discussed in Chapter II and will take up again in Chapter VI). When he learns to turn his observing ego on his own experiencing as well as on the patient's, and to recognize how his own motivations affect the analytic process, the student completes the necessary steps for full comprehension of the circuit of communicating systems. There remains, however, the necessary experience of working through the integration of this comprehension to the level of insightful application in practice. Supervision is an excellent vehicle for this working-through phase of the learning process, a fact which became clear from our transcripts when we saw how much supervisory effort was spent on developing system sensitivity and system responsiveness in our students.

It also became clear that these capacities so significant for the therapeutic interaction were likewise significant for the teaching-learning relationship. The supervisor's empathy for understanding and for appropriate responses operates in two directions, encompassing both the $A \leftrightarrows P$ and the $S \leftrightarrows A$ systems of interaction. This task includes, of course, sensitivity to the intrapsychic processes and tension states of P, A and S himself. He "oversees" the $A \leftrightarrows P$ interaction and thus becomes a "participant-observer" in the treatment process as he influences the student's understanding, his attitude toward the patient, and his technique of interpreting. Functioning as a sideline participant, the supervisor sets in motion in himself the same diagnostic skills in response to the patient which he uses in his functioning as an analyst. At the same time, he assesses what the content, rapport, and therapeutic progress of the communication between analyst and patient have been during the period about which the student is reporting. As his own scanning, hovering attention covers the interaction in the triadic $S \leftrightarrows A \leftrightarrows P$ system, the supervisor becomes a resonating instrument on two levels. As a therapist he responds to the needs of the patient and evaluates the student's interventions; as a teacher he arrives at an "educational diagnosis" followed by pedagogical decisions appropriate to the learning process. Supervisory work requires an even greater span of system sensitivity than is necessary for analytic treatment. Attuned to the patient and the analyst, the relationship between them, and to the progress of the analytic process, the supervisor must also be sensitive to the tension level of the student in relationship to himself. Just as the analyst's empathic perceptiveness and responsiveness are instrumental in establishing a therapeutic alliance with the patient, so the supervisor's empathic perceptiveness and responsiveness are instrumental in establishing and maintaining a *learning alliance*.

Many factors intrinsic to the supervisory situation support the learning alliance or create problems that burden it. Some of these factors belong to the student's side of the relationship. A strong motivation to know and to master is a positive asset which will carry the student through stressful periods of ignorance, uncertainty, and self-searching. Such motivation plus mutual confidence and rapport are fundamental to a good learning alliance. Neither supervisor nor student can expect completely smooth sailing, however, and they must be prepared for disturbances stemming from personality problems on both sides of the relationship. Our transcripts offered many varieties of such disturbing factors. They will be illustrated and discussed in the examples to follow.

It is the supervisor's responsibility to understand the experiential nature of the learning tasks which confront the student and to realize that intense, unconscious forces can be stirred up in the student by the learning situation as well as by the patient. Emotional responses to the supervisor as a person, to his exepectations of the student, and to his pedagogic interventions are all an intrinsic part of the supervisory experience. Sometimes conflicts are generated by realistic appraisals of the negative effect of a supervisor's attitudes or teaching techniques. It is the supervisor's task to recognize what aspect of a given learning problem or tension in the learning alliance originates in reactions to the patient or to something in the supervisory situation. His ability to understand the vicissitudes of the educational process, to manage the complex system interactions within the supervisory relationship, and to integrate the roles of therapist and teacher will determine his effectiveness as a supervisor. These tasks present many difficulties to a supervisor.

Among the obstacles to a clearer comprehension of the educational process is the persisting controversy regarding the double role of the supervisor. There have been heated arguments over whether a supervisor is a therapist or a teacher—as if the two roles are mutually exclusive. This question has occupied psychoanalytic educators since supervision became a formal part of training (see Chapter I). It would seem obvious that a supervisor is a teacher whose special aim is to teach a student-analyst how to conduct an analysis. The difficulty seems to us to be not so much in defining a difference in role as in being able to reconcile the factors that are common to the goals of therapy and education. Every supervisor is also an analyst. His professional identity is that of a therapist who is imbued with a theory of therapeutic technique which, for the most part, avoids the more familiar instructional tactics. However, the objectives of teaching and treating actually have much in common, since both experiences may deal with irrational neurotic obstructions to progress. In fact, close examination discloses that the same basic philosophy underlies both education and therapy—that is, the value of integrating impulse, affect, and intellect for the development of a mature individual.

It is true, nevertheless, that an analyst trained as a therapist rather than a teacher often feels under stress when he becomes a supervisor. The new role is conceived of as a sharp break with what he is accustomed to doing. Indeed, the shift requires many crucial adjustments and development of skills over and above what is required for work with a patient. The analyst who becomes a supervisor must be able to move from a position in which he feels familiar and at home to a role he may even have unconscious resistance to meeting—teaching someone else the skills of his craft. The change involves his relation not only to the student but to the patient as well. As a supervisor, he is no longer the primary therapist in the picture, but must exert his therapeutic influence through another person. This is not always easy and often evokes a sense of helplessness and even anxiety when the student's mistakes seem to threaten the patient's safety.

Becoming a teacher of theory in a classroom is not so difficult. The shift in relation to the student is relatively clear-cut and easily accomplished. The role expectation in the classroom is more familiar, more structured; the task is instruction on a general plane. Problems of intimacy, privacy, and deeply rooted affectful experiences which belong to the therapeutic relationship do not arise in the classroom in the same way. They do appear, however, in supervision where emotional blocks to learning stand out in bold relief. These interferences with the learning process based primarily on neurotic conflict require pedagogic "treatment" for which special teaching techniques need to be developed.

There is another aspect of a supervisor's teaching equipment which is also beyond what is essential for conducting an analysis: a supervisor must have very clearly in mind what he himself considers good technique and how he puts the theory of therapy into practice. This task is not so simple, since so much that occurs between an analyst and his patient takes place on a preconscious, intuitive level, not readily available in communicable language. Nevertheless, a supervisor should be able to objectify his own working habits, to formulate the psychoanalytic process in general terms, to recognize how particular events in an individual analysis are correlated with general principles of technique, and to be able to explain all of this to a student in relation to the student's behavior with his particular patient. How a supervisor develops this knowledge and these skills is a complex question, and we are forced at this point to be satisfied with stressing the need for a supervisor to be as much of a continuous learner about the supervisory process as he is about analysis itself.

In the following example, we want to illustrate the main points presented in this chapter thus far: first, the supervisory situation which can be symbolized as $S + A \leftrightarrows P$ to show how supervisor and student work together focusing on the interaction between analyst and patient; second, the supervisory relationship, $S \leftrightarrows A + P$, to show the varying levels of tension and the supervisory efforts to maintain a good *learning alliance* while at the same time promoting the analysis of the patient; third, the functioning of S as an analytic instrument in relation to P and how, in this instance, her sensitivity to the two systems $A \leftrightarrows P$ and $S \leftrightarrows A$ was reflected in her responses to A in the service of promoting his learning and his development as an analytic instrument himself.

EXAMPLE 2

GB (Case I), Supervisory Session 13 (First Recorded), Analytic Hours 52-56

The patient was an attractive, unmarried white woman in her twenties, with hysterical character structure. She showed good ability for introspection and observation of her own emotions and an unusual capacity to verbalize them. She was referred by her obstetrician, who recognized that her illegitimate pregnancies carried to full term, with the babies then given up for adoption, indicated deep-seated conflicts. The youngest child in the family, she was six years old when her father died suddenly. This necessitated her mother's going to work and probably influenced the asthmatic attacks the patient had had as long as she could remember.

In the first 12 supervisory sessions (unrecorded), S took notes of the significant content and of her impressions of A's interaction with P and with herself. These are abstracted here since they lead to formulation of the diagnosis of A's learning problem.

In the first three supervisory sessions A reported the history. P had talked in a freely associating manner which A had followed with adequate diagnostic acuity. S noted that in spite of his "literary flair," A appeared inhibited in his communication with P and also in the presentation of his material to S. In one of these sessions A expressed doubts about P's commitment to analytic treatment. S differed with him, pointed out her evidence, and noted to herself that A's awareness of P's commitment was impeded by his defense against being involved.

In the next supervisory session A reported "an unusual experience." After the next analytic hour, he had developed an acute vasomotor rhinitis, which he had never had before, but which is one of P's symptoms. After the rhinitis subsided, A recognized that he had tried to solve his problem with S in the same way P tried to solve her problem with him in the analytic situation—that is, by developing symptoms. In this context A revealed to S that he had felt criticized by her in the previous session.

This piece of self-analysis was helpful to A; its frank reporting was helpful to S; it revealed the motivation of the previously noted tendency of A to withdraw from P by inhibiting his empathic understanding of her. The potential over-reaction to P—identification and withdrawal—and the tendency to overreact to S by considering her interventions as threatening represented learning problems. On the other side of the ledger were A's ability for introspection and self-scrutiny and his sincere wish to learn and master his difficulties.

About the twelfth supervisory session the "learning alliance" seemed to function well enough for S to broach the problem of recording the supervisory sessions. A agreed.*

---

* Probably the agreement as well as the almost unnoticeable reaction to the recording machine was the consequence of the fact that S at that time intended to study the material for a special research interest in P's pathology, not for the supervision itself.

Exchange 1

A—The patient first talked about her fantasies about me; she was conscious of her wish that I be in competition with her boyfriend for her, yet she added defensively that she knew that the struggle was inside her. She continued saying that she had been suppressing her feelings of resentment against me because I did not answer her questions. After this she tells me a dream—she calls it a "funny little dream"— of that morning. She was not sure whether she was standing up or lying down. She was doing both in the dream and as she is lying on the couch; she's along this wall in my office, pressed to the wall.

"I was lying this way. Then there was a space and a dresser, maybe like a cliff, maybe a kitchen cabinet or sink; it was white. A cockroach came out at one end, crawling along the ledge. I looked; I just watched to see what would happen next. I was fascinated. The cockroach changed slightly as it went. As it reached the edge of the ledge it did a U-turn, hit my side on my flesh, then it was gone and I woke up. It was so real that I had to touch myself."

I asked her to associate to this. At first she talked about having had cockroaches where she lived, in the same building as her boyfriend. They both had cockroaches in their apartments and in the next apartment there were no cockroaches and she almost missed them.

S—Almost missed them?

A—Yes, because they're a living thing and she was totally alone there. There was not even a cockroach. (Laughs.)

S—Reminds me of Kafka.

A—She brings out she's afraid they will bite her. She says she is afraid of the movement, and then she starts to associate to this and brings out a vague memory from childhood. She thinks of the summer when she was nine years old, standing behind a gate with wooden slats, and seeing into a yard.

S—Seeing what?

A—Looking into a yard. She does not remember what she saw there, but she thinks the fear started at that time.

S—She remembers the feeling which she felt when she looked?

A—She didn't say. She just implied that this was the incident when her phobia of bugs started. It was very vague.

S—It is vague, but I think it is significant. It sounds as if it were a screen memory—she looked at something—she does not know what she saw. These vague feelings of children are significant. I think of a patient of mine who lost his father when he was—I don't quite remember—four and a half to five years old. The patient often repeated in the analysis how he used to look through the window with vague feelings of sadness, watching the rain quietly falling on the gray ground of the yard. In that patient's nostalgic fantasies it was always fall weather and it always seemed like the weather at the time of his father's funeral. It had a tremendous fascination for him, these depressive, nostalgic feelings of his childhood. Why do you smile?

A—I was just thinking—why did I not ask her to elaborate on this? And I just thought of that because I had some sort of feeling about the kind of summer she was talking about, from my childhood: the bees and wasps, the fruit ripe, the idleness of the summer when nobody is around and you wander alone—you know.

S—Yes, this kind of nostalgic feeling is significant for several aspects in the child's development.

A—The age of nine, that was the time when her sister went to work; her sister graduated from high school. When the patient was nine, her sister was eighteen; mother worked, sister went to work, she was left alone. That's when her asthma got bad.

S—The dream that she relates now about the cockroach—that is also the feeling of being left alone.

A—Well, she goes on with this. I asked her what other things she is afraid of. She was also afraid of dogs—the neighbors had a bulldog—she tells a story. The policeman's dog chased her; she became afraid of dogs. Then she said, "As a child I had a repetitive dream of being covered with insects crawling all over my body. It was a horrible nightmare," she says, and she laughed as she said, "Now there's only one insect left."

S—The cockroach?

A—Yes, the cockroach. She says, "The cockroach is a symbol of being with people, of being a part of something, of having a group of friends, a family."

S—(Laughing.) How do you like that personification of cockroaches?

A—I didn't believe it. I think the cockroach must be a part of herself that she does not like.

S—Yes, but when you say you don't believe it, I have the impression that you don't believe that she felt as lonesome, as closely connected with the cockroach, through her anxiety, as she described it.

A—I haven't thought about that. I don't know—you might be right—here she switches immediately. She talks about the movie she went to see; it was the psychoanalytic movie.

S—Even if she exaggerates a little, there must be a reality to her longing, to her lonesomeness. Seeing the psychoanalytic movie might be a defense: she does not want to think of the cockroaches anymore.

A—She said the movie was very good; she brought up a lot of things it stimulated in her. But the hour was over; she did not talk about it anymore. That night she had another insect dream.

S—You see, the insect dream was related to the analysis. It was your couch. In that insect dream she indicated that she was lying with her face turning away from you; going to the psychoanalytic movies she turns away from the internal turmoil that the cockroach symbolizes: her anxieties, creeping fears. The symbol is the admission of the depth of her anxiety which is covered up by all the roles she is playing at work and with men, etc. But within is the crawling, crumbling feeling of anxiety. She mentions the childhood feelings and the anxiety dream repeatedly. This being covered by insects, "crawling insects," may be just the dream manifestation of a remembered skin sensation, but it might be something else too. Next time when she brings it up, try to get closer to her feelings.

Comments: Reading and analyzing the $S \leftrightarrows A$ interaction, we can follow step by step the manifestation of learning problems and S's responses and teaching technique: (1) A reports perfunctorily about P's transference attitudes; S does not respond to them. (2) A reports with much associative detail P's dream; S refers to the feeling tone of the dream; to this A does not respond. (3) But he continues with P's associations, which bring to the fore a childhood memory. (4) The memory indicates to S the connection between the affective content of the current dream and the childhood memory and attempts to direct A's attention to it. (5) A does not respond to this and concentrates on the psychopathology.

All through this, the communication between S and A is careful, almost groping, until (6) S decides to follow her own associative thinking and reveals it to A with the intent of mobilizing A's feelings. This intervention is successful. It breaks through the defensive uninvolvement of A. (7) He smiles and responds with an emotionally charged memory of his own, sharing it with S. (8) S keeps the attention focused on P. (9) A responds by recalling anamnestic data of P and interprets their genetic significance. (10) As if with this interpretation the experience were finished, A withdraws from the emotional currents that motivate P's associations. (11) S attempts to keep A's empathy invested in P by interpreting P's behavior as defense against the emerging unconscious material and to connect the dream with P's reactions to A and the analytic situation. (12) S terminates the exchange with the recommendation, "Next time . . . try to get closer to her feelings."

Considering this sequence of the $S \leftrightarrows A$ interactions from the point of view of the fluctuating equilibria and the teaching task, we can observe the interweaving process in teaching. We can differentiate the teaching tasks posed by the inexperience of A from those caused by his defensive uninvolvement; yet these two ingredients of learning problems act together like factors in "symptom formation." The avoidance reaction is noticeable in the beginning of reporting about transference attitudes of P, and even more in his reaction to P's dream and her recall of a screen memory. In A's report of the $A \leftrightarrows P$ interaction, S recognizes A's growing tension; his associative-diagnostic functioning with P is inhibited, and his response to S is evasive. S responds by recalling her own associative thinking in the current situation to indicate implicitly how A might have functioned. This relieves the intrapsychic tension of A; in response to S's intervention A recalls the memory which would have been his associative response to P if he could have permitted it to enter his mind. As if the intrusion of his own memory would have been confusing to him in the analytic situation, he suppressed it. This intrapsychic block explains the inhibition of his responses to *P* and also to *S*.

An elaboration of *A*'s fantasy as revealed to *S* certainly should not be communicated to *P*. But a more experienced analyst would have permitted the memory to enter his consciousness, even would have perceived its significance for himself, and yet by separating his memory from the memory of *P* would have freed the path to understanding of *P*. *S* could have selected this interesting combination of the effect of inexperience upon the empathic understanding of *A* as a subject for discussion. Yet, responding intuitively to *A*'s sensitiveness about his inexperience and his defensiveness about his emotional reactions, *S* felt satisfied by the result of her intervention and did not disturb the attained equilibrium.

S's avoidance of "intellectualizing" the teaching might have been motivated by her impression that the significant problem in this exchange was *A*'s withdrawal from *P*'s feeling of defended dejection in the dream—her lonesomeness and longing in the screen memory. Indeed, *A* does not "believe" the feelings in their symbolic expression. Thus *S* directs her teaching to indicate the significance of empathic understanding of *P*'s feelings in the dream and in the present and future analytic situation, thus keeping the learning alliance in equilibrium.

The pressure of the material to be presented, of the problems to be discussed, did not permit either *A* or *S* to dwell long on the pleasurable sensation of equilibrium. The student hastened to report the next analytic session.

Exchange 2

A—After the patient talked at first about the cockroach dream, she talked at length about a book she was reading currently. It was Margaret Mead's *Male and Female*. She associated to it: bringing up children, teaching them about sex and elimination. The patient added she has heard that children are proud of their bowel movements and this was very bewildering to her. She talked in detail about the attitude of her family toward elimination and toward sex; everything connected with the body was dirty, forbidden. Then she was silent. She seemed anxious, waiting for me to say something. Finally, almost crying, she said, "I want you to say something." And I still kept quiet for a while. When I felt she really could not take it any longer, I said—I think I made a mistake here—I said, "It seems that you want me to approve of this intelligent discussion that you have made."

S—Intelligent discussion?

A—I said that and she was terribly hurt. She said, "I wanted to know what you think. I know now because you are sarcastic." I told her I was not sarcastic; the discussion was intelligent but there was no feeling in it; it was not relevant.

S—Not relevant? Why wasn't it?

A—This chicken really came home to roost afterwards. She really rubbed this in. I had the feeling while she was telling me all this that she was sort of marking time, intellectualizing. This was what I wanted to tell her, but I didn't think of what I was saying; I said irrelevant, which it wasn't. So she rubbed this in; she said, "Aren't you concerned with what I think too?" So I said, "Well, I think the point is that you want assurance that you are a good patient," and she said, "Yes, I would like to hear that, but I also want to know whether what I say is right or wrong." So I said, "You want to hear, 'well done,' about what you said."

S—Yes, this might be true, but I think it is not a problem now. The problem is that she was very anxious—I think of the cockroach dream; she identifies herself, her internal turmoil, with the cockroaches. Intellectualization can be a defense against her emotions, and your problem is how you could convey this to her without hurting her feelings. She has been hurt already.

A—Well, something about her need to talk in intellectual terms.

S—I would have said, "You talk about these bookish things because this helps to overcome your anxiety," or something like it. She needs approval. But approval is a part of teaching a child; a child learns better, grows better, if the parents approve. If you connect it with the anxiety it sounds different. If you just say, "You need approval," it sounds like a reproach. This girl cannot take this now, even if she sometimes deserves it.

A—Well, she switched again—talked about the weekend and there was a long silence. I asked her what she was thinking and she said, "How nice it is to be quiet." I almost got the feeling that she said, "Well, if I don't have to be a good girl, I don't have to talk."

S—Being quiet, where? What I mean is this: there is a difference. How nice it is to be quiet, not to talk because one is spiteful, or how nice it is to be calm inside so one does not have to talk. You are thinking of her anger at you and her spiteful attitude; I am thinking of the anxiety, her uncalmness within, which she wanted to talk down. The steps were fast: the cockroach anxiety, intellectualization, and now calming down.

A—Yes, she went on talking about how upset she got earlier in the hour when I didn't answer: she had an uncanny feeling, everything spun around, she had her eyes closed, she felt she could not move, she was part of the couch; and she noticed that since then she hadn't moved her left arm. That's the arm nearer to me.

S—Yes, and she can talk about it in past tense. The affects ebbed away.

Comments: The transcript reveals a quick change from the calm $S \leftrightarrows A$ interaction in Exchange 1 to a marked increase in tension, tone and tempo in Exchange 2. This change is not unexpected by *A*. He is aware of the mistake he made and its consequence. Thus he reports (1) the disequilibrium in the $A \leftrightarrows P$ system, "I said that she was hurt; this chicken came home to roost." (2) *S* responds only with questions which underline the inappropriateness of *A*'s remarks. *S* does not even attempt an explanation of the motivations of *A*'s behavior, since the tension, the state of disequilibrium in the $S \leftrightarrows A$ system, causes too much resistance to learning. (3) *A* reports his attempts at reassuring *P*, to repair his analytic posture and to reestablish equilibrium in the $A \leftrightarrows P$ system. (4) *S* is not satisfied since *A*'s comments to *P* have an undertone of reproach. She recognizes that *A* has failed to understand *P*'s use of intellectualization as a defense against her anxiety. She informs *A* of this, pointing out that his technical problem is how to interpret this defense without hurting *P*'s feelings and so increasing the tension and resistance in the $A \leftrightarrows P$ system. (5) *A*'s response to this instruction manifests not only his continued irritation with *P*, but his persisting uncertainty about how to interpret to her. (6) *S* explains how she would do it and implicitly orients *A* to his task of empathizing not only with *P*'s anxiety and defenses but with a regressed ego state which calls for careful dosing of interpretation. In the remarks by *S*, these dynamics and technical tasks are not spelled out as they might be, since such elaboration would be too big a dose for *A* at this time. (7) *A* does not respond to *S* directly but continues with his account of *P*. His irritation with her is still present. (8) *S* again informs *A* about possible dynamics of a calm mood, differentiating a spiteful silence from silence due to lack of internal tension. (9) *A* reports that *P* describes the internal turmoil earlier in the hour and the immobility resulting from her unconscious defensive effort to get closer to *A* and to handle her hurt and anger. These affects disappeared and in this way *P*, rather than *A*, restored the equilibrium in the $A \leftrightarrows P$ system. At this point there was less tension in the $S \leftrightarrows A$ system also.

Considering now the teaching problem posed by *A*'s mistake, what prompted the mistake? *A* seemed to be aware of only one factor, his irritated reaction to *P*'s intellectualizing. But why should that be so irritating? *A*'s reporting reveals that he did not understand the "relevance," the dynamically defensive purpose of *P*'s retreat to her intellect. He recognized the use of her intellect, felt it as resistance, but neither cognitively nor empathically identified her behavior as a defense which might be interpreted with relief of tension. This lack of understanding and of technical know-how created uneasiness in *A* which influenced his inappropriate response to *P*. His uncertainty motivated him to rely on known techniques such as silence. This response only served to increase *P*'s tension and to underline his own sense of inadequacy. The result was to "take it out on *P*" with a critical remark which disturbed the therapeutic alliance. *A*'s not knowing and his lack of tolerance for it are clearly demonstrated here, explained by a mixture of inexperience and vulnerable self-esteem.

In responding to the immediate teaching problem, *S* might have informed *A* of her interpretation of what motivated his untoward behavior. Considering, however, the unusual sensitivity of this student to criticism, *S* did not feel that the emotional climate of the supervisory situation would be conducive to learning if she actively proceeded along the path of confrontation. Instead, *S* took into consideration *A*'s awareness of his mistake, his evident anxiety over S's reaction to it, and decided to handle in another way his resistance to learning.

This example with its two exchanges demonstrates several points about the supervisory process. Here we have focused on the interacting systems in the supervisory situation, on the phenomena of changing tensions, especially in the learning alliance. Illustrated in this example is the system-sensitivity of the supervisor that simultaneously directs his attention toward the problems of the therapeutic process and the learning needs of the student. Here we see a demonstration of the supervisor's activity in diagnosing learning difficulties and learning needs, and in making pedagogical decisions. We also want to comment on the way the supervisor's teaching technique in these two exchanges made use of principles of psychoanalytic technique.

In the first exchange, the learning problem was primarily A's inhibition of his empathic involvement with P. He reacted to P's nostalgic mood but resisted letting himself know what he felt and held back on revealing his experience to S. He was also unable to translate his empathic response to P into meaning relevant to her experience with him (transference) and to integrate this with a technical response. In this instance A was experiencing reactions similar to P's but found it difficult to differentiate his own feelings and use them therapeutically. S recognized A's involvement with himself and that a confrontation with this professionally inappropriate behavior would only increase his difficulty. Exposing his lack of technical skill would probably have increased his resistance to listening to her and would have interfered with learning. S, empathizing with A as well as P, chose to respect A's resistances without interpreting them, to intervene in his self-preoccupation only as far as she felt he could tolerate it, and to wait and see if he could get over this inhibition with this much help. There would be time to go into it further if A's block persisted as a technical and learning handicap. The empathic sharing of experience, freely expressed by S, appears to have benefited both A and P. S not only had used her empathy but also had offered an example which A could imitate. She did not make even a confrontation of A's counterresistance, but she did follow the principle of timing and dosing of interpretations according to the level and degree of resistance in the student. In this respect, she "treated" A's learning problem pedagogically.

In the second exchange, the learning alliance was openly disturbed. S was acutely aware of how A had upset the therapeutic alliance with P. In this instance S empathized more directly with P and communicated her disapproval to A, but again without confronting him directly with an interpretation of his motivations. She again empathized with A as well as P. Diagnosing his difficulty as largely inexperience and intolerance of not knowing, S supplied the gaps in his knowledge and thus relieved some of his tension in the supervisory situation. She also gave him an example of how to interpret to the patient. Giving him information and a model to follow relieved his sense of inadequacy so that learning and the analysis could proceed. The teaching technique again closely adhered to the principles of psychoanalytic diagnosis and interpretation in the sense of providing new information.

The analysis of this example illustrates how the trained system-sensitivity of the supervisor, his dynamically oriented understanding of preconscious motivations, and his system-responsiveness serve the several purposes of teaching. With these analytically trained capacities he senses meanings communicated by the patient which are not appreciated by a student-analyst; he establishes and maintains a learning alliance; and he directs the self-observation and the self-analysis of the student.

Impressionistic and elusive as the supervisor's activity appears to be in the actual teaching process, the study of our transcripts enabled us to dissect the interweaving processes of the supervisory situation and to differentiate a variety of objectives in the supervisor's activity. Independently, both investigators recognized in each record (whether it was a case supervised by herself or by the other investigator), (1) the general and particular problems of learning and how the supervisor dealt with them; (2) the student-analyst's immediate response in the interaction with the supervisor; (3) the effect of the supervisor's teaching upon the student's responses in interaction with his patient.

Viewed from another level of abstraction, in the short-term interaction of one supervisory session we could differentiate further the following phases which represent the sequences of movement in the supervisory process: (1) A communicating to S about P; → (2) S responding diagnostically to this information differentiating what belongs to P from what belongs to A; → (3) S responding pedagogically, focusing on selected teaching targets; → (4) A responding to S from (a) himself, (b) his experience with P, and (c) his reactions to S; → (5) S responding to the information from (4) diagnostically and pedagogically; → (6) A communicating directly or indirectly to S his responses to previous supervisory sessions and their effect on his work with P; (7) S evaluating A's overall progress and responding accordingly.

Phases 1 and 2 constitute the beginning of the process of interaction between A and S and the collecting of information which forms the basis of further action. Phases 2, 3, 4 and 5 make up the active teaching-learning interactions. Phase 6 provides a measure of progress in learning whose degree and pace influences phase 7, where S evaluates himself as an effective teacher as well as A as an adequate learner.

Classifying the events in these phases, we were able to abstract a general pattern of the aims and teaching tasks constituting the supervisor's teaching activity. We organized these data into a chart (Chart I) which has been mentioned earlier and will now be discussed in more detail. The

Chart I.—Model of Supervisory Activity

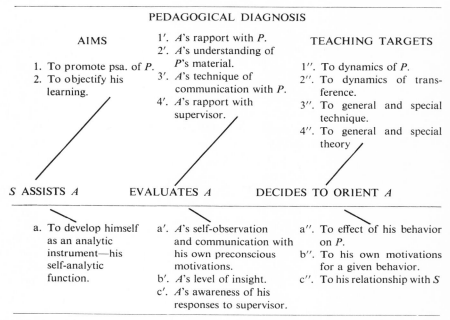

PEDAGOGICAL DIAGNOSIS

AIMS

1'. *A*'s rapport with *P*.
2'. *A*'s understanding of
   P's material.
3'. *A*'s technique of
   communication with *P*.
4'. *A*'s rapport with
   supervisor.

TEACHING TARGETS

1. To promote psa. of *P*.
2. To objectify his
   learning.

1''. To dynamics of *P*.
2''. To dynamics of transference.
3''. To general and special
   technique.
4''. To general and special
   theory

S ASSISTS *A*   EVALUATES *A*   DECIDES TO ORIENT *A*

a. To develop himself
   as an analytic
   instrument—his
   self-analytic
   function.

a'. *A*'s self-observation
   and communication with
   his own preconscious
   motivations.
b'. *A*'s level of insight.
c'. *A*'s awareness of his
   responses to supervisor.

a''. To effect of his behavior
   on *P*.
b''. To his own motivations
   for a given behavior.
c''. To his relationship with *S*

chart is composed of three main columns, overall aims, pedagogical diagnoses, and teaching targets, each of which is divided into a upper and a
lower area by a line which extends horizontally through the whole. On
this line, the supervisor's functioning *to assist* the student-analyst by way
of *evaluating* his analytic behavior and *orienting* him to theory and correct technique is represented in relation to the three columns. The line
itself is intended to call attention to the fact that the content of the $S \leftrightarrows A$
transactions includes both conscious and preconscious aspects, both interpersonal and intrapsychic processes.

Chart I is designed in such a way that by reading along the horizontal
line and following each phase of supervisory functioning into the respective columns above and below the line, one can find represented the general varieties of teaching activity which may occur in any one supervisory
session but which should occur repeatedly at some time or other during
the course of a supervised analysis. For example, starting from the left,
moving to the right and above and below the line, we find that *S* assists
the student to attain a given aim. In order to do this, *S* continuously evaluates the "material presented," which should include the student-analyst's
participation in the analytic process and in interaction with *S* (see Chapter
V). To this information, whose meaning is only partially conscious in the
reporting analyst, *S* responds on the conscious level with a diagnosis of

A's prevalent learning need and with a decision to orient A to what S considers to be either a corrective aim or one which expands A's knowledge. Within his own intrapsychic system at the same time, S responds to preconsciously perceived cues, his own marginal, peripheral thoughts and impressions, since, even though his decision to orient A becomes explicit, the decision is rarely arrived at by conscious deliberation. More frequently, it is the result of an intuitive understanding of what is "needed" to promote the psychoanalysis of P and to develop A's insight into the analytic process, including his part in it.

Throughout the multitude of exchanges between himself and A, S keeps in mind the overall (long-term) aims of the supervisory experience (Chart I, left-hand column): (1) to promote the psychoanalysis of the patient; (2) to expand the student's knowledge and help him objectify his learning; (3) to assist him in developing himself as an instrument in the psychoanalytic process. Aims 1 and 2 are placed above the horizontal line since they refer to teaching goals achieved mainly by cognitive processes and deal with knowledge more consciously available. Objectification of learning (Chart I, 2) is accomplished partially by the student when working up his case in preparation for supervision (see Chapter II). It is evaluated by S on the evidence of how well A utilizes supervisory teaching and according to his ability to formulate problems relevant to the clinical process or to theoretical implications. The relation between specific patient material and the general theory which it exemplifies is subsumed under this overall aim. The third aim of supervision—to assist A to develop himself as an analytic instrument—is placed below the line and designated as the letter a, rather than numeral 3, to differentiate the unconscious, intrapsychic aspects of this aim. (The same shift from numerals to letters is followed in the middle and right-hand columns below the line.)

The middle column of Chart I includes the areas of information which S uses in evaluating A's work with P and the progress of his learning. Listening to A report about the analysis, S picks up cues which help him assess A's competence and come to a pedagogical diagnosis of the learning problem. Difficulties may appear in any of the four areas above the line or the three areas below. Areas $1'$, $2'$ and $3'$ indicate A's adequacy in maintaining the therapeutic alliance, and in using his empathy to understand and to respond appropriately to P. Area $4'$ refers to the learning alliance and gives indications to S relevant to A's motivations for learning or his manifest resistance to it. On the basis of his evaluation of A's rapport in the supervisory relationship, S decides whether the learning difficulties, if any, lie in that area primarily.

Below the line, area a' refers to A's capacity for self-observation and introspection, basic to the functioning of his self-analysis and use of himself as an analytic instrument. Area b', A's level of insight, refers to the results of his analytic work on himself and indicates his relative freedom from intrapsychic obstacles to working as an analyst. Area c' gives a measure of A's awareness of the way he works in the learning alliance, how conscious he is of his responses to S which promote or retard learning (see Example 3). Evaluating A's functioning in these areas (a', b' and c'), S diagnoses the presence or absence of a learning problem which requires attention directed toward self-analytic functions or which indicates more formal analysis.

The evaluative task of the supervisor (just described with reference to the middle column of Chart I) requires further comment before proceeding to the topic of teaching targets. Study of our recorded material revealed that this activity went on continuously and, most of the time, intuitively. It was such an integral part of the supervisory work in the course of every supervisory session that it would seem one might take it for granted as one does the diagnostic-evaluative functioning which occurs in the work of an analyst with his patient. There, however, the activity concerns only the patient and the therapeutic goal. In supervision, a supervisor's diagnostic evaluations involve a more complex series of personality factors.

These factors are relevant to a student's aptitude for analytic work, his unanalyzed resistances to learning in general or to learning from a particular patient or supervisor, and the development of his capacity for self-analysis and skilled responsiveness. Assessment of these factors contributes to the decision regarding his competence to analyze independent of a supervisor's "overseeing" eye.

Included in this assessment, although usually on an even more unconscious level, is the complicated network of motivations within the supervisor, such as his preconceived expectations of a given student and his investment in teaching. (The latter can often be compared to the exaggerated therapeutic ambitiousness of a student.) The supervisor's ability to become aware of his own defensive reactions to a student's resistance to "being taught" is another aspect of a supervisor's self-observation. It cannot be taken for granted that a supervisor's teaching interventions are always free of inappropriate emotional responses or even "blind spots." Our experience demonstrated again and again the necessity for a supervisor to listen to and evaluate himself in interaction with his student; and it is our opinion that the more aware a supervisor is of the various aspects of his educational role, the more effective he will be as an object for identificatory learning and as a developer of students in general.

A clear picture of his responsibility for evaluating performance, diagnosing learning needs, and making pedagogic and administrative decisions about them is what we would like to establish at this point. We have stressed the point of view that the personality of both student-analyst and teacher-analyst provides assets and handicaps for the respective therapeutic and educational tasks. What we wish to emphasize here is the necessity to take into consideration a complex of overlapping factors. In making an "educational diagnosis," each factor should be balanced in relation to the others before coming to a pedagogical decision.

Some factors, such as *aptitude* for analytic work, are more basic than others. One usually assumes that, before beginning supervision, the judgment has been made that aptitude is present. This is not always the case, however, as our experience and the records of any institute can testify. Another factor almost equally fundamental and even more pervasive is the amount of *experience* which a student has had in analyzing. A first case naturally causes more anxieties and defensive reactions due to inexperience than a fourth case does. Inexperience with certain types of pathology or therapeutic problems may be of significance even after a student has analyzed several cases successfully. The specific learning difficulty should be weighed against aptitude and experience and also against the *level of theoretical learning* which a student has achieved. This last factor is especially relevant to the theory of transference and of technique, both being somewhat empirically treated in the literature and in the classroom. When aptitude is adequate, a supervisor evaluates not only the amount of experience and theoretical knowledge to which the student has been exposed, but also how well he is able to apply this learning in practice.

In supervision, as in the analytic situation, the diagnostic task does not lead to a syndrome with a label, but to a formulation of the multifaceted complex of surface behaviors in relation to deeper psychic functioning. In the supervisory process, such a formulation may focus on the patient or the student or the analytic process, or it may turn to the supervisor and the interaction between student and teacher (see Examples 2 and 3 in this chapter). This aspect of supervisory work is not only a large part of what a supervisor does in trying to understand what is happening in the analytic and the supervisory situations, but he also needs to understand how he arrives at his diagnostic conclusion, since this becomes a part of the content of what is taught. It is closely related to the first step in the sequence of activity required for arriving at an interpretation (see Examples in Chapter VI, section on Technique of Interpretation). A supervisor's mind is trained to organize his observations in the multidimensional frame of reference of psychoanalytic theory, and students expect to learn from their supervisors how to achieve this skill.

Each step in the supervisory process requires the operation of the supervisor's system-sensitivity and system-responsiveness. Each communication he makes to his student involves all these functions and is determined by his selection of an area in which he thinks the student demonstrates a learning need. This learning need may represent either a deficiency of knowledge or experience or it may represent an error in analytic behavior.

Whatever the diagnosis of the learning need, the supervisor proceeds to do what he thinks is indicated. He calls the student's attention to the problem in one way or another and sets up the opportunity for the student to look at it with the diagnostic-interpretive processes already described. Each step in the supervisory process (the teacher-learner interactions) is only one of a series, just as in the analytic process. One step may include only a small fragment of the interaction between analyst and patient or in analyst or patient alone. Each step moves from one level of learning to the next, more advanced, more complex, including a larger fragment of the total process, encompassing more events and more levels of meaning.

The supervisor is usually the one to select the event to be focused on for immediate examination. He also selects the mode of viewing. By this we mean that the supervisor determines how the analyst proceeds to study the event selected. If, for instance, the supervisor offers his own description and formulation as in Example 2, then the student starts his learning by passively looking at the diagnostic processing of observations by another person's mind. This kind of experience is similar to looking at a picture projected on a screen. In the given instance, the boundaries, composition, and focus are set by the supervisor, but the student may also be drawn into the action of diagnosing when the supervisor omits several parts from the larger picture and calls his attention to the gaps which the student-analyst is expected to fill in from his own perceptions and introspective work (see Examples 2 and 3). The student-analyst's own associative and interpretive functions become actively involved: his own analytic instrument sharpens the focus, establishes relationships and builds the meaning of the whole event. Thus, the segment to be examined and the method of examining it determine the complexity of the learning task in a given moment of supervision. The supervisor's choices are a reflection of his pedagogical diagnosis of the student's level of experience, his particular learning difficulties, and his capacity for using his self-analytic functions.

In Chart I, we have listed these targets of a supervisor's teaching efforts in the right-hand column. Since it is impossible to itemize all of the various problems on which a supervisor concentrates attention, we have combined them in very broad areas with both specific and general import. Items 1″, 2″ and 3″ above the line correspond roughly to items 1′, 2′ and 3′ in the middle column, since they have to do with understanding the patient and using proper psychoanalytic technique. Item 4″ is a target chosen when the student's level of knowledge and experience permit or when the patient presents questions of special theoretical interest.

Focus on general aspects of technique (3″) or theory (4″) requires a capacity in the student to translate experience into concepts and, in turn, to use the concepts to widen the field of experience. These two teaching targets, insofar as they deal with general theory, are beyond the learning problems posed by a given case and relevant to the correct diagnostic-interpretive work with that patient. They are even beyond the learning needs having to do with fundamental habits of analyzing, such as the posture of freely hovering attention, continuous self-inquiry, etc. For this reason, we have termed this teaching target "surplus teaching." Our study demonstrated that it occurred more often in advanced cases or with students who had mastered the elementary aspects of technique and who had good empathic communication with their patients (see Example 15). They also were not burdened by resistances to learning but demonstrated curiosity about theory and an investigative interest which permitted the supervisor to bring in areas for discussion in addition to the immediate necessities of the given therapeutic process. Such interest in theory which extends farther than the purely technical "how-to's" should be basic attitudes in all psychoanalysts, whether their primary investment is in practice or research. When it is possible to provide "surplus teaching," the supervisory situation has proved to be a valuable research training experience.[34] These discussions stimulate questions not answered by what is "known." Formulation of such questions expands scholarship and the scientific range of students and supervisors and adds a dimension of intellectual creativity to the experience of both.

Selection of a teaching target from among many alternatives is influenced by all of the factors that go into making an educational diagnosis. In any one supervisory session, there is much that could be discussed, but the time is limited and S must decide what learning problem takes priority, considering also the effect his intervention may have on the learning alliance. We have represented in Chart I this decision-making activity by the phrase "decides to orient A." To orient is a general term that includes clarification, explanation, instruction—in other words, to teach regarding the varieties of topics in the right-hand column of Chart I.

Decision thus involves not only the target but the pedagogical technique. When we reviewed the teaching techniques which we observed in our transcripts, we were able to group them under four headings which seemed to describe a range of supervisory tactics: (1) clarification or calling A's attention to some gap in his information or understanding of the patient; (2) confrontation, or calling A's attention to a countertransference or a mistake in technique; (3) demonstrating S's analytic work habits; (4) prescribing or telling A what he should do.

Each of these general patterns of teaching technique seems to include several possibilities, such as simply calling attention to an event in the analysis, questioning its meaning or correctness, explaining something beyond A's level of experience (see Example 2) catalyzing his own analytic apparatus, or recommending a course of action (see Example 3). Closer examination of the differences in these tactics show how a choice of one or another possible tactic is influenced by the pedagogical diagnosis and the supervisor's effort to advance the student's learning. For instance, as demonstrated in Example 2, if S thinks A's aptitude is adequate but his experience is insufficient, he may indicate a failure to take some factor into account in understanding a particular event and explain his own understanding of the event, or he may simply raise a question and leave it to A to fill in the gap with his own recall of peripherally perceived cues that can now be fitted into new meaning. This aims at developing A's diagnostic or interpretive skills and at compensating for a lack of experience or knowledge. Confrontation[21] rests to a greater extent on S's diagnosis of flaws in A's analytic instrument which need correcting, whether they be rooted in defensive counterreactions or more serious countertransferences (see Chapter VI and Chart III). Depending on his estimation of A's insights and ability to introspect, S may actively participate in catalyzing A's self-analysis at certain points (see Chapter VI, section on Self-Analysis). If both experience and system sensitivity are in question, S may resort to demonstrating his own chain of associations to P's material or interpretations he might have made were he the analyst of P. Then, again, if there seem to be serious doubts about A's aptitude or his countertransference resistances, S might prescribe an interpretation to be made by A, or prohibition of an acting-out behavior in relation to the patient; or S might strongly recommend more analytic work for A, a change of supervisor, or even withdrawal from training.

These different teaching tactics seem to be based on a fundamental strategy of teaching which follows three principles: first, that the teaching-learning process is similar to the psychoanalytic process and takes into account the necessity for diagnosis, interpretation, and the working through of resistances by both student and teacher; second, that the supervisory process progresses through numerous short-term tasks but in an orderly progression through objectives of increasing complexity to a long-range goal, the development of the student-analyst as an analytic instrument; third, that to achieve this long-range goal the supervisory experience trains and exercises the self-analytic faculties of the student in relation to the patient without attempting to analyze his personal conflicts.

This brings us to the teaching targets below the line in Chart I. Depending on his diagnosis of the learning problems and its cause, S may decide to intervene (to orient) A regarding: a″—the effect of his behavior on P; or b″—his own motivations for a given behavior. These two targets are clearly related to a′ and b′ in the middle column under the line. Supervisory interventions call attention to learning problems in these areas, exercising in one way or another A's self-observation, his skill in introspection and integrative functioning. Teaching tactics in these two target areas are also directed toward bringing in sharper awareness A's understanding of the psychoanalytic process (a'') and his participation in its progress (b''). Further discussion of these points will be found in Chapter VI, especially in the sections dealing with the technique of interpretation and self-analysis.

The third point on teaching targets that are concerned primarily with some difficulty in A himself is indicated by c''. Supervisory effort takes the form of explicit interventions in this area when the tension in the $S \leftrightarrows A$ relationship rises to a high level. This condition is usually accompanied by a strong resistance to being taught. It corresponds to the educational diagnosis which Ekstein and Wallerstain[29, p. 139] have categorized as a "problem about learning," differentiated from a learning problem. The latter refers to the difficulties with aptitude, experience, knowledge, and the counterreactions which are more manifestly defensive and not as deeply rooted as other countertransferences (see Chart III). Learning problems of this sort can be dealt with in a variety of ways and supervisory teaching tactics do not encounter the resistances which they meet when the countertransferences involve the supervisor as well as the patient, or are more specifically directed toward the supervisor for whatever reason. Both of these last instances indicate more deep-seated conflicts, less accessible insight, and a need to maintain a defense against anxieties associated with childhood conflicts. When the supervisor becomes the transference object, learning can proceed only with the greatest difficulty, if at all, and the supervisor is usually forced to focus actively on the disturbances in the learning alliance and bring them to the conscious attention of his student. What happens after that depends on many factors.

The following example illustrates a segment of a complex, emotionally charged supervisory situation in which the student was openly defensive against the supervisor's teaching method, which he interpreted in terms that appeared to be transferences of characteristic defenses. Discussion between S and A compelled the supervisor to examine her method and her own possible blind spots. Introspective exploration of this experience was profitable for both student and teacher. Thus, this example illustrates the supervisory process in full circle.

EXAMPLE 3 (Unrecorded on Tape)

AF (Case III), Supervisory Session 15, Analytic Hours 140-150

The patient was a defensively provocative postgraduate student who attempted repeatedly to manipulate A by finding "compelling" reasons for changing the schedule of his analytic sessions. On the occasion described here, he implied that A might reduce the number of weekly sessions from four to three. These requests mobilized A's countertransference, which came into clear view at this point.

On previous occasions when *A* granted these requests, *S* had called his attention to *P*'s guilt reaction over this success, which represented undeserved power over father or mother. *A* was well acquainted with this pattern of *P*, yet he could not perceive *P*'s guilt in this instance because of his own anger that was directed not only toward his demanding, manipulative patient but even more toward Institute regulations. In order to help *P* keep his academic schedule and also to see him four times weekly, *A* had to make several changes in other patients' appointments; all this could have been avoided if the Institute had not required that supervised cases have a minimum of four analytic sessions weekly, or so, it turned out later, *A* thought to himself. *P* knew of *A*'s dilemma and half hoped that *A* would decrease the sessions so that *P* could save money. *A* could also have used the free hour for another patient who paid more. All of this blocked *A* severely.

Two weeks before, when *P*'s request to change the analytic hour came up in the supervisory session, *S* had asked if *A* had questioned the reality of the need and had tried to explore the meaning of the request with *P*. This had not been done.

Exchange 1*

In the material presented in the fifteenth supervisory session *P* seemed less guilty and continued his manipulation of *A* by talking about future schedule changes necessitated by his class schedule in the spring quarter; he entered into a contest with *A* over silences. *A* perceived this but could not intergrate it into a clear diagnosis. He made pieces of interpretation without any follow through to the point of bringing *P*'s pattern into clear focus, such as his alternating pleasure and guilt when he felt he had made *A* speak.

S (1) pointed out *A*'s behavior, (2) then formulated the problem, and (3) tried to stimulate *A* to associate to what the more complete interpretation might have been (if he had made it). This brought the learning block and the resistance against learning into clear focus. *A* resisted associating and revealed that he thought *S* was making a competitive guessing game out of the supervision.

S felt the incongruity in the student's behavior. His performance was not up to the level of his intelligence, his knowledge, his perceptiveness or his demonstrated analytic ability. The resistance became more clearly focused in terms of an identification with the patient in his manipulative and limit-testing behavior. In this identification, both *A* and *P* seemed to be acting out a childhood pattern.

As *S* tried to explain *P*'s dynamics, *A*'s resistance to her became more manifest. He distorted what had been said in the previous supervisory hour and reported a feeling that he could never satisfy her. Gradually, this feel-

---

* The steps in diagnosis and teaching tactics are not as clearly exemplified as they would be if this supervision had been recorded on tape, but notes were made immediately following this fifteenth session.

ing was translated into his sense of never being able to keep up with her, get ahead of her, or achieve equality, and that his failure was because S would never permit equality. A based his feeling on a teaching tactic which S frequently used. [This tactic consisted of asking a question about the material and then asking A to associate to what had stimulated her particular question.] When S asked about what that particular way of questioning meant to him, A brought out two patterns of response to this teaching technique: (1) he thought if he would guess and was successful, S would be pleased and would approve of him; (2) he felt S wanted him to identify with her.

Comments: These two patterns of reacting to S's method of teaching reflect childhood patterns of relating to an ambivalently loved parent. They could be interpreted as transference reactions to S. The first pattern reflects the relationship of a child who wants and needs love and approval but who has trouble knowing just what behavior on his part will bring it. In this student's persistent clinging to this meaning of the $S \leftrightarrows A$ relationship (and with other supervisors also) there is revealed his feeling about authority figures. It is as if he says, "You don't really want me to learn and to grow up to become your equal; you only want me to guess what you are thinking as a kind of confirmation that you are right, an admiration of your all-seeing eye. Only then will you love me and let me progress to another case."

The second pattern attributes to S an even more sarcastic motivation for teaching in the way she does. Again, A could be saying, "You don't really want me to learn except to become a minor edition of yourself. I am supposed to do it as you would do it to gratify your self-satisfaction, not to develop myself." The negative feeling toward learning by identification cannot be denied here. Its roots in this student's past experiences were not known; only the fact of some compulsive repeating (transference resistance) was clear in his current behavior.

Exchange 2

What S did in this situation was to point out a third level of response to her Socratic teaching technique. She first acknowledged that all A said might be true under certain circumstances, but that in this instance, her conscious intent was quite different.

She pointed out that there could be another response which included awareness by A of the need to develop his own equipment so as to be able to use it independently. She defined his equipment in this situation as his associative and interpretive ego functions which he used constantly in his analytic work. She described her Socratic method as giving him an opportunity to "exercise" this equipment in order to increase his skill by practice. She compared her question, "What made me ask that?" with the question every analyst asks himself (and sometimes asks the patient)—for example, "What made him (P) say that, say that now, or in that way, or ask that question, etc.?" She explained that the step of asking himself these questions might not be done consciously, but it was part of the process of introspection which resulted in empathic understanding of the patient. She described how this was preliminary to arriving at any interpretation to be made to the patient. *A* understood all of this intellectually, although he admitted that he had never thought about it this way before.

Comments: This $S \leftrightarrows A$ interaction illustrates a situation in which it became necessary for *S* to explain the goal of her teaching and to elaborate on her method in order to involve the student in the supervisory process. In this instance, the student, because of his accumulated resistance, put himself "outside of the supervisory situation." He did not feel or act as a "participant" but as a subject," passively exposed to an authority with whom he could not cooperate, whom he only suffered. In order to "bring him back," his resistance had to be dealt with. This was achieved through *S*'s understanding of the psychodynamic pattern expressed in *A*'s accusation and by her response to it which used "conceptual teaching" to enable the student to observe and objectify in order to understand the motivations which blocked his learning.

S recognized that *A* was operating on a child-parent transference level in the supervisory situation, but instead of pointing this out, she explained the meaning and goal of her Socratic approach. Her directness and self-examination focused *A*'s self-observation upon his own anger. She drew parallels to similar phrases used by *A* in the psychoanalytic situation and showed him how his phrases served to activate the patient's associative and self-observing processes. In this way *S* attempted to catalyze *A*'s self-analytic functions. He began to see supervision in a different light and to differentiate the supervisory relationship from the level of child-parent transference on which he had been operating. Success in this achievement did not occur overnight and *A* realized that the persistent repetition of this transference distortion might require more personal analysis for him. In other words, in this instance there was a serious question about the adequacy of his self-analytic functions to overcome this resistance to learning and professional development.

S served the double role of a supervisor very explicitly. She remained the teacher of the student who needed to learn something about technique, while at the same time she "treated" the learning block by interpreting it through clarification and confrontation, attempting to catalyze his self-analysis.

This experience confronted *S* with a need to do some self-analysis herself. She knew that she used the Socratic method as a frequent pedagogic technique in classrooms as well as supervision. She realized she had taken for granted its value as a stimulus to participatory thinking through of a problem to be solved, as in supervision, or in arriving inductively at understanding a theoretical concept. She also realized that she had taken for granted that her students not only understood this value of this teaching technique but that they also "identified" with her in valuing it. This presumption of "alliance" went so far as to assume without question that her students in supervision realized that her question, "What do you think made me ask you that?" had an analogue in the therapeutic situation and that the catalyzing, exercising purpose of such a question was clear. She had assumed that its usefulness for these purposes was agreed to by the person questioned. Her experience with this student necessitated reevaluating all these assumptions. It became necessary to question her motivations and to ask if she really did expect a student to imitate and to identify with her. The introspected answer was yes, but not for the purely narcissistic satisfaction which was attributed to her by this student.

This question highlights the meaning of learning by imitation and identification, the dangers involved in "providing a model" as a method of teaching. It highlights the necessity for the teacher to be just as constantly alert to the mixture of realistic and transference responses from students as it is necessary for a therapist to be alert to the same mixture of responses from patients. Quantities of ambivalence and of transference distortions can be hidden under an exterior of what looks on the surface like "good motivation for learning," a "cooperative student," a "good learner," etc. This is not to say that imitation and identification play an insignificant role in learning, or that providing a model should be avoided by a teacher. This is impossible, anyway. This example, however, illustrates in sharp focus the care which needs to be given by a teacher to avoid an authoritarian attitude and to recognize the possibility of negative transference reactions which can treat the teaching-learning process as a caricature of parents and teachers.

Four supervisory hours (two months) later, the student opened the session with a smile of pleasure by saying, "What we talked about a few weeks ago is very clear now. What you told me I was doing with you is just what he was doing with me."

This example documents many of the points discussed in this chapter. When we follow the supervisor's activity in making an educational diagnosis, we see that S became aware of A's resistance to learning by responding first to the problem manifested in the $A \leftrightarrows P$ interaction. The analysis was stalemated, P was repeating the same pattern again and again, and A was missing it. He was not able to use the explanations and suggestions which S had given in previous supervisory sessions. We see here a movement in the supervisory process as S responds to a clue from the therapeutic material which stirs up resistance in the $S \leftrightarrows A$ system. From there S uncovers some of the elements of a supervisory transference which constituted a problem about learning which S proceeded to "treat" by further confrontation and explanation, giving A an opportunity to ventilate his feelings toward her at the same time.

In this example we can also observe one of S's teaching tactics: the questioning technique aimed at stimulating A to utilize his diagnostic, interpretive, and self-observing functions. For some time this technique was relatively unsuccessful, causing S to make further evaluations of the learning problems and the learning alliance and, consequently, to shift the focus of the teaching target from P to A. It became necessary to deal directly with resistances disturbing the $S \leftrightarrows A$ alliance and to confront A with the evidence for "flaws" in his analytic instrument. S began this supervisory work by explaining something about the ego functions instrumental for analytic work. She proceeded to point out how A's counter-reactions disturbed the analytic process and made some effort to catalyze his self-analytic functions. A, in this instance, was able to achieve some insight and consequently a recommendation for return to analysis, which S considered, was not urged.

Illustrated here also is the fact that supervisors must follow the principles of analytic functioning which they recommend to their students. A supervisor's sensitivity needs to be turned on the student as well as the patient and the disturbances of equilibrium in the learning alliance need to receive as much self-examination by a supervisor as is expected from a student.

To summarize, we should like to quote Bateson[7] who said, "In any given learning situation one learns not only what one is supposed to learn but also something about the process of learning itself." Bateson spoke of this phenomenon as "deutero-learning." As a counterpoint of this idea, we will add that in any given teaching situation, the teacher becomes aware not only of what he is supposed to teach, but also of the process of teaching itself.

– V –

The Supervisory Process: Initial Phase

IN THE LAST CHAPTER WE DESCRIBED THE TRIADIC RELATIONSHIPS OF the supervisory situation and how, within the framework of its system interactions, the process of teaching and learning develops. We discussed how the supervisory process evolves within the supervisory situation just as the therapeutic process evolves within the psychoanalytic situation. Based on a learning alliance, the supervisor and student-analyst work together to clarify and sharpen the effectiveness of the student as a skillful instrument in the therapeutic process.

In this chapter and the two that follow we intend to elaborate on the activities of the supervisor in facilitating the supervisory process as it moves through a sequence of teaching-learning experiences that, like the therapeutic process, manifest initial, middle, and end phases. These phases have been defined according to a sequence of learning objectives which roughly correspond to the sequence of operations which an analyst goes through in his functioning as an instrument in the therapeutic process. In each phase of an analysis, these operations become more complex as the treatment process proceeds through the transference neurosis and working through to termination. Each phase of therapy presents the analyst with more complex problems of diagnosis and technical response. These changing learning needs also confront the supervisor with more complicated problems of educational diagnosis which necessitate corresponding changes in teaching objectives and teaching techniques in each phase of the supervisory process.

We want to emphasize that separation into phases does not imply clear-cut or rigid boundaries between them. What a student needs to learn and when he learns it depends to such a large extent on his endowment, on the quality of his personal analysis, and on the level of maturation he has achieved that an ideal sequence of learning may not be possible. Such variables influence not only his learning problems but his accessibility to teaching, requiring that a particular difficulty be given precedence over other learning needs. In addition to these factors, various aspects of the patient's structure and pathology confront the student with the need for skills which he may not yet have mastered, so that ideal progression of his psychoanalytic learning is disturbed. Normally, his competence and ease of learning should improve between elementary and advanced cases, but this may be irregular too, depending, for example, on the style and expectations of his various supervisors as well as on the patient.

The phases of the supervisory process which we propose are by no means of equal length, nor are they characterized by an equally smooth course. Learning needs overlap phase boundaries and a particular objective may offer greater difficulty to one student than to another. For example, a student might have special difficulty in recognizing transference implications, or he may fail to understand the dynamics of the regression involved, so that teaching effort must be spent on this problem for a longer period of time than usual. Nevertheless, in each supervisory experience we studied, the process of teaching and learning could be divided roughly into three phases and three corresponding groups of objectives.

It is a principle of educational psychology that optimal learning moves ahead from a foundation of what has already been learned, and that basic knowledge and skill must be acquired before the next step can be mastered successfully. Applied to psychoanalysis, this means that the teacher must know what is basic, and the student must grasp the fundamentals of the psychoanalytic process and acquire skill in basic operations before he can easily progress to more complex levels of learning, such as understanding the dynamics of transferences and the nuances of interpretive techniques.

In formulating basic learning objectives for psychoanalysis, we have combined our experience as analysts and our study of learning deficiencies as they appeared in the students we supervised. These basic objectives represent the first steps in the use of the analytic instrument and can be stated as follows:

First, to learn to listen with free-floating attention. This is the "posture" of an analyst and one of the fundamental skills. It reflects his attitude of receptivity and of associative scanning of the multiple determinants of his patient's behavior. It makes use of his empathically perceptive and synthesizing functions (Chart II, 1′).

Second, to learn to make for himself inferential interpretations of meaning that is beyond the awareness of the patient but is explanatory of his behavior. These inferences are not usually communicated to the patient, since this is a diagnostic step in understanding, which makes use of the introspective and integrative capacities of the analyst (Chart II, 2′).

Third, to learn to estimate the patient's level of anxiety and resistance. This objective involves the analyst's capacity for empathy with the affective and regressive state of the patient. Based on system sensitivity it indicates the degree of communication with the intrapsychic system of another person (Chart II, 3′).

Fourth, to learn to judge timing and dosing of responses in tune with the equilibrium in the $A \leftrightarrows P$ system—in other words, to develop the tact

Chart II.—Supervisory Experience

Therapeutic Material as Presented to S by A	Learning Objectives in Relation to Functions Active in Psychoanalytic Work
1. Patient's associations (verbal, paralinguistic, nonverbal communications).	1'. To listen with free-floating attention → develop associative processes → self as instrument (receptive, perceptive, synthetic functions).
2. Analyst's associations and inferences toward diagnostic meanings.	2'. To make diagnostic interpretations to self → introspection → synthetic and integrative functions.
3. Analyst's responses to patient (interventions, interpretations).	3'. To estimate resistance and anxiety → empathy with affective and regressive state of patient ("system sensitivity").
4. Analyst's self-questioning or responses that intrude from himself.	4'. To judge timing and dosing—sensitivity, empathy, responsiveness (in tune with system equilibrium).

5. Phenomena of transference and countertransference.
—identifying transference distortions
—identifying repetitive patterns with their genetic roots
  —in patient
  —in self
	5'. To become aware of transference and countertransference
	—in patient
	—own behavior as causing patient response
	—need for self-analysis

6. Phenomena of psychoanalytic process —in patient —between A and P —from hour to hour —from phase to phase	6'. To recognize dynamic lines, their shifts in relation to stimuli inside and outside the analytic situation—process of analysis.
7. Evidence for insight and growth in P and self.	7'. To recognize movements toward transference neurosis, working through and termination.

or "system responsiveness"[68, p. 195] required for skillful interpretation (Chart II, 4').

The first three objectives will be discussed and illustrated as we focus in this chapter on the initial phase of the supervisory process. The fourth objective, complicated as it is, will be commented on in relation to problems of initial interpretations, but a more detailed approach will be presented in the next chapter on middle-phase objectives and problems.

These basic objectives become targets for achievement by both student and teacher in the initial phase of the supervisory process, and a supervisor's success in performing these teaching tasks is dependent upon the information which the student-analyst provides (Chart II, left-hand column). The beginning of supervision is largely devoted to helping the student learn how to communicate with the supervisor, how to report the

material of the therapeutic experience in order to make the best use of
the supervisor as an assistant with the patient and as a teacher for himself. This material is the vehicle that carries the supervisory process
through its various tasks. The content and the pattern of presenting the
material is the foundation on which the relationship between student and
supervisor evolves since this is the source of the information necessary for
understanding the patient and the analyst as they interact with each other
in their analytic work. On the basis of this information, the supervisor
makes his educational diagnosis and his pedagogical decisions.

Thus, the content and pattern of reporting by the student serves three
functions in the supervisory process: (1) it reveals the story of the patient
and the analyst's understanding of him; (2) it manifests the signs of tensions in the learning alliance; and (3) it indicates the learning needs of
the student. The presentation is not only the means of communicating to
the supervisor, but it represents the result of the analyst's processing of
the psychoanalytic data and permits evaluation of his understanding, tact,
and communication with the patient. It constitutes the material for the
learning experience by which the initial objectives are achieved.

In the beginning of his first case, indeed in the beginning of each new
supervisory relationship, the student is eager to give and the supervisor
to receive detailed reports of the communication between patient and
analyst. The story of this communication paints a picture for the supervisor of the patient's pathology and personality structure. Since he very
rarely sees the patient himself, he must be able to obtain from the student
a picture clear enough for him to feel some confidence in his own diagnostic understanding. The supervisor responds to the clinical material as
if he were the analyst of the patient. By way of his own inferential associations, and at the same time by comparing his understanding with what
he assumes to be the student's understanding, the supervisor can follow
the therapeutic process parallel with the educational process.

This is not a simple task since the information provided by the student
is often inadequate. To be adequate, it should include not only the patient's verbalized associations but also significant nonverbal and paralin-
guistic behavior (Chart II, 1). It is these latter avenues of expression
which convey so many of the clues to preconscious and unconscious meanings and which point the way in the psychoanalytic process, and it is this
kind of information which the student-analyst often misses altogether or
to which he does not give its proper meaning. Elements of the experience
may remain on the periphery of his awareness and not be reported, or
they may be communicated to the supervisor by a tone of voice which
imitates the patient but of which the student is not cognizant. He may
unconsciously mimic the patient as he reproduces the analytic moment.*

---

* Arlow[2] offers an interesting example of how a student revealed his unconscious
involvement with his patient, a situation which called for a supervisory intervention.

When these items are incorporated into a student's report, even if he is not conscious of their meaning, they become clues for the supervisor's trained ear and permit him to help the student recognize their significance.

Selection of what to report takes place in the analyst as he sifts the patient's material and processes it to discover latent meanings. A potentially good analyst will show talent for this and will naturally include his own associative thinking which occurred while with the patient (Chart II, 2). A student less talented or less experienced will often be able to tell the supervisor what he thought about the patient's material as he studied it in preparation for his supervisory hour, even if he had not been fully aware of the derivative meanings of what the patient was communicating at the time. What he managed to register on the periphery becomes accessible later and falls into place in the puzzle more easily when the student can look back on the experience, at a distance from the tensions of the therapeutic hour.

Clearly, the basic task—to listen with "evenly-hovering attention"—is fundamental for establishing the analytic situation. This attitude is necessary not only for receiving messages from the patient, but also for sending them—messages that reveal in words or other cues that the analyst is receptive to whatever the patient has to communicate and that the analyst can be trusted to receive it uncritically. This first objective, listening with an analytic ear, is essential to the establishment of a therapeutic alliance and to getting the analytic process under way. Freud contributed to our understanding of this analytic posture in several papers. In the *Encyclopedia Britannica* article[45] he described how "the attitude which the analytical physician could most advantageously adopt it to surrender himself to his own unconscious mental activity, in a state of easy and partial attention, to avoid so far as possible reflection and the construction of partial expectations, not to try to fix anything that he heard particularly in his memory, and by these means to catch the drift of the patient's unconscious with his own unconscious." He also differentiates between a state of receptivity and one of reflection where critical faculties operate; advises "making no effort to concentrate the attention on anything in particular, and in maintaining in regard to all one hears the same measure of calm, quiet attentiveness—of 'evenly hovering attention'."[42]

In addition to receptive, perceptive faculties an analyst makes use of his synthesizing function. What he takes in with his analytic ear, he processes by "vicarious introspection," as Kohut has so ably described.[59] As an analytic instrument which probes below the surface, using signals to which only a trained ear is attuned, the analyst's mind links together meanings of which the patient manifests varying degrees of awareness. This inferential activity is the first step in interpretive use of the analytic instrument and is first directed toward integrating for himself the many levels of meaning revealed in the patient's communications (see Chapter II).

These diagnostic interpretations precede verbalization of responses to the patient, a diagnostic activity which usually goes on preconsciously in an experienced analyst and also with a beginner. It is important, however, for the student's learning about the analytic process and himself as an analytic instrument for him to become aware of his own diagnostic thinking. This important teaching objective is approached in these ways: the student spontaneously reports his diagnostic associations to the supervisor and only corrective teaching is necessary; or the supervisor attempts to discover what they were by a series of questions leading the student's peripheral associations into consciousness; or failing with this method, he spells out the stimulus-response sequences of the dynamics himself. All these types of supervisory communication undoubtedly occur in every supervisory session, depending on the sensitivity of the student and his sophistication regarding the analytic process. When given spontaneously, they offer indications of the student's ability to use his synthesizing and integrative functions in empathizing with another person's experience. When these diagnostic associations are absent, the supervisor needs to find out why. It may be a matter of the student's not realizing their importance for both the therapeutic and the supervisory process. On the other hand, they may be left out because of other motivations (see below). In any case, absence of these communications is a clue to the existence of a learning problem which then becomes a focus for the teacher's attention.

A good student will thus report to his supervisor both the patient's behavior, verbal and nonverbal, and his own diagnostic thinking (Chart II, 1, 2). In addition he will reveal his own responses to the patient (Chart II, 3) and the patient's reactions to them. This interpretive activity adds a dimension to the analytic process in that interactions between analyst and patient come into play—a different level of communication. Focus on intrapsychic dynamics brings into view the internal struggle of the patient, whereas focus on interpersonal dynamics permits observation of the analyst's struggle with the patient's resistances in an effort to help him with his internal conflicts. As this material of the analysis is discussed in supervision, the part the analyst plays as an active instrument becomes clearer, blind spots become visible to both supervisor and student, and other forms of countertransference can be seen to interfere with the therapeutic work.

The interactions between patient and analyst are obviously a vital part of the student's report to the supervisor. They reveal the depth of communication, the quality of rapport, and the balance in the therapeutic alliance. The student may demonstrate understanding of the patient's message and empathy with his affect and his state of regression, but interpretations may be precipitous, off target, and not in tune with the dynamic-economic balance within the patient at a given moment (Example 2).

It is on the basis of information about these interactions that the supervisor assesses the system sensitivity and system responsiveness of the student-analyst (Chart II, 3', 4') and determines what he needs to be taught about the technique of interpretation. This area of learning always presents some difficulties in the initial phase of the supervisory process although their severity will depend on the student's talent and the habits previously learned in his residency or practice of psychotherapy. Many of these habits are not appropriate for psychoanalytic technique and have to be corrected in analytic supervision.

Another kind of information is significant for the supervisory process (Chart II, 4). It includes any intrusion of fantasies, sensations, or impulses into the analyst's mind that do not appear to be connected with the analytic work of the moment. He may recognize that they are incongruous with the therapeutic material, or he may have vague impressions that somehow they are responses to something from the patient. Whatever their origins, these intrusions should be reported to the supervisor since they can be useful in shedding light on a problem of the patient only half understood until then. These phenomena are signs of preconscious activity still under the influence of a counter-cathexis by the analyst's ego. Evidence of this kind of mental functioning adds still another dimension to the student's understanding of himself as an analytic instrument in the analytic process. An experience of this sort is often puzzling and even anxiety-producing, especially before he has learned to listen to these intrusions and incongruous responses as clues that can lead to insights beneficial to the patient and himself. The majority of students, however, need to be taught that such experiences are useful and frequent in the work of an analyst. Successful efforts to discover the meanings of such intrusions often bring conviction as no other teaching does about the need for continuing self-analysis.

As the supervisory process gets under way and as the patient and the therapeutic interaction come into better focus, the learning alliance develops and becomes the foundation on which the teacher bases his teaching efforts and the student achieves his learning. Usually, a supervisor needs to give special attention to the learning alliance with a beginning student. He comes to his first case and his first supervisor with anxieties stemming from his ambition, his feeling about being a student, and his insecurity about his competence with an analytic case. He knows from his residency experience that supervisory teaching of therapeutic techniques is a very different experience from that in other learning situations. He knows that the treatment of a patient demands more from him, touches him more deeply, stirs up emotional reactions, and even threatens his equilibrium in various ways. This knowledge stimulates defensive tensions in his relation to his patient and to his supervisor. The inevitable identification with his personal analyst and the fact that now he is assuming the role of an analyst undoubtedly reinforce insecurities and anxieties from other sources.

Any insecurity present is intensified by the student's awareness that he is expected to lay bare to the supervisor the details of his interactions with his patient. These details will include not only what is explicit and conscious, but the student knows they will reveal to the supervisor much that is implicit and of which he himself is only vaguely, if at all, aware. To enter such a situation takes courage and a strong wish to learn new things, not only about a new procedure but also about himself. It requires a tolerance for not knowing and a degree of trust in his teacher which is unique in formal learning experiences. The not knowing includes his ignorance of theory and technique which his experience in psychotherapy can only partially counteract. It also includes his unawareness of the motivations of his responses to his patient and his underdeveloped sensitivity to the impact of his own behavior on the patient.

His fear of exposure may be a simple "examination" anxiety, but its resolution requires an entirely new level of orientation toward being exposed and toward the person who sees the exposure. A student-analyst is prepared to some extent for exposing himself to his supervisor, since he has been through a similar experience in his training analysis, but there is an understandable and significant difference in the kind of "threat" posed by these two individuals. Spitz in a discussion about analytic supervision described this anxiety with the remark, "The supervisor is more threatening for the student than his training analyst was. The latter was threatening in the unconscious of the student-patient, but was protective realistically; whereas the supervisor is realistically threatening to the status of the student-analyst."[86]

Within the scope of this book, we will call attention to many different conflicts which, if they remain unanalyzed and unresolved, become interferences either in the therapeutic relationship or in the learning process, or both. Interference in one situation often reverberates to produce problems in the other. It is not our purpose, however, to attempt a complete inventory. To cover the wide range of individual variations is impossible. Consequently, we will mention only a few conflicts which seem to us significant and fairly frequent in our experience.

Probably the most frequent anxiety behind the student's reluctance to present a full account of the therapeutic interactions is his fear of being found wanting, his shame over failure and anticipation of humiliation. Such feelings stem from the secret fantasy of childhood that he could perform as an adult "if only. . . ." Some student-analysts are in the midst of this problem in their training analyses when they start supervision, or they have not succeeded in integrating childhood reality limitations with childhood wishes nor in differentiating childhood hopes from adult reality limitations, so that the position of learner is felt as a narcissistic blow to be defended by secrecy and obscurity.

Another common and related conflict might be described as a reversal of a primal scene conflict—that is, the projection of primal scene curiosity onto the supervisor, who is then defensively denied the satisfaction of looking on at the student-patient interactions. A modification of this problem is an acting out of a childhood wish to separate the parents. The student comes between supervisor and patient either by confusing the patient's material or by leaving himself out of the transaction in a defensive reaction formation. He may also thrust himself to the fore to the exclusion of the patient. The problem of loyalty to his training analyst should not be overlooked. Many a student repeats an adolescent conflict when he feels his interest in his teacher and the new learning experience is a disloyal and even threatening separation from his training analyst.

Sometimes these difficulties are resolved by the student-analyst when he can recognize them. Of course, if they persist, continuing personal analysis is indicated. It is to be hoped, however, that a student's analytic experience has produced enough insight to prevent these conflicts from recurring in the supervisory process and that the experience has prepared him for beginning his first case by developing his capacity for self-observation and self-analysis. His work in supervision will reveal whether or not the professional objectives of his training analysis have been achieved. The supervisory experience will extend and expand what he learned as an analytic patient.

Assessment of these questions begins with an evaluation of the student-analyst's pattern of reporting. The pattern reveals an individual style in presenting material which depends on the student's innate intellectual and psychological endowment and, to a large degree, his previous clinical experience. More significantly, however, it is influenced by character-determined attitudes toward learning from supervision. The pattern and style of reporting provide the supervisor with signs of initial tensions in the learning alliance and of the unsolved personal conflicts mentioned above that show themselves in various forms of resistance to learning and especially to being taught.[29] A supervisor is cued in many ways to the underlying difficulties—for example, by extreme defensiveness or exaggerated compliance. Indeed, the pattern and manner of presenting the psychoanalytic material to the supervisor reflects the student's personality like a projective test and offers a profile of his learning strengths and his learning needs, their changes over time, and his professional growth.

We offer five examples of different patterns of reporting the therapeutic process. These examples are selected to portray a continuum in the student's accessibility for, or defense against, supervisory teaching. They are arranged in a descending series from a pattern of openness and adequate content that sets the supervisory process in the direction of freely moving teaching and learning, to a pattern where abundant content is inadequate for supervisory purposes and covers a severe learning block. We have tried in this set of illustrations to differentiate a basic character factor from the usual fluctuations in learning responsiveness brought about by changing tensions in the $S{\leftrightarrows}A$ system. For this purpose, we have added selections from the first phase of three students other than the two who were the principal contributors to our investigation. Needless to say, not all of the supervisory sessions of these students followed the pattern illustrated here. These examples are taken from the early hours for the most part; three were from elementary cases and two from advanced ones.

EXAMPLE 4

HB (Case II), Supervisory Session 5, Analytic Hours 20

(See Example 1, Chapter III, for details regarding the patient.) This student was analyzing his second case. He begins the session by informing S about the number of hours to be presented. Then he succinctly summarizes the therapeutic theme and its discussion in the previous supervisory session. Thus he follows the continuity of the psychoanalytic process by sharply emphasizing the dynamic lines and their shifts when P changes the theme. There is a tone of involvement in both the $A{\leftrightarrows}P$ and the $S{\leftrightarrows}A$ interactions; he seems able to integrate his role as an analyst with his patient and as a student with his supervisor, and ready to reveal his interventions between himself and the patient. He reports naturally what each one says, but with it reveals some of his own interpretive thinking and technical decision making. HB's "openness" is apparent in the freedom with which he can talk about himself with the supervisor, the mistakes he is aware of, his disagreements with her, his reactions to her criticism of him (see Exchange 2).*

This transcript is offered primarily as an illustration of a pattern of good reporting. It is clear, however, that it shows learning problems and strains in the $S{\leftrightarrows}A$ system. References will be made in subsequent chapters to appropriate parts of this example as particular learning problems are discussed.

Exchange 1

A—I have three hours this week because he didn't come yesterday. He thought that yesterday was the first day of his week's vacation. Now, last

---

* The same quality of 'openness' can also be recognized in his more inhibited first recorded supervisory session (Example 1) in his response to a slip of the tongue ("us"). This slip revealed his tendency to identify with P which forecast a countertransference problem, grappled with on many occasions.

week we ended on the theme in which we discussed his feeling that he was sexually confused—his words—and we briefly discussed his formulation that it wasn't homosexuality that troubled him but rather his difficulty in relationships in general. We ended on that theme; you and I thought this was a very good formulation.

So he comes; this is last Tuesday and the first material is as follows: he describes his feelings of guilt and apprehension and the feeling of being caught in the act as he leaves the office every day to take the bus to come down here. He's afraid people will stop him and talk to him and ask him where's he going to go, and somehow they will mill around and he will inadvertently tell them. So he's going though mildly elaborate cautions by walking around the back of the building. And this day, the twentieth hour, he was telling me that he increased the elaborateness of his precautions by walking, not around the building and out to the bus stop, but he comes to the bus stop one block away from the office. He's afraid he will "be caught in the act."

S—What do you think?

A—He tells me he thinks that it means first that he'll be thought neurotic by others, but "being caught in the act" means that he'll find out it's true, he is neurotic.

S—So why do you think—that for this man being neurotic is such a thing that one has to hide in shame?

A—Because obviously the meaning of being neurotic, to him, is what we were talking about—his sadistic impulses.

S—His sadistic impulses? And what is implied in the sadistic impulses, because he behaves as if he were committing a crime?

A—Yes. Well, we go back to the dream that I reported to you last time in which there is a baling machine, putting hay in bales. It comes down with a chopping motion and is intended to kill cows—his mother. And his interpretation of the dream is that he realizes that what he's tried to do is to protect his mother from his father's brutality.

S—Did you interpret the dream to him in that connection?

A—No. I did not take up the theme: well, what does neurotic mean to you? So, obviously also whatever neurosis means to him must be very guilt-provoking, because with the next association he says he realizes that he's accusing—these are his words—he's accusing himself of homosexuality; he's accusing himself of neurosis. I thought of repeating the word "accusing" to him—but I don't know, I just didn't. And he feels that he's a bad character. He realizes that this is an exaggeration. He is not actually a bad guy, but he feels like a bad guy. That is what he says. Then he goes on to say that he needs to impress people, that he's been doing this in the following way: by using psychiatric terminology, letting me know what he's learned in college; that he has also false modesty—that he didn't tell me about his scholarship offers right away at the first interview when he wanted to tell me about them, but he waited until the third interview. And that when he was talking to Mr. Seton at the factory last week in relationship to a period of work there, he boasted about his hobbies which make him seem to be a well-rounded man—that is, he plays a horn and he's also been an athlete: football, baseball, etc. Then the next material deals with his feeling that he must discuss further how he feels about fellatio and cunnilingus. Marcia is the first girl friend with whom he had any sexual activity. After they got over the necking and petting stage, he urged her to perform fellatio. She did, and they had such a sexual practice for a rather long time because this satisfied her need not to have sexual intercourse with him. He went along with it because he really wanted to protect her virginity, and he also needed to shy away from intercourse. He said that he felt selfish, that this is enjoying himself but not letting a woman enjoy herself. He also had cunnilingus with Marcia and felt ashamed because of it. The next association deals with his affair with a kindergarten teacher—last year. She was 20 years older than he, and he tried to get her to perform fellatio. She refused and they had intercourse and he had a premature ejaculation. The subject of premature ejaculation is beginning to come up now.

Comments: In this exchange, the supervisor stimulates *A*'s thinking about meanings and assists *A* to question the manifest content and to associate to latent possibilities. The rapport between *S* and *A* is good. The interaction is largely question and answer definitely directed by *S* to activate *A*'s diagnostic processes rather than to gather clarifying information for herself. This is only the twentieth analytic hour, but *S* apparently feels she is adequately acquainted with the patient up to this point.

Exchange 2

A—I was interrupted by the telephone for a moment and it brought up an aspect of his feelings which might not have come up for a while. It was an emergency; it was a referring physician who wanted me to get on a case immediately, so I talked for a moment or two, got the patient's name written down, told the referring physician that I could see the patient tomorrow and that he should call the patient's father and tell the father that . . .

S—That all happened?

A—While the patient was in the room. It took a moment or two. I said to the patient as I left the phone, "This is an emergency, Hanson." These are my exact words. He said that this is what he felt while I was talking on the phone; nothing that I said was meaningful to him because it was routine, giving an appointment, etc., but his heart fluttered when I called him Hanson because this meant that this was purely a patient-doctor relationship and it was not personal.

S—So what should you call him?

A—Exactly what I asked him, and he said, "I prefer that you call me nothing because then if you call me nothing, I don't have to categorize you as a friend or an enemy or something else." But he's so sensitive to clues from me as to how I might feel about him and what pigeonhole he can put me into.

S—Yes. What did you answer?

A—Well, let's see. Oh, I answered—now I realize, not apropos—I said to him, "I asked you what you want me to call you because I was interested in whether you have thought and felt about this subject before. Instead of following his lead—which is, "I don't want to classify you as a friend or enemy or anything"—instead of following that up, somehow or other at the moment I thought I was teaching him something about the analytic method, that if you have fantasies about something like this, or feelings . . .

S—Yes, but actually what did you do?

A—I cut off his flow of associations.

S—Not only did you cut off his flow of associations but you defended yourself against analyzing his transference reaction. When he tells you, "I wish you wouldn't call me anything," that means, "I wish that you would not become for me something, but would remain nothing, nobody, just an institution—analysis." Now that doesn't exist. You have to become somebody. You were just as afraid of the closeness as he was. And so you responded to his feeling, "O.K., you leave me alone and I'll leave you alone," and so on.

A—I didn't follow up what we thought was so important last time: his formulation of his relationship problem.

S—Well, relationship is the major problem for everybody. I think that you actually cling to that, defending yourself against how sick that boy is. He's afraid of his sadism and criminality, homosexuality and otherewise, and you say, "O.K., that is all a relationship problem." You always protect yourself against how ill that boy is; this time you really defended yourself against his transference reactions to you. You accept his defenses. Now, you see, there is nothing wrong in accepting his defenses, but you have to think why you do accept his defenses. Why are you so afraid of his illness?

A—All right. I've been thinking about that because you mentioned in the first supervisory hour that you thought he was very ill, and in my deepest feelings I've been disagreeing with you over the last month and I've been asking myself why I didn't agree with you and I talked it over with some people in these terms: that I come to the Institute and I meet the supervisor and she says this patient is really ill, and then he leaves the office, or others come in after him or before him who are really ill and they're so depressed or they're so borderline that they have to go in and out of the hospital. My feelings from doing work with a lot of hospital patients is this: that those are the sick patients. This fellow is healthy.

S—That is, I think, naive.

A—Naive?

S—Because those patients are sick because they are already in the hospital, or coming in and out—depends when you get the patients. This patient is not in and out of hospitals yet and it may not be true he will be in and out of hospitals. The danger of this case is that he might commit suicide when he gets himself involved in a situation which is criminal or sadistic, or the other danger might be that he becomes psychotic and then you will realize it. So that actually the fact is that this boy who comes to analysis in a state in which the defenses are still holding up, when you begin to analyze him, you work through the defenses, then you will see what happens when these defenses break down. That is the reason why I said the last time, not so much that the relationship is the primary problem but rather that we have to see whether we can work with his unconscious and try to reorganize it without breaking down his defenses.

A—I see.

S—That is what I emphasized the last time. Now for you it seems that it is easier to say, "O.K., this is not true; the supervisor tells me I have to defend myself because I am afraid of the analysis of a very sick person." You are afraid of analyzing somebody whose instinctual urges are so confused and threatening, as the instinctual drives of this man are threatening to him. It is threatening to him and it is threatening to you. And he tries to defend himself and you try to defend yourself. That's all right to some degree. But you have to see how much your defense against it is a protection for him. That is all right if you can see through your own defenses. It is a very complicated situation.

A—Because at times it seems to me from what he was saying if I insisted on defending myself—at that point it would no longer be supportive to him in terms of something he could defend himself against, but it would perpetuate whatever problem he had.

S—You see analysis is not only support. That is the situation. You, personally—you, yourself—are a person who grasps things intellectually, and as long as you can hold on to them intellectually you can say it. So actually you protect yourself against emotions. I'm not talking now just about your emotions, but also the emotional impact of this patient, whose emotional impact is very strong. If this patient were not an intelligent fellow, not a person with whom one can relatively easily identify, then, of course, you would not need to defend yourself against him so much.

A—But it's too close to home.

S—Too close to home. And that is what we have to deal with, with this young man.

A—I think that's probably one of my faults. When I begin to talk a little too much, what I'm doing is using my intellect to defend against feelings. I can notice it in other cases too. When I get a little verbose, then I begin to wonder what I'm doing, and I think, in a sense, that I wasn't verbose here, but my words were inappropriate, really.

S—Talking about what?

A—That I dealt with the process of analysis rather than what the patient was saying. O.K. So then he goes on. His last associations of the hour are to tell me his feelings on first meeting me. One, he thought that I was older than he had expected I would be. This surprised me. I think it surprised you too; yes, because we thought it would be otherwise.

S—It's a denial of what we expected. I don't always believe what the patient says to you.

A—I know that this took me aback (laughing) when he told me. This is the first time that a patient has ever said to me, "You're much older than I thought you would be"—the first time.

S—He wants—you see, this man now somehow changes his own protectiveness by saying, "I will tell him that I like him; I will reassure him."

A—Ah, because he felt from what I said that I needed reassurance?

S—Because you didn't accept him—withdrawal.

A—Friend or enemy.

S—He says, "O.K., I placate him; you are older." So . . .

A—But he gets in a backhanded compliment because he says, "Now I realize"—he said, "I was worried because I knew I was coming through the auspices of the Institute, that I was to be sent to a man who was just beginning practice, just beginning analysis." And he said, "And I see that you have an active practice, and I know that probably this case will require supervision and that it will consequently be meticulously handled just like surgeons more carefully operate when an older man is watching them over their shoulders." And he said, "Then, too, I often have a feeling of prestige that the Institute thought that I was a good case to be analyzed." And he ends the hour on this theme.

Comments: This second exchange in the $S \leftrightarrows A$ system is an account of complicated emotional interactions of high intensity. As happened with the patient of GB (Example 2), a telephone call answered by A produces a disturbance in the $A \leftrightarrows P$ equilibrium. The patient verbalizes less of his reactions to the interruption because A does not give him a chance. Instead, A chooses to intervene with an active renewal of contact with patient by explaining the emergency. This is manifestly aimed at relieving any feeling of being left out, although A does not really know that P feels left out. However, when A called him by his last name, P responded with a feeling of being rejected. P actually wished A to call him by his first name; but, apparenlty, both A and P had to defend themselves against this wish for closeness.

A realizes that he missed the point and reports what he intended to do—that is, orient P to the need to verbalize associations to such interruptions. This is a common problem for beginners in such situations. However, they do not always realize the nonanalytic effect of their well-intended efforts. With the help of S, A in this case is able to see that he stopped P's flow of associations, but he has difficulty recognizing his own defensiveness against the same problem: that of emotional closeness in the transference. To make a gesture of closeness but on a superficial level, calling him by his famliy name, was a defense against the transference demands both positive and negative.

S confronts A with this behavior. A responds with an intellectual formulation which S interprets as the same kind of defensive action. S vigorously elaborates A's problem as she sees it. The positive equilibrium between S and A definitely is disturbed as A begins to defend himself against S. The interaction continues with evaluative judgments on both sides expressed in highly emotional terms, especially by S.

The equilibrium between S and A is restored by effort on both sides. S focuses on the primary goal for both of them, the successful therapy of P. She points out how A's defensive needs interfere with the promotion of the analysis and A is able to accept what she says and elaborate on it. He identifies with both P and S at this moment, begins to introspect and analyze himself. As we will see in subsequent examples, this experience with P and with S had a powerful impact on A. It brought him to recognize a personal problem stirred up by this patient, which later made him decide on his own to go back for more personal analysis.

This exchange demonstrates the strain that can develop in the equilibrium of each system in the supervisory experience. In the $A \leftrightharpoons P$ system here, disrupting tensions are managed by an intellectual focus and other distancing techniques used by A and P and which A permits to continue. Here the equilibrium is maintained on a positive basis at the expense of the therapeutic process.

The learning alliance between S and A is put under great strain as S recognizes A's mistakes and the effect they have on the patient's therapy. She reacts emotionally to this situation in the supervisory relationship and proceeds to pursue the problem with what looks like unnecessary forcefulness—unnecessary because of A's fundamentally earnest investment in learning and his capacity to examine himself as he becomes aware of his mistakes and their defensive motivation. A is under a double strain since something in P's interaction is obviously making him anxious and stimulating activity which has a negative therapeutic effect. This situation with his patient needs to be revealed to S, who necessarily evaluates it. Even anticipation of her criticism could create tension in A and put stress on the learning alliance. When it comes, A responds with defensiveness against S as well as against P, although each stimulus for this kind of behavior is determined by different factors. It is clear that S presents her evaluation of A in penetrating fashion and stirs him to self-examination, even though she does not attempt to interpret the conflict or its genetic roots. Handling this obvious countertransference, S limits her activity in this exchange to confrontation of A with his lack of awareness to the effect of his behavior on P, and to the presence of unconscious motivations in himself which need attention if he is to treat this patient well and to become a competent analyst.

This exchange demonstrates a problem for the supervisor. She has some responsibility for the patient's welfare and is naturally concerned when the analyst makes mistakes. Here the problem was how to protect the patient and at the same time teach the inexperienced analyst how to correct his mistakes. When A's difficulty was clearly a neurotic problem of his own, then S was faced with an increasing sense of helplessness. She could not treat P herself and she could not analyze A. In this instance, disappointment in *A* was an added factor to intensify her frustration, helplessness, and tension, which found an outlet in the emotional manner and the vigor of her interaction with *A*. This is an illustration of a frequent occurrence in supervision which does not always have as constructive an outcome.

Exchange 3

S—What happened then?

A—Then the next hour, he comes and he tells me that Natalie is coming to town. He's put this visit off with Natalie for about a month and a half; finally she's coming. And he has a feeling of expectation and he says he doesn't think he's going to try to limit his sexual activities. There's an urgency and here's a chance to express it. Then he discusses that he is going home for a week, and he mentioned this at the beginning of the week—that his schedule called for having about a week, a week before January 1 and a week before July 1—and so we fully discussed it and I told him about my vacation, that it would be longer than usual. So I told him when I would be gone. So he said, "Now, remember, I told you that I would be taking a week off," and I said, "Go ahead and have a good time." Then he discusses that he doesn't like to go home because he doesn't know what to do with himself when he's home with his people, but he's going to go anyway; his mother nags him; his father insists on discussing things that only his father is interested in. He returns to Natalie, stating that this would be a chance for sexual release, that he's been limiting himself lately: there's been no masturbation now for about two weeks and intercourse in frequency has been cut down—once with Betty and once with Bea—and then he says that Natalie is the most attractive one to him, and then he laughs and says, "She is the most oedipal."

S—Oedipal—what do you think it means?

A—Well, it means to him that she's more like a mother than the other girls are. She's older, she is a mother, and so on.

S—Oedipal from his point of view?

A—Yes. Then he mentions to me four thoughts that occur to him all at once: (1) feelings about his impotence, (2) feelings to superiors, (3) feelings to inferiors, (4) a homosexual dream of childhood which he had when he was about eleven years old, which he recalled several days ago and somehow or other couldn't remember to tell me. Then he says that he'll discuss his impotence because he feels that most at the moment, and he says that there's been two occasions, one when he was with Marcia and one when he was with Natalie, and both times he felt guilty because he was hiding from both Marcia and Natalie his affair with the other one, saying to both of them, "It's all over; I broke it off," and then he would be impotent at that point.

He feels that impotence is a punishment and that if he were to marry at this time, that he would be impotent because he is so fickle. He wouldn't be able to be constant with his wife, with one woman. And then he feels that—he hopes that analysis will turn out to be a prophylaxis against the occurrence. Then he tells me the dream that he had in childhood that he recalls now. It is a dream in which he is with Don, who is one of the friends with whom he had a lot of mutual masturbation and mutual handling of genitals, and he is putting his penis into Don's rectum and he says that the dream is one in which it seems as though the rectum were a funnel, and the funnel was filled with milky fluid. And this is the dream that he feels is a homosexual dream of his childhood, and in discussing it he feels—he remembers that at this time he clearly had the impression that women had penises and testicles and that somehow or other this dream indicates to him how curious he was about finding out about such things, about conception, about intercourse, about male and female anatomy, etc. And then he returns to the first dream which he had in analysis here, the dream of his immediate superior showing him a film in which Marilyn Monroe is being examined physically. He has a voyeuristic pleasure from it and he discusses then his interest in stag movies when he was in college, because even when he was in college he was not sure of just what was there. And then he discusses—he tells me an anecdote of his feelings about how he was correct in a business decision, and his immediate superior was incorrect. Our patient's feelings were benevolent to the boss: "Well, you can make a mistake. You know these things happen." He says that he could only be this way because he felt superior to his superior, and that's the gist of the story.

S—Do you have the feeling that this is true?

A—About his feeling of benevolence to the boss?

S—What about that?

Comments: P, having been more directly involved with A in the last hour, takes a different tack in the next and talks about his sexual affairs. He takes note of A only to tell him he is going away for a week. There is a slight provocativeness communicated in the way A reports this interaction to which A seems to respond by informing P of his own vacation. This is not followed by any further analysis and S does not ask about A's reasons for his activity here. P seems to be moving toward a provocative rivalry with A which is not made explicit by A or by S. P moves away from the rivalry to a safer position by discussing his impotence and referring to homosexual childhood curiosity. Then he moves back again, recounting a competitive episode with his immediate superior. A gives no information on his associations to the meaning of this material, and when S prods him, he backs away. S does not press the point.*

Exchange 4

A—Well, I don't know what to say about it. I'll just have to put it in the back of my mind. Then he discusses after this his feelings about inferiors—namely, the mechanics, shop men. He discusses them the following way: he says that "the foreman, he's tough; he makes the mechanics do the work

---

* Many other comments could be made regarding this exchange, but we decided to focus only on these.

they should do." He himself, is not. He resents their attitude and he leans over backwards to be. My interpretation of this, myself, is that he's obsequious really to superiors and that he's a martinet to inferiors and this is bending over backwards to try to be what he really isn't, he pretends to himself that he's a mild, nice guy. But I said nothing to him about it; I didn't know what to say. Then he tells me how he goes to great pains to avoid father's anger. At this point something clicks in my mind. He's been talking recently—not recently, all along—that he also goes to great pains to avoid women's anger. So I point out to him—I remind him that he often talks of women in the same way: "You try to avoid your father's anger, you try to avoid the women's anger, and this, perhaps, ties in with your formulation last time that your trouble is with relationships in general." And he says at this point that he just doesn't remember ever having said that he had trouble with relationships and he's a little bit angry at this point.

S—You make too much out of that statement because you think that that says something. Everybody has some trouble in personal relationships; this man just has too many and too deep.

A—Yes, and I think the difficulty of clinging to it is it's going to give him a verbal defense which we're going to have to work away, because I can see it forming in the second hour—yeah. So the next hour is this: he discusses his anger at a friend who is probably going to get a job patient would like. This makes our patient very angry and he says, "At least this time I was able to let my friend know that I was displeased that he was telling me this information. That he knew I was angry—I couldn't inform him of this." Patient says, "It may be sour grapes," but he thinks he would prefer another job anyway. The boss in one job is easier to contact on a personal basis, which the patient prefers. And he says, "After all, maybe what I really want is a superior—a warm, father-like figure whom I can get close to." Then he apologizes for not remembering what he said yesterday about relationships, that on the way home he remembered his very words in which he formulated that maybe his trouble wasn't with homosexuality but with relationships with men and women. And he said, "I was afraid that you would be angry with me and that then I'd have a third category of people whom I'm afraid to anger: women, my father, and you." (Supervisor laughs.) So he wanted to come forth with his feelings, even though I may be trying to block him. And he doesn't (buzzer rings; A says, "Our time is up?" S replies that they still have five minutes.) And then he discusses how he's not wanted to anger the boss and how this year at the office he feels more in-group. Last year he was very out-group. In fact, last year the others used first names; he couldn't. He felt very uncomfortable.

S—It comes back to that first name business—how you called him—because he wants to get in closer relationship to you.

A—Then he says in a rather intellectual way, "Is there a similarity in my feelings between girls and father? That is, trying to avoid anger? I try to get girls to fall in love with me and I try to get my father to fall in love with me." He said, "I can express my anger better with my mother than

I can with my father, and I can express my anger with my father only after he's been very drunk and he's meek on the next day, meek and worn out, and then I can't even express it directly. I can only be cold and sulky and not say exactly what I feel." And he complains that his father never was a buddy to him, never tried; he always begrudgingly played a little catch with him, but never a real companionship. And he says that he's always been afraid of his father because his father always has been so unpredictable. He tells how if he would come home late—knew he was going to be late for supper—he was afraid to tell father, he'd tell mother and mother would tell father that he was going to be late, and he would keep his fingers crossed that the old man wouldn't be angry. Then he says that he was encouraged last week by our work on the dream of the cows. He said, "There was something that you said and how you said it that made me feel like I was really working well in treatment, and it reassured me because I don't know if I'm saying the right things or if I'm working right." Then he says, "After all, I have had relationship trouble, not only with superiors but with peers and I've always felt let down." I think I would like—one final last thing because it deals with the relationship between me and him—as he gets up at the end of the hour, he says, "I've been wanting to ask you all these weeks questions, but I hold them back." And he said, "The question I want to ask you is, am I doing all right? I don't feel that I am doing all right." I say, "Why not ask me what you feel like asking me?" "Well," he says, "I feel that this would not be the right technique." So I said to him, "Look, don't worry about the technique; this is my area. Maybe you have some feelings, you think you want to be your own doctor here."

S—you went farther in giving that interpretation than I would have gone; I would not have told this last thing. You see, I just would have said, "Why don't you ask me?"

Comments: The material on relationships with men, superiors and inferiors, continues. *A* associates that *P* is describing himself as the opposite of what he really is but admits he does not know how to communicate this to *P*. Instead, he makes a generalization about relationships and stimulates *P*'s anger. *S* sides with *P*, and *A* tries to recognize the difficulty.

In this exchange, *P* appears to be working at his task and demonstrates the to and fro quality of his associating. He moves closer and then farther away from *A*; he begins to demonstrate some self-observing function; and he makes connections between present and past—all important for the developing psychoanalytic process. But *A* responds to a direct question with a defensive distancing which seems to be compounded of inexperience and a personal conflict. He tries to orient *P* to the role of analytic patient but he interferes with the therapeutic alliance. *S* picks this up and points out the mistake in dosing of his interpretations. Her teaching technique is to offer what she would have said.

The next example illustrates a notebound pattern of reporting which is very common, especially in beginning students. This pattern may or may not represent a serious learning problem. Whether or not it does depends to a large extent on the defensive function of the student's dependence on notes. A beginning student who takes very full notes in the analytic sessions often behaves as if he is compelled to read each word to the supervisor, reporting in the "he said-I said" style. Each detail has equivalent value; underlying themes are not abstracted; and no sense of dynamic process is revealed. The quantity of detail fills the supervisory time with no room left for discussion or other teaching. Such a pattern may be largely due to inexperience, lack of knowledge about what is pertinent for psychoanalytic reporting, or some form of tension in the supervisory relationship. It may be a defensive screen to cover more serious and deeply rooted resistance to learning, such as reluctance to give information about his own thinking or responses to the patient. Such a student may use his notes to keep the supervisor at a distance and prevent his intrusion into a private relationship (Example 8). Whatever the cause, the supervisor needs to discover it and try to help the student overcome it. The noteboundness and the dependence on detail may be easily remedied with some simple explanations. The supervisor's task is to decide whether the problem can be traced by technique of supervisory teaching alone or whether it requires more analysis for the student.

EXAMPLE 5

GB (Case I), Supervisory Session 14, Analytic Hours 56+

(See Example 2, Chapter IV, for details of the patient.) In this session, *A* is reporting almost verbatim from his notes. According to his report, he said very little to *P* during the two analytic hours covered by this exchange. He reports what he said, but his comments could be characterized as interventions for clarification and orientation to the treatment goal rather than as interpretations designed to mobilize or make conscious unconscious motivations.

Exchange 1

A—I think I had gotten up to the point where she had been talking about how she had changed her attitude towards her boyfriend. She wasn't going to be so dependent on him. So the next day—that was on Tuesday—she had seen him the day before and they had discussed her analysis and afterwards she felt like a naughty girl, and she realized her prototype for analysis was "Lady in the Dark" with Ginger Rogers. She said Ginger Rogers was in this movie she saw recently, "Oh Men, Oh Women," and she had such a different part that she, the patient, suddenly recognized it's not necessarily like "Lady in the Dark."

S—That she is not like "Lady in the Dark," or it is not necessary to be like "Lady in the Dark," or what?

A—Well, that not every analysand is like the character in "Lady in the Dark." Then she said that her boyfriend told her of a dream he just had, and the dream was that a little dog followed him everywhere he went, and talked to him. And she said—her reaction to this was to be sorry for him because he is so poor at communicating with people and he can't express his feelings, especially any anger. It never occurred to her that this little dog might be herself. (Laughs.) And she just talked about the fact that this is a flaw in him that he can't show his feelings, how she gets angry about some things even if she doesn't show it, how he wouldn't even get angry if they were out together and another man made a pass at her, and her sister says he's weak, but she says, "No, he's not effeminate; he's just unable to show his feelings." She wonders, if they got married, whether she could stand this. She says how all the other men she had to do with were—she's using my word now—ruthless, and how she's not afraid of Peter when she used to be afraid of the other men if she was attracted to them; how this fear was part of the attraction. She says, if they had a child, she might resent the fact that Peter is so passive; how her sister said that she really needs somebody to take the reins, to take control. Then she said, although it sounded ridiculous to her at the time, she realized that I had been right the day before when I said her troubles in the office were not the real problem, because today there's no problem in the office. Then she starts to ruminate why she discussed her treatment with Peter and decides that it's because he said that he can't pay a lot of attention to her now, that she had to prove to him that she could get along without him and so she had to demonstrate that she is making progress in analysis.

Now, the next day she tells me something very interesting—this is on Thursday. She says, "A week ago, last Thursday, I had the worst asthma attack since starting treatment." She had forgotten it several times, "I have to tell him," and she then forgot. She says her period had started on Wednesday and on Thursday evening she was supposed to go to a high school reunion which she had promoted, but she came late and was locked out. So she went home and she started to have abdominal cramps, which is not usual with her period, and she had diarrhea and she was bleeding, and the menstrual blood was bright red and she became very frightened and became aware of the fact that she couldn't breathe. And she had to take medication, and even the next day she had some asthma. She was very weak, had to go home from work. She wonders why she forgot to tell me about this. Decides perhaps the weekend is her time and what happens during those three days she doesn't tell me.

S—There's something else she didn't tell you either—because what caused the asthma? Of course, it was very bad weather, but . . .

A—She finally gets on to the fact that her Thursday hour of the previous week had been very disturbing; she was quite angry with me. That's when I told her what she said was irrelevant. And how also at that time she realized that really she wasn't fighting me, she was fighting something in herself. Really, quite a bit of time had gone by, so I asked her why she's so intent on discussing this event of a week ago, today. And she repeated that she has made some discoveries. First of all, she's not fighting me, but herself; secondly, this treatment is not mysterious or not like voodoo, and so she's not so afraid of it anymore. She's beginning to see what it consists of. Then she tells me a story that she's been afraid to call the dentist because she had been referred to him by Dr. Dean; she had gum trouble during the pregnancy and she's still single, so he'll realize what the story is. She was very embarrassed but this day she finally called him, after postponing it. Then she says, very often with Peter she's very childish, behaves like a four-year-old. She asks utterly silly questions, "Why is a ball round?" and this kind of stuff. (Laughs.) And he used to wince whenever she did this. The other day she stopped in the middle and she was too embarrassed to make this kind of a statement. She feels she has greater self-control about it. And she says she used to rattle on about something that was on her mind to him and he was obviously bored, and then she'd try to win his interest—as if he were an audience and she an actress, or a lecturer, she said. But now she tries to think of what will interest him in the first place and not talk about her own concerns so much.

So I said, "Well, that's very useful socially, but not in the treatment." And she laughed and said, "This is a result of the treatment." She said she realized that it's not possible to solve problems through advice and that help is not the same thing as affection, that the people closest to you cannot help you. She says it's funny how her own feelings about the kind of person she is change from day to day: one day she will think of herself as a fighting person, can stand up for herself, and then the next day she does not recognize that character, and she says how she leans on other people until she suffocates them. When she said these words she became quite startled, realizing the reference to her own symptom: how Peter complains about her being overly dependent and she didn't know what he was talking about until very recently. Now she knows. She says she called the dentist when she realized that there would be an advantage to getting the work done because of the income tax. Now she has a lot of medical expenses anyway. This material consideration was more important than the pain she was suffering, pain wasn't enough. Then she says, "I have a headache now." Then she says that as she took off her coat, coming into the office, she got clumsy and hit herself on the head with the coat hanger—big wooden coat hanger, and the thought flashed through her mind, she'd just had her hair done, very attractively done, and that she was punishing herself for splurging. This was Thursday.

Monday she came in and she said that morning she had slept through her electric alarm clock which rings for about half an hour, and she awakened at exactly the moment when she was supposed to be at work, and she was not surprised at all. She had had a presentiment that this would happen.

S—Yes. She wanted it, so she knew.

Comments: Since this is an excerpt from the beginning of the four-teenth supervisory hour, the supervisor has already acquired a picture of the patient. In this exchange, the notebound manner of presenting the analytic material is clear. A's reporting has another limitation which makes the analysis resemble a soliloquy rather than an interacting process: for the most part, A omits a report of his own thinking regarding the meaning of what P says or the motivations of his own communications to her—his technical decisions.

Another point illustrated by this exchange, and evident in later hours also, is his lack of interaction with S. S says very little but she is obviously listening, as her three remarks would indicate. No direct response is called for from A. However, he proceeds with P's story as if there had been no interruption by S. The last remark of S is an interpretation to which he might at least have given some recognition. Instead, he proceeds as usual to continue his reporting in an almost non-sequitur fashion.

Yet this "bland" reporting is in marked contrast to the vivid exchanges which he described in the previous supervisory session presented in Example 2 (Chap. IV). There, A revealed his sensitivity to both S and P, and was able to use S's instruction immediately by gaining insight into his own associative processes and using them for better understanding of P's genetic material. It can be assumed that the resistance manifested in this pattern of reporting reflects, to some extent, a reaction to the previous supervisory session, with a need to maintain some distance from S and from P. Why this is so is not available to S and it seems that A is unaware of what he is doing. At this point in the supervisory hour, S recognizes A's defensiveness and responds by waiting rather than by challenging it. Since A does not always report in this way, S knows that some current factor has upset his equilibrium. She gets her clue from his dependence on notes and his failure to include himself. She prefers to wait a while and listen emphatically to A as well as to P before she can determine the cause of the trouble and what teaching activity is indicated.

This example of temporary noteboundness is in contrast to situations in which this pattern is prolonged. In such instances, the "educational diagnosis" and the teaching remedy would be different.

In the next example, the pattern of reporting demonstrates a different problem. Here, the student's conscious motivation was "to tell all," but at such an abstract level of out-of-context generalizations that the supervisor felt shut away from the analytic experience and therefore unable to follow the ebb and flow of the analytic process. The difficulty was clearly one of communication with the supervisor—not due to inexperience, since this was the student's fourth case, nor to lack of knowledge about the analytic process. It represented a problem in communicating evidence of the process. The student reported his inferences as to the meaning of the patient's associations (Chart II, 2) but did not give the evidence for these inferences—that is, the patient's associations in the sequences of the $A \leftrightarrows P$

interaction. It became clear in these early supervisory sessions that the problem lay in choosing what to report and was rooted in the student's strong desire to impress the supervisor with his "scientific" attitude and knowledge—a kind of supervisory transference. The motive obviously interfered with the learning alliance and prevented the supervisory work from progressing smoothly. The supervisor felt it necessary to concentrate on modifying this pattern of reporting before any other teaching could be achieved. Hence, she confronted the student with the difficulty early in the supervision, and they had a frank discussion about her position in the supervisory situation, a student's role in providing information, and how the kind of information provided indicated not only progress in the analysis but also his level of learning.

EXAMPLE 6

MF (Case IV), Supervisory Sessions 3-5, Analytic Hours 20-32

This example is composed of excerpts from three supervisory sessions which cover the supervisor's diagnostic thinking and her efforts to improve communication in the $S \leftrightarrows A$ relationship.

The patient is a married man of 35, an executive in a small business, whose work took him out of town for a few days occasionally. He is the youngest of two boys whose father died after a long hospitalization when the patient was 10. Anxiety attacks and phobic symptoms are P's chief complaints. Further details are not contributory to the purpose of this illustration.

Exchange 1

A—Let me now trace back some other things, including what I think is his main transference development—talk about my interaction with him too. First of all, when I talked to you last, he'd been on the couch one session. In the next three sessions, the theme of competitive struggle, interaction with men, tended to predominate. He portrayed the world of men as composed of those whom he can dominate and those whom he submits to. It's a fairly straightforward notion of a hierarchical world, and he's had a pattern of having chums at college, high school, whom he could dominate. These people are still very important to him. The fact that a high school chum married, fairly recently, and now isn't as close to him as before, has a bearing here. I mention this because in the early sessions the dreams and much of the material has to do with competitive struggles with men, and some hint at reversal of roles, with definite transference implications that I'm a dangerous person but that he encapsulates me somehow, too. I'd like to demonstrate that, as I understand it, by a dream and discussion of one of the dreams in an early session.

This is the third session on the couch. He had two dreams the previous night. In one he was at a race track with his wife's brother, his wife, and his brother, and he was—he seems to be losing, couldn't get a winner, but then he got a horse to place, and he told his wife and his brother that he had bet on this horse, and they kind of laughed, thought it was kind of silly, but the horse did come in second and he had a pleasurable experience of I-told-you-so.

Then he had another dream; it was more of a nightmare, and in this dream he and his wife were visiting his mother and stepfather in Montana and they were sitting around a table. His wife and he were to drive to Chicago. Then the scene shifted entirely and he and his brother were in a room, and it was a squared-off room, and there were bins all around the room, and there was a bin, he said, "in the proximity of where your seat is," as if the room in the dream was my office. He said, "A snake was coming out of that bin, but also this snake coming out of right there," and he points to a place right next to him, on the wall, right where he is, there's a snake coming out too. And he said he kept pushing them back—he was frightened—pushed one, pushed the other, but that the one that was to the right of him did come out and that was why he was frightened; he seemed to have handled the other one but the one that was next to him did come out.

Now, in the day residue there's an important experience that tied into that; he had gone for the standby reserve physical examination the day before. This has many meanings: being an officer, the discipline, experience is important, discussion of his brother who was also in service and was not an officer. So this was an area of some victory over the brother. It has partially that context, but also in the physical examination he felt embarrassed, especially when they had to take clothes off, and be examined by the doctor for hernia and cysts, etc. He was frightened, but it's interesting that he describes his fear that he might get an erection and be embarrassed. He talked of it in terms of being easily sexually aroused, but saw it here mostly in terms of he "had seen a pretty girl beforehand," and being afraid that he might think of her. There's a tendency to describe it in heterosexual terminology and not to see it in a homosexual content, at least immediately. And this led to long associations about sexual feelings, embarrassment, seductive mother, and how she would excite him and how then other women would excite him in a similar sort of way; smoking, masturbation, etc., etc.

And practically the only comment I made about the dream was that there seemed to be two snakes, and what explanation did he have about that? That he'd been talking in terms of himself, his embarrassment, and something coming out from inside him; what about the fact that there were two snakes and that his brother was in the dream? This led into much association about the brother and this brought out the fact that he and his brother slept in the same bed for a long time, that he had vivid memories of his brother approaching him in kind of a quasi homosexual act—that is, he would be asleep and his brother would cuddle him, hold him, and lick his ear, etc., and that he was frightened, although he doesn't deny that at times it felt good. Then he talked more about his brother's development.

This brother has not done as well as he has, and he has in effect won a victory over his brother by his marriage, the army work, etc.

This was the major line. There are many, many more details. One important thing about this man is that he takes to free associating. I said this last time and I still think it's true. It's the precision of it—and he's observing, very active in this free associative process—tremendous amount of material. I feel, though, that the significance of these dreams is in the fact that I am the dangerous person in the snake dream, and yet the fact that he started treatment and then was able to start with a relatively low fee, I think somehow reassured him at this stage that I wasn't quite as dangerous and that the danger was more from something else. I think there's some of that and that there will be repeated testing of just how dangerous he feels I am. At this point he doesn't quite know how to place me in his rather rigid hierarchical system. [A goes on like this until the end of the supervisory session. S does not interrupt because she keeps hoping the picture of the therapeutic process will get clearer. She finally suggests that next time A give more sequential detail.]

S—So, next time, let's begin from where you see him today. Let's start with that one hour on Saturday and go through the material hour by hour. That may sound like a contradiction from me. . . .

A—No, it doesn't; I know what you mean.

S—. . . because I'm so often heard talking about "don't give me the details hour by hour." But I can't follow the process here, and that's what I want to be able to do, both for the sake of the patient and you. So let's do it that way. We can't do it word for word, naturally, but I want to see the sequences in the hours—see what follows what—not just what precipitates the dream during the day, but how did he get to the dream in the course of the hour—this kind of thing.

A—What would you say about the connection with the material in the process? I have a feeling about it—I don't know—first few hours, there was some kind of a feeling of victory and mastery in that he unexpectedly said that he was concerned that I wouldn't let him start: the business about the arrangement on the low fee. And some ambiguity about where to place me and yet . . .

S—Yes, I understand this, but this is your interpretation; this is not the data.

A—Oh!

S—You see what I mean?

A—Yes, I see the difference.

S—I heard you tell me these things, and as far as I know they're perfectly correct and they make good sense, as far as I can tell, but I have no data to make any kind of consensual interpretation. I don't see what you made your interpretations from—the dreams, yes, but these, again, were presented as isolated phenomena.

Comments: The problem can be seen clearly here in A's urge to summarize themes and to present dream material isolated from the context in which it occurred. This pattern of reporting does not give S adequate information to establish any empathy with P or with the interactions in the $A \leftrightarrows P$ system. For a student analyzing his fourth case, this represents a serious learning problem. The tentative "educational diagnosis" lies between lack of aptitude for doing analysis or for learning from experience, or a learning block generated by some kind of transference reaction. Since he was analyzing three other cases under supervision and had progressed at the usual rate from one case to another, the diagnosis could not be entirely a lack of aptitude. S confronted him with her difficulty, explained what needed to be done and recommended a specific modification of the pattern of reporting for the next supervisory session.

Exchange 2 (*Supervisory Session Two Weeks Later*)

A—O.K. You want me to go into the sessions in some detail in the material. Before we do that, let me give a brief outline of what I think is taking place. I've seen him five times since last time I saw you. He was away one week. Most of the material in the first session has to do with cues about what being away meant to him, and it's even more clear in the second session, in which the concern that I would be angry about this began to emerge as an important factor. He tells of having a headache, some material in a dream, and some other thing that I'll talk about. Then in the material during last week I think the struggle over the commitment to treatment becomes a crucial issue, and it's again stimulated by the Memorial Day holiday. By the third day, there was definite evidence of increased anxiety related to concentration of sessions for him, as we saw a few weeks ago, which I think still indicates the struggle over commitment to treatment. It comes in the form of an intensification of his anxiety over examining some certifying papers. I think this is related to the phobic structure, but it's used protectively and has been interpreted by me as protective already. What he attempts to do is say, "Well, I guess I should look beyond this and look back on the past." I interpreted that that too is looking away from the here and now, what his feelings are about me and the treatment, and so this elicited a good deal of reaction and I think showed some of his fears and anger. I'm beginning to think this is a nuclear conflict here, at least one of the nuclear—that is, his fixation at an early level of the oedipal period in which it is both the comparison with his father, the wish to destructively incorporate, and yet some fear that in the incorporative process that something terrible would happen to him, beyond just the retaliation for the destructive wish. The fact of father's illness as something bad and dangerous comes into play, and what especially stimulates me right now is there's a great deal of material through here of memories of being frightened by father, by other patients on the ward with father, by the hospital, by memories of being terrified that a patient would come in to the elevator as he went up to see father, and a number of other things which, I think, will emerge as an important problem in the transference if it hasn't already. I think some of the fear emerges already, around the issue of how I'll react and about his wanting to get away, and a number of other things like that. This is the basic line of the material. In terms of my activity, let me sort of summarize that to you just before I go into the sessions. In the first session I realized that I was rather quiet, so towards the latter part of the session I was, I think, also trying to get my bearings and see what the material meant, and the only interpretation I made was a comment showing how his behavior indicated a fear that he was like father. This was a rather dramatic moment in the session when he was imitating his father's slurred speech and talking of symptoms that he had, which are quite obviously related to the father's symptoms and symptoms of other patients in the hospital. In the second session much of my activity was involved in a dream interpretation, but also in bringing him back to look at the meaning of the headache that he rather casually said that he had when we started with the session, which was a way of trying to relate the dream, and other feelings to the here and now within the session. In the third session there was more work on the meaning of the headache and what this had to do in terms of his concern over my anger. And in the fourth session much of what I did was related to showing the use of his anxiety of examining the papers as protective and as resistance, and then beyond that how he wanted to retreat from that to the past, again without fully looking at the meaning of how his anger to me was related to the headache. This is a little out of context.

Comments: Only a sample of *A*'s pattern of reporting at the beginning of this supervisory session is given here. It underlines his tendency to talk in terms of abstract generalizations which give no information about the analytic process. Even the abstracted process is separated into the patient's "activity" and the analyst's "activity," thus isolating one from the other.

Following this introduction, *A* proceeded to give more specific material, but the same learning problem persisted. *S*, unable to meet in the available time the teaching tasks she felt were indicated, asked *A* to come for a two-hour session in two weeks.

By this hour the educational diagnosis leaned more in the direction of a transference reaction which *A* had resistance to recognizing. It seemed to be directed more toward the supervisor than toward the patient. Was it a general character defense or something more specific to *A*'s feeling about this supervisor? Exchange 3 gives us a few more clues and an idea of how *S* dealt with the problem.

Exchange 3 (*Next Supervisory Session Two Weeks Later*)

A—Could we start with the learning problem that came up last time or would you rather I talked about the patient?

S—Well, suppose you tell me what you think about your learning problem.

A—Well, from the other case on which I worked with you, I remember the way I summarized. It was somewhat abstract, as if isolated, as if not really representing a process, best illustrated by the time that I didn't see you for a month, that I listed a series of dreams and was showing the process by a kind of flow of unconscious material from the patient without bringing it into interactional focus—that is, in the sense of what was going on between the patient and me. What I reported was material taken out of context. I had tried last time to change that. This is a conscious attempt on my part and I did not succeed, so it means that it's more than a learning problem; it's something else. Actually the feeling that I have about this case, intuitively, is that he's ideal for analysis, and he's moving in the direction of developing a transference neurosis. I think I can specify that, but still it doesn't mean I'm able to describe the process or describe my activity in process terms.

S—Well, I can illustrate, I think, very clearly from last hour. You recall you said at the beginning of the hour, "Let me summarize," and then you gave me some rather high-level interpretations of a large block of his dynamics, and then you said, "Let me summarize my activity too."

A—Rather than . . .

S—Now this, I think, is a clear example of a tendency, perhaps only under certain circumstances, to separate yourself from the patient, and both of you, in a sense, from the analysis. You see what I mean?

A—I see.

S—Now, I don't know whether that's with the patient too or whether it's only with me. I have a suspicion it's only with me, or whatever I represent.

A—The point is very clear, because I remember that, consciously, as I was summarizing what was going on in the first part, I did attempt to put it in process terms with something that I was involved in in terms of the transference figure and in terms of some action that I took in regard to his being away or not being away or in regard to a certain crucial interpretation, but I see the separation has to be there because of the way I reported it. My mode was to talk of "here are some special techniques that I used," but to separate it—in other words, to try to focus on these special technical aspects. I didn't appreciate your point. The point is, why couldn't I talk of that in the same sense?

S—You see, you're there with the patient, and in the analysis, and you're there the next hour, and I'm not. There are two weeks intervening between the times I get there, and in order for me to really perceive what goes on in the analysis, you have to bring me in. I can't get there by myself. This pattern of yours, "Let me summarize," doesn't tell me what happened, how he got to that association, or how you got to that inference. Then you say, "Let me summarize my activity too." You shift to a different angle. An analysis is a simultaneous interaction and the best way to portray it is to give an account of the stimulus-response sequences.

Now, he comes in the next hour, after your last supervisory hour. There should be some evidence of the bridge between the previous analytic hour and the next one. If there is an obvious bridge, this in itself is evidence of a process going on within him which has to do with disturbances of his old equilibria and some realignment. Sometimes the evidence for this can be given right out of the mouth of the patient, so that it is obvious to me too, without your interpreting it. For example, whether this is an increased resistance or a decreased resistance, or what theme he is working on, what kind of a problem, and then comes your evaluation of this: interpretation and technical decision, and how he struggles with this, and how he interacts with you. How does he draw you into the picture, and what do you do about that? And then what his response is. If you can give me an account of these things, you tell me the process as you see it. Only after we get this kind of material is it profitable to discuss the dynamics in more conceptual terms.

A—I had an insight while you were talking, and it's this: that I think my need to prove myself to you, what I can do, plays a role in my isolating in just this kind of way, in making this kind of fractionation, which really works against it, as so many needs do—that is, to talk about the process and then emphasize, look at me. Look what I'm doing to hasten, to facilitate this analysis. I expect all this comes in and works against just that goal in the need to show it to you, an important authority to me. I realize that is the way that I did think about it too, last time.

S—Yes, but you see what you're eager to show me is not the analysis but your interpretation of it, and that's not the same thing; that's more like a student who is trying to demonstrate to the teacher how much he knows, how much he knows about the things that the teachers are supposed to know. You're putting it on the blackboard all by yourself, and I can listen, and I can say, "Well, that's a fine formulation," but I have no way of knowing whether it's correct or not.

A—There may be some who, in actual contact with the patient, have an intuitive awareness of this process. At times I think I approach that; the capacity to translate it is hard and I realize I have trouble with it.

S—I can't always help a student get to the point of recognizing this problem.

There's one other thing that seems to be involved: an ability to reexperience the analysis as you tell me about it. Now, if you can do this, then you're letting me in on what happened right there in that analytic office of yours. I think that there are many students with the difficulty that we're talking about who have a great reluctance to do that.

A—I know what you mean.

S—For both narcissistic reasons and neurotic ones. In a way one could accuse me, you see, of having a neurotic interest in getting in there and looking on, etc., etc. But whether or no, this is something that makes for a vividness of the analysis of a patient, your part and his part, which makes it alive for me and which makes it possible for me to understand, and from where I sit to try to help you see things that you may not have been able to see, or interpret something from a different angle. This is where I think the supervisor is an instrument that is important and valuable in not only your learning, but in the analysis of the patient. So the question is how to relive the two weeks in your report to me.

A—You know, I can feel this—like last night I was going over the notes, and I felt it some last night, and the question is, could I share with you here today as freely as I shared with myself in going over it?

S—That's the problem. I think, too, that success in this is a measure of success in analyzing. You see, if you can do this with me, then I'm sure you can do it with the patient: this kind of sympathetic sharing of his experiencing. If you can do this, it seems to me it is a measure of your empathy and your ability to understand the patient, not only in a perceptive way but also in a responsive way.

Comments: Here we see an active interchange between *A* and *S* about the learning problem. *A* has given it much thought and is eager to talk about it. *S*, in response, elaborates on what goes into reporting an analysis so that another person can understand it. *A* follows with his immediate associations leading to some insight into his motivations toward the supervisor and his awareness that his way of satisfying his transference need actually defeats his purpose. *S* takes this self-observation a bit further, implying competitive as well as exhibitionistic impulses. She does not press this point, however, but tries to keep the focus on the supervisory goals. She emphasizes the role of empathy in making a vivid case presentation and thereby participating in the supervisory process more effectively. In this teaching exchange, *S* drew on the capacity of *A* to empathize with her, to put himself in her place, and he responded with developing insight and a feeling of collaboration with *S*, a working together for the sake of *P* and for his own learning.

It becomes clear in this exchange that a transference reaction to the supervisor is the principal factor in the diagnosis of this learning problem. It is also clear that the transference elements in the difficulty can be faced and self-analysis can be stimulated in the supervisory process without any necessity for *S* to become involved in "analyzing" *A*. With this much confrontation by *S*, *A* was able to make a good beginning at resolving his need-tensions toward *S* which blocked his progress in learning.

The three examples given so far present patterns of reporting not uncommon in supervisory experience. HB, in Example 4, demonstrates a better than usual openness and system sensitivity in spite of other learning difficulties. His previous experience with one analytic case and in psychotherapy does not account fully for his good performance in providing information to the supervisor. He reveals good endowment for analytic work, an endowment developed further by his personal analysis. Both HB and GB, in Example 5, show clearly that it is not the abundance of information but its quality that makes the difference in the supervisory process. In these first two examples, the information given permitted an understanding of the patient's dynamics by both the analyst and the supervisor, and a grasp of the evolving transference. HB's freedom of communication with himself and with the supervisor permitted more active participation by her in both the therapeutic and the teaching work without having to give as much attention to the learning alliance as was necessary in the other examples. The restricted information of GB and his defensiveness in Example 5 focused the supervisory effort on understanding the immediate cause, but it did not represent a deep-seated resistance which seriously and persistently interfered with learning. Other cases of noteboundness are often manifestations of problems more difficult to overcome. MF, in Example 6, on the other hand, demonstrated even more clearly the difference between quantity and quality of information. He presented an overabundance of his own diagnostic associations out of context with the process of the analysis.

The special transference motivation for this method of communicating with the supervisor is not at all clear, compared to Example 7 which follows. In the latter, AB obviously demonstrated transference expectations of *S* which were transferred from the relationship with his mother. In Example 6, some elements of a mother or father transference were undoubtedly present. Yet, closer to the surface seemed to be a transference from earlier relationships with teachers who had valued rote learning or the abstraction of a scientific report. The stereotyped character of MF's communication to the supervisor seemed to result from superimposing an old learning experience on this one, whatever the more personal roots might be. The problem was dealt with at this level rather than a deeper one, since the condensed abstractions seemed to interfere more with learning than with his therapeutic work. The tone of this transference reaction, however, was positive and both supervisor and student were able to meet the challenge without disrupting the teaching-learning situation.

In the next two examples, more serious and more negative resistances were manifested through the pattern of reporting. They confronted the supervisor with more difficult problems to diagnose and to deal with pedagogically.

EXAMPLE 7

AB (Case III), Supervisory Sessions 1-6, Analytic Hours 1-46

This illustration is composed of summaries of notes made by the supervisor during and after each session. The student, AB, was analyzing his third case. He was intelligent, psychologically well-endowed and very ambitious. Unfortunately, the supervision was not electrically recorded, so that it is difficult here to give direct evidence of the factor in his pattern of reporting which indicated both his learning problem and his resistance to learning.*

Exchange 1

A spoke slowly with grave and ponderous utterances as if every word had the utmost importance and the listener should be admiring and awestruck. The patient, a young businessman, similarly ambitious, reacted to A's manner of speaking with irritation. His covert ridicule was obvious to S but not to A.

During the first and second supervisory sessions, S attempted to call A's attention to P's message. A, however, had poor tolerance for not-knowing. He felt unjustly criticized and responded with hurt feelings and withdrawal from S. S made a note that "A's ambition to do well with me causes him to concentrate more on me than on P." In the third and fourth supervisory sessions, she tried to facilitate A's ponderous, pedantic speech. A frankly resented her efforts and said that he considered her "too demanding." S let this go by in silence waiting for a more propitious moment when A's defensive resistance would be less and his self-observation better able to operate.

In the fifth supervisory session, A reported a complicated dream in which P was ridiculing his choir leader. In his report, A recognized that the choir leader was a symbolic representation of himself, but he did not perceive the theme of ridicule or recognize the transference meaning of the dream. S probed his awareness of these things by questioning, since a spontaneous report was lacking. When S confronted A with this evidence of a "blind spot" regarding the way P was perceiving and reacting to him, the already tenuous equilibrium in the $S \leftrightarrows A$ system was further disturbed. A, with more hurt and surprise in his voice than anger, said, "But I was an only son and could do no wrong with my mother." Unaware of P's transference reaction to him, A was also unaware of his own transference reaction to S, who, recognizing the intensity of his resistance, decided not to confront him with the transference nature of his response. Instead, she soothed his hurt pride with praise for his good understanding of the dynamics of the case in general and told him that, under the circumstances, she could understand his reaction to feeling criticized. This time, however, she went on to point out not only his sense of frustration in trying to impress her, but how P frustrated him also and how he responded with counterreactions. She outlined the evidence that P interpreted the analytic situation as one in which he felt he must submit to the analyst, that his defensive protest made him strive to "get to the interpretation" before A did, that this behavior frustrated A's need to be first and most important, and that he was reacting by blinding himself to P's critical, ridiculing communications. A began to recognize his own difficulty in yielding to the supervisory situation, following which he demonstrated more empathy for P.

In the sixth supervisory session, A told S he had discussed his problem with his analyst. S thanked him for the information but did not ask for

* Ekstein and Wallerstein[29] would call this a "problem about learning."

more details. *A* continued his report of the analysis and *S* noted that a "therapeutic alliance" was developing. Since the hour of the ridiculing dream which led to a crucial supervisory hour, *P*'s tension in relation to *A* had been increasing. *S* had discussed with *A* the possibility that *P* would run away from the analysis. With the analytic work *A* did on his reactions to "criticism" by *P* and *S*, he was able to respond more adequately to *P*'s material. Using what he had learned in the two previous supervisory sessions, he helped *P* to accept the role of patient in the analytic situation. *P*'s tension was relieved and *A* was convinced that there were things he could learn from *S* without feeling damaged. *S* added to her notes, "The learning alliance is developing also." *A*'s "perfectionism" persisted but was not expressed in the defensiveness initially presented.

Comments: This learning block which showed itself in *A*'s pattern of reporting and of relating to his supervisor was diagnosed by *S* very soon, but her supervisory work was more difficult to accomplish. She chose to regard *A*'s resistance to learning as she would regard resistance in the early stages of a therapeutic situation. Recognizing the contribution his transference to her made to the learning block, she continued to focus on the interference of this block in his professional work, making a well-timed confrontation with the evidence from the analytic material. There was no need, in this case, to make explicit a recommendation for analytic work on the problem, since the student brought it up spontaneously with his analyst. The pedagogical problem would have been even more complicated had the difficulty persisted much longer or if the student had not been in analysis. It seems clear, in this instance, that this area of narcissistic conflict had not been sufficiently worked through by the time this student began his third case. These clear-cut transference resistances to both supervisor and patient needed more analysis and could not be handled pedagogically. In this case, however, it can be assumed that the supervisory experience played an important role in mobilizing enough anxiety and in focusing the conflict, so that the student brought the problem to his training analyst with benefit to all concerned.

With this student, as with MF in Example 6, the learning difficulty has to do with lack of self-knowledge and self-observation (Chart I, below the line). These deficiencies represent flaws in himself, in "the instrument" he needs to use for analytic work. Ideally, their "cure" is taken care of in the training analysis and the student-analyst comes to supervision with most of the work on himself done, so that his self-analytic function can operate in the service of the patient and the supervisor can focus on other problems. In AB, Example 7, more work needed to be done on "the instrument" before his introspection and empathy could be effective in the therapeutic process. Basic skills could not be taught until "the instrument" could participate in the process (Chart II, 5, 5′).

In the next example, the pattern of reporting demonstrates resistance against learning which was expressed in a most subtle way and which at first was very hard for the supervisor to diagnose and even harder to "treat." As in AB, the problem had to do with "the treatment." More analysis for the analyst was indicated, but the outcome was not as fortunate as in the case of AB.

EXAMPLE 8

DF (Case II), Supervisory Sessions 1-5, Analytic Hours 1-30

The electrically recorded material of this supervision is summarized here in order to make it possible to trace the development of the supervisory process, while avoiding the redundancy of these transcripts.

This was A's second case, an intelligent married woman working in an allied profession and seeking analysis for her marital problems.

Exchange 1

A reported in great detail and gave much information about P. This information, however, was limited to descriptions of P's appearance, body language on the couch, and biographical details. These details were reported freely and repeated in several variations as if A were eager to include S in the room with himself and P. All of P's family were filled in elaborately. Nevertheless, in spite of these rich and vivid observations, S soon missed any account of A's responses to P or of his diagnostic thinking about the meaning of P's associations and other behavior. S was impressed by A's keen "perceptiveness," but became uncomfortable with the suspicion that some of the minute detail repeated over and over did not come directly from P but stemmed from A's fantasies or associative elaboration without being labeled as such. S was quiet during the first supervisory session except to indicate at the end of 60 minutes, which had covered only three hours of material, that too much time was being spent on these details and A should get on to the establishment of the analytic situation.

In the next supervisory session, this impression was intensified for S by A's pattern of reporting not only new details but many of those already told, as if A felt S needed to be reminded of the previous material. It soon became apparent that A was not trying to be helpful to S, who might easily be expected to have forgotten some things during the interval of a week, but that this pattern was a defensive maneuver which stood like a shield between A and S. How P kicked off her shoes, how she lay down, her posture on the couch, etc., was repeated several times and the pattern of reporting made a caricature out of both the analytic and the supervisory process.

In the second hour S tried to break through the shield by focusing on the latent meaning of a dream. A listened to what S had to say, categorically contradicted it, and without pause returned to his "stream of perceptions." S noted A's resistance, but said nothing, feeling that she needed more time to observe this strange behavior in order to evaluate its significance. It was clear that P seemed to possess an unusual ability to observe her own experiencing and A had a need to show S that he "perceived" it all, but descriptions of his perceptions was as far as he could go. In the third supervisory session it became clear that A possessed an intense empathy with P that interfered with his ability to keep enough distance from P in order to objectify his observations and give them "meaning" in the analytic situation. Toward the end of this session, S attempted to test A's interpretive functions by asking a question about the transference. A responded with disquieting vagueness, leaving S uncertain as to A's understanding of transference in either a conceptual or behavioral sense. The detailed pattern of reporting occupied so much time that none was left for adequate discussion. A suggestion that more supervisory time might be necessary met with resistance and was not pushed by S.

A brought up the transference question in the next session, but his remarks were so ambiguous and contradictory that S felt further explanation on her part would only involve them in an unprofitable intellectual discussion and probably stimulate A's resistance to greater intensity. S preferred to wait without calling attention to the resistance function of A's behavior. She assumed that the pattern of reporting and A's manner of relating to her had multiple meanings and at this point in the supervisory process she could not be sure whether underneath this excessively empathic perceptiveness was an unusual, albeit undisciplined, talent or a serious personality problem. This learning block could be a manifestation of both. It presented a difficult pedagogical problem, and the pedagogical strategy would be dependent on the relationship between the psychological aptitude and the personality problem. To be able to understand how and why this student was using his aptitude as a defense would take time.

Another supervisor in a similar situation might have decided simply to point out to A: "We cannot proceed in such detail. I know now how this patient behaves with you. You should present what went on between you and the patient, so I can understand that too." Such a tactic would have defined the student's task for him. He could have followed it or not and his attempts would clarify the learning problem. If this had been A's first case, such a procedure would have been indicated without doubt. Since it was a second case, however, and since some of the same difficulties had been reported by the first supervisor, it seemed to S necessary to proceed slowly. As the analysis went on, it became clear through the smokescreen of detail that P was growing more and more anxious and seemed to be reacting to a feeling of distance and rejection from A who, if his report was accurate, was carrying "abstinence" to the limit in his lack of response or interpretation to P. It also seemed clear to S that A, while aware of P's growing anxiety and worried about it, did not understand it well enough to interpret it. S became more active and explained to A her understanding of the $A \leftrightarrows P$ relationship and how A's close listening in silence made P afraid of revealing herself while at the same time stimulating a longing for further closeness. S indicated she thought A must be insecure about something with P. A said very little in response to S and did not appear to have grasped the meaning of S's interpretation of P's conflict and anxiety. S tried again in several different sessions to make clear how A's behavior with P raised P's level of anxiety, and in turn this increased A's insecurity. S explained that the resulting spiral of emotional interaction could be counteracted by a more objective understanding of the process, first by A, and then, through interpretation, by P also.

In the teaching exchange, S decided not to open up countertransference problems either in the analytic or supervisory relationships without first concentrating on A's understanding of the $A \leftrightarrows P$ system. She felt that A was deficient in observing his own functioning in relation to P, and that if this improved, A could develop a better understanding of the transference-countertransference reactions without feeling so threatened by them, either in the analytic or the supervisory situations. Slowly, the work went on with temporary improvement. A consulted with his analyst, to little effect. Eventually, the supervision terminated without good therapeutic results or learning achievement.

The first examples given in this chapter present patterns of reporting not uncommon in supervisory experience. They illustrate the kinds of information fundamental to a good teaching-learning experience: a clear vivid picture of the patient to which must be added the analyst's diagnostic thinking and self-questioning, plus an account of the analyst-patient interactions (Chart II, 1, 2, 3, 4). As stated earlier, an adequate report gives evidence that the student-analyst is able to use his receptive, perceptive, synthetic, and integrative functions in the service of psychoanalytic work, and that he possesses good system sensitivity and system responsiveness (Chart II, 1', 2', 3', 4').

These examples also illustrate variations in reporting which influenced the supervisory process in different ways. Deficiencies in any one of these four basic areas of information produced tensions in the learning alliance alerting the supervisor to the manifest learning difficulty. Evaluating this problem in relation to the four fundamental learning objectives mentioned earlier, the supervisor attempted to determine the cause and set the student on a more productive path. In two cases, Examples 7 and 8, the matter of the student's preparation of himself as an analytic instrument seemed to be in question. AB, Example 7, was able to profit by more analytic work on the personality characteristics which so clearly interfered with his professional work, whereas DF, Example 8, was not able to do so. It was clear that both of these students needed more development of their self-observing functions before learning could proceed in supervision. In AB and DF, the necessary help could not be provided by the supervisors. HB, Example 4, presented another variety of professional handicap, caused by an unsolved conflict, which required more personal analysis in spite of his earnest self-observation and his capacity for introspection. Learning, however, proceeded parallel with his investigation of himself. GB and MF, Examples 5 and 6, were able to exercise their self-analytic functions enough to overcome the learning difficulties demonstrated here. They possessed "instruments" adequate for beginning an analysis, so that the supervisory experience could concentrate on basic objectives and then could move on to the more advanced objectives of the middle phase of the supervisory process.

— VI —

The Supervisory Process: Middle Phase

IT IS IN THE MIDDLE PHASE OF AN ANALYSIS WHERE, AS IN A CHESS game,[42] the variety of therapeutic problems multiplies. The opening moves may be fairly constant. The end-game may be predicted with some confidence if all goes well in the middle phase. The flow toward the end-game may be described in general terms but the variations caused by resistances, regressions, and the impact of current life situations on both patient and analyst cannot be foreseen. Only "living it through" in a situation where the experience can be simultaneously objified will enable a student-analyst to understand the psychoanalytic treatment process and develop his equipment for meeting its myriad challenges.

When one examines the middle phase of an analysis, the phenomena of regression and transference stand out, interwoven with each other in the complex movement to the level of a transference neurosis with all of its primitive affect and irrational resistances. A student-analyst must learn to identify these phenomena in the behavior of the patient and to facilitate their development and working through by skillful interpretation. The intensity of erotic and aggressive affect, its incongruity with the immediate present, and the patient's use of the analyst as an object for reworking his infantile conflicts test the analyst in many areas. They test his tolerance of aggression and frustration, his impulse control, his empathy, and his ability to listen with understanding. The regressive content of the patient's behavior, especially the unrealistic aspects of transference expectations, arouse deep-seated impulses and wishes in the analyst, which may set off a chain of anxiety reactions and various other manifestations of conflict, such as defensive guilt or shame. These stresses touch an analyst more deeply in the middle phase than in the beginning and are more likely to reach his vulnerable spots, with consequent stimulation of counterreactions.[51] If they persist, these reactions interfere with the analytic process and block the student's development.

The prevalence of such reactions in the middle phase defines the more advanced learning objectives in this phase and influences the focus of supervisory teaching. The student-analyst's system sensitivity is called upon to penetrate to deeper levels of meaning as the regressive transference develops. With the successful initiation of the psychoanalytic process, the surface resistances of the early hours are modified, the multiplicity of behavioral determinants becomes more observable and changes from one defensive position to another become more rapid. Thus, the increasing complexity of behavior in the $A \leftrightarrows P$ system makes increasing demands upon the diagnostic and interpretive functions of the analyst. First, however, he must learn to recognize the patient's behavior as manifestations of the different aspects of transference and he must learn to identify his own countertransferences (Chart II, 5'). This task of applying explanatory concepts to behavioral observations confronts him in all phases of his work but it is more complicated and difficult in the middle phase. A large share of the supervisor's teaching effort is directed toward helping the student reach this objective.

Learning to correlate theory of transference and regression with clinical manifestations should ideally precede learning how to facilitate their development. In other words, diagnostic understanding of these phenomena naturally comes before interpreting them to the patient. Such an ideal learning sequence is hard to provide for a student of psychoanalysis because of the demands of the clinical situation. The immediacy of the interaction between analyst and patient often calls forth a therapeutic intervention before full understanding of the situation has been achieved. Steps in the process of observing phenomena, understanding their meaning and choosing a therapeutic tactic proceed in rapid succession compared to the relatively slower pace which is possible in other clinical fields, such as internal medicine. There the diagnosis which determines the choice of therapy is often delayed pending laboratory tests, and both the therapist and the student have a chance to consider the matter more deliberately. In the analytic situation such deliberation is frequently not possible, especially for an inexperienced student, and an interpretation is often evoked prematurely. To diagnose transference phenomena and to develop interpretive skill (Chart II, 6') are two learning objectives prominent all through supervised training. However, they become especially important in the middle phase of the supervisory process. Ideally, the student should master the fundamentals of diagnosis before proceeding to the technique of interpretation, but because of the special transactional nature of the situation with the patient, the student-analyst cannot approach them separately.

It is the supervisory situation which provides this opportunity through a retrospective scrutiny of the analytic events. The student's trials and errors can be compared with what the supervisor thinks and what he might have done, in the light of his more extensive practice in thinking in terms of psychodynamic processes. The supervisor can focus on the student's learning needs one at a time and thus help the student to identify the various facets of conflict, defense, transference, and genetics removed from the urgency of responding to the patient. Retrospectively, the effect of the student's therapeutic interpretations can be examined in relation to his diagnosis of the analytic moment. The result can be compared with what he was consciously aiming toward and he can see how far off target he might have been. Review of these therapeutic events with the supervisor teaches the student to differentiate his mistakes in understanding from the nuances of the way he expresses his interpretation to the patient. His tone of voice or the affective valence of a word may not be congruous with his target and the patient may respond to these nonverbal elements instead of to the message the analyst wishes more consciously to communicate (see Examples 2 and 13).

Learning to assess the dynamic and economic effects of an interpretation presents many difficulties, as will be brought out later in this chapter. However, the supervisory study of the oscillations of resistances and the movements within an hour, from hour to hour, and from phase to phase of an analysis (Chart II, 5, 6) teaches the student the meaning of psychoanalysis as a dynamic process (Chart II, 6') with all its ups and downs and gradual progression toward changes in intrapsychic structures.[63]

As the supervisory process progresses and the student's self-observing functions become more active in his analytic work, the area of self-analysis claims more teaching attention. This area is intimately tied in with teaching the technique of interpretation since proper responses are prevented when character resistances or neurosis stands in the way.[42] In the middle phase, the supervisor is in a better position to focus on blind spots, since they become more observable in relation to specific interactions in the therapeutic work and the student can be more successfully confronted with evidence of "blindness" or other effects of his internal anxiety and conflicts. He can more readily see how they interfere with his interpretive skill. Indeed, in the initial phase, the supervisor's concentration on the student's perceptiveness, his self-observations, and the importance of communication with himself (Chart I, a') now bears fruit and leads easily to a more advanced level of learning: the various layers and directions of the unfolding psychoanalytic process as it includes himself as well as the patient are comprehended. The student can begin to see *how* and to understand *why* his patient's behavior produces an effect on himself which generates a response that in turn affects what happens next in the patient.

In this respect the diagnostic analytic attitude of the supervisor functions parallel with and in the service of his distinct role as teacher. As teacher, he instructs the student about the various facets of the psychoanalytic process as they transpire in the interactions between patient and analyst, but he knows that such theoretical teaching would remain ineffective for the progress of the analysis, as well as for the student's development as an analyst, if the supervisor were to avoid confronting him with the effects of his behavior or orienting him toward self-observation and examination of his motivations.

A detailed discussion of the many variations of transference-counter-transference interactions is not pertinent to our topic. Here our aim is to point out that supervisory teaching must consider from its beginning and through all of its phases the preconscious-unconscious motivations of the analyst's behavior with the patient (Chart I, b″). This does not imply that the student is "in analysis" with the supervisor, since the supervisor does not attempt to interpret unconscious conflicts of the analyst or to assist in working them through to their genetic roots. The supervisor simply trains the observing ego of the student to observe not only the patient's behavior but also himself in interaction with the patient (Chart II, 5, 5′). Study of our transcripts and examination of our supervisory experiences, both as supervisees and as supervisors, lead us to the conclusion that development of the student's self-analytic function is probably the most important objective in supervisory learning. Other objectives can be learned in other situations, and in supervision are subsidiary to and dependent upon successful self-analysis. It is for this reason that we put so much emphasis on the supervisor's efforts to cultivate a student's associative and intro-spective faculties by active teaching techniques in the initial phase of the supervisory process. Moreover, the young analyst, when he has finished his training, will have to depend on his self-analytic function to guide him through the unpredictable vicissitudes of his analytic work. His self-analytic efforts will of necessity have to serve the corrective roles of both personal analyst and supervisor. Independently, he will work well and creatively according to the effectiveness of his self-analysis. On occasion, the most significant learning experience will be the recognition that he cannot accomplish the necessary working through by himself and will then seek analytic help (Example 9). To be able to know when this is neces-sary is an important accomplishment for a student-analyst.

It was clear in our study of transcribed supervisory sessions that not all deficiencies in the student-analyst's functioning were countertransfer-ences and not all countertransferences were generated by the same dy-namics. We were able in our material to differentiate motivations and levels of counter-reactions in the $A \leftrightarrows P$ system with widely differing sig-nificance for the therapeutic process which, consequently, called for dif-ferent teaching techniques. It was fortunate that these principal contribu-tors to our research were different in their characteristic way of learning psychoanalysis. In this respect they provided demonstrations of individ-ualized difficulties which made it possible to identify specific "problems about learning" motivated by their character structure and manifested in the relationship with the supervisor as well as with the patient.

Both of our two project students showed aptitude for analytic work, and lack of theoretical knowledge was not a frequent problem. The chief cause of difficulty was inexperience in applying theoretical concepts and in using oneself as a therapeutic instrument. In general, the learning problems which required special teaching effort in the middle phase were found in the following areas: (1) in recognizing the shifting nuances of transference, (2) in technique of interpretation, (3) in self-analysis.

Illustrations in this chapter will concentrate on these three areas of learning needs. These needs are correlated with middle phase objectives which proceed from the basic objectives (Chart II, 1′, 2′, 3′, 4′) and involve a more refined and skillful use of introspection, system sensitivity, and system responsiveness. Understanding of the growing complexity of the transference, and increasing insight into countertransferences (Chart II, 5, 5′) become more focused objectives in the middle phase. The shifting cycles of the psychoanalytic process should become more observable in this phase (Chart II, 6). The student should learn to recognize dynamic lines which form continuing themes progressing toward new integrations (Chart II, 6′). The learning objective of this phase is a gradual movement toward a view of psychoanalytic therapy as a process of changes moving in a goal-directed fashion over time.

To illustrate middle phase objectives, we have attempted to dissect the teaching activities in relation to learning needs as they were demonstrated in the four cases we studied intensively. In such a dissection the parts cannot be separated completely, since nothing is that divisible in either psychoanalysis or supervision. We have tried, however, to differentiate and classify the events in the supervisory process according to the focus of the supervisor in a definable moment of interaction with the student-analyst. In a fragmented, cross-sectional study of this kind, we are dealing with transactions lifted out of the middle of an analysis, and we realize that the few lines of reference available for the reader may make his task difficult. However, any supervisor is familiar with this problem since his intermittent contacts with the therapeutic process necessitate a tolerance for "suspended knowing" as he gropingly listens for orienting continuities. In our examples, isolation from the on-going flow of the analytic and/or teaching process is more apparent than real, but the mass of material and limitations of space create this artifact. It requires the reader to concentrate on the immediate situation being illustrated and to examine it as standing not alone, but on its own, as a representative of a difficulty commonly met in this phase of learning. A more longitudinal view of progress in a student as he struggled with the ups and downs of both his therapeutic and his learning work will be presented in Chapter VIII.

Transference and Regression: In Chart III we have presented a classification of learning problems referable to phenomena of transference

Chart III.—Learning Problems Relevant to Transference Phenomena

A. *Failures of Recognition and Diagnosis* (due primarily to inexperience and deficient theoretical knowledge)	B. *Transference-Countertransference Reactions by the Analyst* (due to unsolved conflicts in the analyst)	C. *Transference Reactions to the Supervisor*

1. Misidentification of *A* with someone from the past.
2. Affect towards *A* (hostile or erotic) as a defense against the opposite affect
3. Regression to a defensive relatively conflict-free developmental position.
4. Regression to a position of conflict.
5. Shifts from one transference relationship to another as a defense against anxiety aroused in the first (e.g., father transference to mother transference).
6. Recognition of remembering childhood events as a screening defense against more anxiety producing events or against a regressive fantasy.
7. Erotization of transference relationship.
8. Resistance function of transference.
	1. Transference to *P*.
	  a. Identification of *P* with a transference object from *A*'s childhood.
	  b. Overidentification with *P*'s transference expectations (e.g., dependent longings).
	  c. Repetition of defensive character attitudes by *A* (e.g., generalized arrogance).
	2. Counter-resistances to more specific behavior of *P* which produces anxiety in *A*.
	  a. Defense against *P*'s affect.
	  b. Defense against *P*'s regression.
	  c. Defense against *P*'s transference expectations.
	  d. Defense against *P*'s transference identification (i.e., *P*'s contrasex image of analyst which arouse his, or her, anxiety over sexual identity).
		1. Generalized character patterns.
		2. Reactions more specific to a given supervisor (e.g., competition or compliance).
		3. "Problems about learning."

and regression. They fall into three large groups: (A) Failures of Recognition and Diagnosis; (B) Transference–Countertransference Reactions by the Analyst; (C) Transference Reactions to the Supervisor. These headings and subheadings represent our attempt to identify learning deficiencies and to differentiate them in relation to significance and cause. We will not try to discuss each instance listed in the chart, since this would take us into the theory of transference and away from our focus on the teaching process. To a large extent the items in Chart III are self-explanatory. Moreover, the chief value of putting them in chart form lies in bringing together the various kinds of difficulties seen in supervision in this most important area of learning. It is our assumption that educational remedies can be more easily instituted if learning problems can be differentiated in relation to etiology. A number of illustrations will be given in this chapter, and cross references made to examples in other chapters with special emphasis on correlated teaching techniques.

The first group of learning difficulties (Chart III, A) involves diagnosing the transference meaning in the patient's behavior. A knowledge of the concept of transference, its dynamics, economics, and genetics, its structural aspects, and its role in psychoanalytic therapy is fundamental to the recognition of behavior which expresses transference and the diagnosis of its various forms, but even excellent theoretical knowledge cannot insure correct application of concepts. This fact was borne out by the many instances in which our students failed to understand their patients' communications because they were uninformed or unpracticed in identifying multiple meanings and diagnosing transference phenomena.

In this first category of difficulties due to inexperience with phenomena of transference and regression, our students could recognize transference as a misidentification (Chart III, A 1) of the analyst, but they had more difficulty in understanding its dynamics: how a given transference reaction was serving as a defense against the breakthrough of more ego-dystonic impulses, fantasies, feelings, etc. (Chart III, A 2, 3, 4). How the patient used the expression of hostile feelings toward the analyst to cover up his positive feelings about which he had more anxiety was something our students had difficulty with even on their advanced cases. Their diagnostic skill was often taxed as they were confronted with having to differentiate the levels and dynamics of regression as the transference neurosis developed. Alexander[1] made a distinction which we found useful in classifying learning difficulties. He distinguished between regression to a relatively conflict-free developmental position and regression to a position of conflict (Chart III, A 3, 4). In the first type of regression, the patient retreats defensively to a preconflict position to avoid the trauma of reliving an infantile conflict. For example, a mother transference may persist, but the content expresses a wish to be fed rather than to be permitted more genital contact. In such an instance, regression proceeds to an oral level of maternal relationship which is less conflictful and more ego-syntonic at that moment. The patient is protected against the more frustrating and anxiety-laden reproduction of the heterosexual conflicts of the oedipal phase. The beginning student understandably has trouble with following the shifts from one regressive position to another, especially when the affect becomes negative and the childhood ego state manifests the primitive affect and distorted reality sense, which the patient's adult ego has held onto up to this stage of transference neurosis.

The dynamic significance of a sudden shift of transference relationship, for example, from a mother transference to a father transference, to defend against erotic fantasies belonging to mother, was frequently missed (Chart III, A 5). Here the meaning of castration anxiety as a protection against the anxieties inherent in heterosexual wishes on a genital level was not difficult to understand intellectually but presented a problem in diagnosing specific patient behavior with such dynamic determinants. In this kind of transference phenomenon the degree of regression is often less; the patient remains on a genital level but shifts objects in an effort to balance the high cost of continuing in a mother transference. The shift may be very rapid and the student has difficulty recognizing there has been one, let alone understanding the dynamics and economics involved.

Often coincidental with this kind of error was the failure to recognize a regressive fantasy underlying the memory of a childhood event. The mistake lay in not recognizing the "screening" function of remembering an event to ward off recall of other events or fantasies about the event—fantasies often more significant than the event itself (Chart III, A 6). The student would follow along with the patient's efforts to recall genetic material, failing to see this as a resistance to expressing a fantasy about the analyst which, if brought out, would arouse anxiety. The student often encouraged recall of childhood rather than focus on the fantasies and affects of the "here and now" experience. In many instances of this kind, the fantasy was almost conscious and a subtle erotization of the analytic experience was accomplished (Chart III, A 7) by permitting the patient to experience affect in the present and talk only of the past. The resistance function of such a pleasurized transference repetition of childhood fantasies (Chart III, A 8) was especially difficult for a student to identify in patient behavior. The concept of transference resistance could be defined, but the in vivo manifestations of it were even more difficult to see and understand. All of these difficulties in category A seemed to be caused more by insecurity due to lack of knowledge and experience than to some personal conflict in the student-analyst.

The second group of learning difficulties was composed of transference or countertransference reactions by the analyst to the patient (Chart III, B). These reactions seemed to be due to unsolved conflicts in the analyst. They also played a role in the failure to recognize transference meanings, but in this category the transference nature of the analyst's reaction was more significant than his inexperience in causing the learning problem. The degree of difficulty varied with the type of reaction in the analyst and the strength of his resistance need. Supervisors often see instances of transferences from analyst to patient. In such instances, the analyst clearly misidentifies the patient and reacts to him as to someone out of his own past (Chart III, B 1, a). These transferences, both positive and negative, produce serious interferences with empathic understanding and professional work.

An instance of true transference from analyst to patient was not observed in clear-cut form in the cases we studied intensively. Other students provided several. In one, the analyst identified the patient with his brother toward whom he had had sadistic fantasies in childhood. The student-analyst, in this case, was unaware of his transference identification for a long time but was troubled by the occurrence of sadistic thoughts toward his patient during the analytic hours. Until he finally overcame his reluctance to report these thoughts to the supervisor, the latter had been very puzzled by an apparent stalemate in the analysis. With the revelation of A's brother transference to the patient, the stalemate could be explained and remedies instituted.

In other instances, an overidentification with the patient can be seen (Chart III, B 1, b). In Examples 9 and 10 to follow, the patient's dependent longings aroused similar feelings in the analyst, so that in his identification with his patient, the student first defended himself against this regressive pull (Chart III, B 2, b) by ending the analytic hour early. Later in recounting a dream, the identification broke through in a gesture and a confusing use of the pronoun "I." For a moment the supervisor could not tell whether the analyst was quoting the patient or referring to himself. In this case the problem of overidentification came close to being a true transference. The following example also illustrates how the supervisor handled the problem pedagogically.

EXAMPLE 9

HB (Case II), Supervisory Session 23, Analytic Hours about 100

The conflict in A caused him to distance himself from P in order to defend himself against the tensions stirred up by P's increasing need for closeness. Both A and P have intense ambivalence and anxiety in this area.

In this segment of material P is talking about his fear of women and his tendency to depreciate them. A interprets the latter as a protective move and P opens up with his awareness of his fear of A, his wish to be free and spontaneous but his fear that if he does he will cry. This theme is elaborated over several hours, moving from similar situations involving many persons in addition to the analyst in the present and both mother and father in the past. The self-depreciation which accompanies P's hostile identification with the depreciated woman is manifested in detail while at the same time he is able to verbalize his longing for a close and spontaneous relationship with A and his stronger fear of it.

Exchange 1

A—I asked him, "What will come out if you are spontaneous with me?" He replied, "I don't know. I am afraid." At this point I terminated the hour. After he left, I realized I had let him go ten minutes early. So I asked myself what was going on here.

S—Who's afraid?

A—I used the ten minutes before the next patient arrived to jot down my immediate associations. I realized I was afraid of his longings and that I must have ended the hour in order to avoid the tension of the situation. I have another patient whose hour ends at the time I let him go. This patient is fighting hard against both paternal and maternal attachments to me. I concluded I had confused the two patients. I guess I understand the other one better and have some conflict about understanding this one.

S—I agree. Of course, we know there is tension here. It has shown itself before, and I know it is hard on you.

A—At other times the way I worked it was to become more rational than he. This time it was an actual withdrawal.

S and A discuss the problem of how to deal with the slip in A's behavior in the analysis of P. Neither A nor P said anything about it the next day. A was silent because he was in conflict over how much to tell P. He considered "confessing" his error and the reason for it. A, however, waited to discuss this with S, who assured him that there was no need to expose himself to P but that there was need to stand the tension so as to expose the related fears in P. S explained that these problems were not uncommon, especially in inexperienced analysts, and that A needed to bring up the mistake, find out how P felt about it, and handle his response analytically.

Comments: In this excerpt from the twenty-third supervisory hour, the sincerity of A's wish to understand himself in this anxiety-producing situation with P is obvious. His professional self-image has been shaken, but in addition he realizes there is a deeper problem which has more far-reaching consequences and demands more analytic work within himself if he is to master it. The relationship with S is clearly positive as he turns to her for assistance with his problem. There is no hesitation to report the content of his bit of self-analysis.

In listening to this material, S accepts what he has to say, but chooses not to move out of the teaching role into the role of analyst for A. With this choice, she communicates her confidence in him and implicitly encourages his efforts at introspection on his own. S focuses her explicit remarks on the technical problem with P.

She makes another pedagogical decision at the same time. As S listens to A's account of the incident and his introspective work, she wonders if she should advise him to see his analyst. She knows that he is not currently in analysis, and she realizes that the problem he is facing is one which probably will require more interpretive work than is possible in supervision. Up to this hour she has confronted A many times with his intellectualizing defenses and pointed out his fear of P's transference affects. A has accepted these confrontations without withdrawal from S, but in this episode it is obvious to both of them that there is a more deeply rooted problem here than can be handled in this way. *S* decides, however, not even to raise the question of more analysis for *A*. She is rewarded for her patience and her confidence in him when he tells her, after the summer vacation, two supervisory hours later, that he made arrangements to return to analysis.

EXAMPLE 10

HB (Case II), Supervisory Session 32, Analytic Hours about 150

In this supervisory hour, the persisting problem of *A*'s countertransference reveals itself again in a subtle form which *S* recognizes through perceiving an incongruity in *A*'s reporting and a simultaneous hand gesture which signals the countertransference. This is an illustration of the unconscious influence of a countertransference and also of the usefulness of a supervisor in assisting the analyst to become aware of such unconscious activity in himself.

Exchange 1

The patient is telling of a married woman he is playing at having an affair with. In reporting the patient's dream, *A* says, "It was a very open dream: 'Mother, Father and I' . . ." (pointing to himself).

S—(Interrupts.) "You mean, 'mother, father and analyst'?"

A—No, I made an error here that I think we have to look at for a moment. When I said, "I," I was reading from my notes, but actually it's the identification between the two of us.

S—(Interrupting again) The identification is visible, because you pointed to yourself as you said, "Mother, father, and I." Hence, I ask my question and you correct the error; so what happened in the dream?

A—You and I understand that I struggle with these problems myself and it makes it harder for me to see the issues in the patient, but I think I can still see them well enough. So the dream is this . . . .

Comments: Here, again as in Example 9, *A* is confronted with his countertransference but *S* keeps the focus of the teaching relationship on the analysis of the patient without delving into the dynamics and the genetics of *A*'s identification of himself with his patient. Of course, by this supervisory hour, she knows that *A* has returned for continuation of his personal analysis.

Examples 9 and 10 illustrate also the supervisor's evaluative function (Chart I, middle column) of making an educational diagnosis of the countertransference problem and then deciding what to do about it. When the learning problem is primarily a lack of information or inexperience in understanding multiple meanings, the choice of teaching moves is relatively simple. In such instances, the supervisor needs only to indicate, to explain, or to demonstrate his own interpretive processing. However, in the case of a character defense or a persisting neurotic conflict in the student-analyst, the supervisory task is more complicated.

In the examples mentioned here, A was not conscious of the residue of conflict nor of its intensity until he was confronted by his "slips" in behavior. In one instance he became aware by himself that a problem existed. In the second instance awareness required supervisory help. S recognized the problem here as involving an unresolved conflict in A which probably would need more personal analysis to work it through to a point where it would not interfere. This diagnosis was made early in the supervisory relationship (Example 9) but the pedagogical decision was to wait and see if A could handle it by himself once the supervisor indicated the problem. This student's eagerness to learn, his demonstrated empathy and capacity for self-observation, and his receptivity to teaching efforts by S determined her procedure in his case. She chose to be patient, to encourage his introspection, and to let him arrive by himself at a decision regarding his own therapy. With another student, more resistant to observing himself and to undertaking the necessary introspection or more reticent in the learning relationship, the supervisor's task would have been different and might eventually have led the supervisor to choose to make an explicit recommendation for more personal analysis.

Probably the most frequent countertransferences are the analyst's defenses against the anxiety produced in him by some specific behavior in the patient. For the most part, these reactions are stimulated by a patient's affect, regression, or transference expectations, which touch on some unsolved conflict (Chart III, B 2) and automatically arouse a defensive maneuver. It is these reactions that are most commonly diagnosed as blind spots, since the analyst is unaware of both his own response and the meaning of the patient's communication. He is "blind" in two directions: his empathic understanding and his self-observation.

Other transference reactions by the analyst to some behavior in the patient can be discerned as stemming from character traits with built-in adaptive as well as defensive functions for the analyst (Chart III, B 1, c). Most of these repetitions of character attitudes are not specific to the analytic situation but can be seen in any relationship which makes the individual concerned feel vulnerable. The attitude has a general defensive function—for example, an air of superiority—which covers feelings of inferiority. Gitelson[49] makes a valuable distinction between this type of character-rooted defense transference and other forms of countertransference. It confronts the supervisor with difficult teaching problems, since the trouble usually originates in the student's narcissistic need to keep his image of himself intact. His counterdefense is therefore often directed against the patient's attack on his self-esteem, a constant threat in any analysis. If this problem occurs frequently and is a serious interference with therapeutic work, it is rare to find the remedy in supervision alone. Since it is also rare to find an analyst who does not present this problem in some degree, the supervisor's educational diagnosis becomes especially important (see Chapter IV). An example of this learning difficulty has been given in Chapter IV, Example 2. The problem shows through in many other illustrations in conjunction with other difficulties.

Examples of defenses against personal conflict were very much in evidence in our material, something to be expected in any student. Primarily, these defenses were manifested in distancing techniques which protected the student against some aspect of his patient's transference that produced unmanageable tension in him for various reasons. GB's need to push off his patient's wish for closeness has already been noted (Example 2). Both GB and HB found it necessary to protect themselves against the pull of their patient's regressive longings. Both students defended in various ways against hostile affects.

Of special importance for the development of an analyst (Chart III, B 2, d) is the ability to recognize the shift from the regressive maternal transference on an oral libidinal level to an aggressive erotic maternal transference on a genital level. This seems especially difficult when the sex of the analyst is opposite to that of the transference imago. It seems to occur because the patient's fantasy of genital satisfaction with a transference object of a sex opposite to that of the analyst threatens the analyst's sense of sexual identity. Until he (or she) has lived through this experience with insight into both the patient's dynamics and his (or her) own reactions to this form of transference misidentification, much counterdefense transference can reinforce the patient's resistances to reexperiencing this level of childhood conflict (see Example 18).

A third group of difficulties (Chart III, C) involved transferences to the supervisor which interfered with learning and in some cases with analytic work also. This type of reaction usually comes into focus early in the supervisory relationship and has already been illustrated in Chapter V with Examples 7 and 8.

Each of these categories of learning difficulty carries a different significance for the supervisory process. The educational diagnosis must take into account the factor of inexperience and weigh it against the signs of reaction to narcissistic injury. Such character defenses can be contrasted with more transient responses to anxiety stirred up by reactivation of an old conflict which would be maintained in good equilibrium if the patient's affect of the moment were different. The supervisor in assessing the educational problem is often confronted with evidence of resistance against insight as strong as any transference resistance in a patient. If intense resistance is manifested even when the problem is pointed out, the supervisor begins to question how much insight the student has achieved (Chart

I, b') and how well his self-analytic functions have developed. Such estimations play a large part in determining the educational remedy. In many instances, the consistent attitude of the supervisor in directing the student's attention to the effect of his interaction with the patient or to an incongruous bit of behavior in his manner of reporting is sufficient to mobilize his self-analysis and unblock the therapeutic process. In other cases, all that is required is careful teaching through exercise of synthetic and interpretive functions, so that transference meanings can be identified. With some problems of countertransference, however, return to formal analysis is indicated.

The following examples are taken first from the early phase and subsequently from the middle phase of the supervision of HB. They clearly illustrate problems in recognizing transference phenomena and being able to deal with them. These problems, which are manifest in all phases of analysis, often bcome more acute in the middle phase. The excerpts demonstrate the supervisory techniques used in these instances and how they varied from simple instruction in dynamics to making an interpretation, including attempts to activate the student's self-observation and recognition of the process nature of analysis.

EXAMPLE II

HB (Case II), Supervisory Session 6, Analytic Hours about 25

This is an illustration of A's sensitivity toward the transference need of P and his insecurity about his response to it.

P returned after a one-week interruption (he had been visiting his parents) and began the analytic hour with resistance and resentment toward A.

Exchange 1

A—P said, "Your calling me Hanson filled me with panic and excitement and a feeling of rejection." I said nothing about it because I thought I had said enough the first time he brought it up, except that I thought to myself, what could this mean? Really, this corroborates the formulation I've had from the very first few times in which I saw him in anamnestic interviews. I felt then that this man is really looking for a warm father. What is building up here in my mind is that he is beginning to deal with the frustration of the treatment situation.

S—The problem is whether you are aware of how much significance it has for him that you, for some reason, are avoiding being the warm father. One has to investigate this. Why don't you want to be the warm father?

A—Well, I thought that over, too, last night while I was going over these notes. I thought that if I gratify his wish, his anticipation of treatment in terms of getting a warm father, can I ever help him to become aware that this is a strong motivating factor in his relationship with people in general—the striving for a warm father?

S—Yes, this is right from one aspect, but one could investigate that from the other side. What do you think about the countertransference side?

A—Well, the first thing that comes to my mind is, can I be a warm father, or should I be?

Comments: A here expressed his inexperience in finding a solution to the dilemma of frustrating the transference demand (Chart III, B 2, c) and yet not increasing P's resistance unduly. S perceived A's tension and insecurity; her pedagogic decision wavered between the formal, theoretical approach and the consideration for the analyst as an "instrument of therapy." On the basis of the theory of the psychoanalytic process the answer to the question, "Should I be a good father?" was simply, "No, you should not; also, actually you cannot be." This probably would have relieved A for the moment but would not have helped him to evaluate himself in the interaction with P.

Exchange 2

S—In the beginning we discussed that this man, although younger than you, considers himself your contemporary and you consider him as a contemporary of yours, even a peer. This motivates your insecurity, "Can I be a warm father?" You correctly say that he wants you to be a warm father, but he wants more. You sense the intensity of his demands and withdraw from it. You can see that you freeze up when he says, "Why did you call me Hanson?" After all, one could say something about that, couldn't one?

A—Yes, surely.

S—One could say something like, "I called you by your family name as one would address a colleague, or person at work. This is not necessarily colder than if I called you by your first name."

A—Holding up the reality to him.

S—Yes, but somehow you seemed afraid of his demand. It is, of course, important to know that you are afraid, and what you are afraid of.

A—Mmm—afraid might not be the right word, but I was wondering whether it is a kind of awareness that perhaps I'm inadequate to the role of being a warm father to him.

Comments: S, responding to the growing tension of A, withdrew the pressure and elaborated on how A's awareness of his problem with P could be utilized to P's advantage much more than if he were to "be warm and get involved." S pointed out that the technical problem is not whether he should or should not gratify the transference demands. She explained the dynamics of the spiral of conflicts which could arise from being a "warm father" and repeated the necessity of self-observation in order not to get involved.

This very brief episode in the sixth supervisory session illustrates that the analysis of P's transference reaction could not be separated from A's reaction to it; consequently, in order to develop the student's independence in directing the analytic process he had to learn to take his counterreactions not as a threat, but as a part of himself which he has to investigate in order to be aware of his functioning in the analytic process.

In the next supervisory session, there was opportunity not only to teach about transference, but also to illustrate the emotionally charged analytic interaction and A's spontaneous self-analysis which, in turn, facilitated S's job of elucidating what was going on in the $A \leftrightarrows P$ system and in each of the participants.

EXAMPLE 12

HB (Case II), Supervisory Session 7, Analytic Hours about 30

Exchange 1

A reported that P related a recent experience. In summary, while traveling on a train he saw two little boys about five to seven years old, traveling alone. He considered one the ideal independent, self-reliant boy; the other he considered passive and dependent. P projected a great deal of emotionally charged fantasies onto those children—his envy of and anger toward the independent one and his repudiation of the dependent child. As P was spinning these fantasies in terms of his current life situation, he appeared to be picturing himself more and more as a dependent child who wanted someone, a mother, to regulate his life, make his decisions and take care of him. He asked questions of A about trivia: how should he act toward a woman at work, etc.

S—What does this mean?

A—I couldn't figure it out.

S—What do you think it means?

A—Well, we're talking about people doing some basic things for him; it may be that he is asking me a very basic thing, "How do I relate to people?"

[A had indicated that he understood P's regressive fantasies, his wish to be a little boy; yet when P projected these fantasies by asking childishly for advice, A did not recognize that P was projecting onto him the role of the mother. Questioning by S did not help; A veered away from the transference.]

S then repeated some of P's questions and added, "P asks these questions because he wants you to encourage him. I don't say that you should encourage him; you should interpret his behavior. You could say, "You are asking me like a little boy would ask his mother, 'Can I go out and kick that boy?' "

A—Well, when he asked me those questions I decided not to say anything because I wasn't sure of my ground.

[Here S avoided confronting A with his avoidance of the transference (Chart III, B 2, b, c). In both instances (Supervisory Session 6) and in this one he was aware of P's transference need. In the previous session it was the role of the strong father from which he withdrew; in this session he was aware of P's regression but felt helpless in interpreting it.]

After *S* pointed out in an indirect manner how he could have called *P*'s attention to how his fantasies were being projected onto him, *A* continued.

A—I didn't say anything and my silence made him pose the question again and he added that he should try to find out why he feels the way he does. I thought he was working in the analysis, so I said nothing. There was only a moment's silence and he was in a depression. He said he is no good, he is no good as an engineer, he is no good in science, would not be good in business; he had no reason to be angry at the co-worker—he was the one who did not do his job. After he depreciated himself for a while, he felt better and began to intellectualize. Then again he goes on in a very vague way to analyze what he's been saying, and he says, "There is also something I'm feeling about you: I am not angry, I am not worried; I feel up a stump and I am panicky because I can't think of anything to say." And he says, "Can you help me with what I'm feeling?" And I said something like, "I wish I could." But at the moment he was so vague that I didn't know what he was getting at. He responded, "It is like fighting with something that you can't see; it's so nebulous." And he says, "I have a little boy feeling right now," and he begins to reminisce about being close to his mother and that ends that hour. Somehow or other, I was dissatisfied with my response to his request. I felt that it was not adequate, somehow, or other.

S—Why do you think you are dissatisfied with this?

A—I don't know. I'm more satisfied now as I said it to you than when I thought it over last night.

S—You are more satisfied now because you face it. You hear your own honest statement to *P* and you know I am in agreement. But why could not anything else come to your mind? I believe that you had the same kind of feeling he had—namely, you were dissatisfied with the fact that you could not bring out more in him and in yourself in relationship to the problem at hand.

A—You mean I was dissatisfied because I felt frustrated?

S—Not by him but by yourself.

A—Yes, that is right.

S—By yourself, by the fact that you could not help more. Now the problem is, how could you help more? In the given situation, interpretation of the regression step by step, how it happened and why, would have been a kind of intellectualization. I think it's just as well. You can let him feel it, but the fact is that you must feel it too.

A—Yes, that's right.

S—There is no harm in that. You will see what will come.

Comments: *S* did not elaborate about the significance of such mutually meaningful experiences in the analytic situation; neither did she ask why he could not help more. The opportunity for such confrontation, followed by pointing out *P*'s regression and by calling *A*'s attention to his response to *P*'s regression, seemed to be a natural supervisory teaching in this situation. Calling *A*'s attention to his own regression in empathic response to *P* was not "psychoanalysis" of the student. In such interventions (as illustrated in Example 3) S did not attempt to establish the intrapsychic motivation for A's reaction. She only called his attention to the phenomenon in order to develop his ability for self-observation and for improvement of his intrapsychic controls.

It is, indeed, an implicit task of supervision to observe and develop the student's empathic understanding which involves his own capacity for partial regression and the control of it. He must be able to take distance from his empathic position and deal with it on a cognitive level in the service of the psychoanalytic process of the patient.

EXAMPLE 13

HB (Case II), Supervisory Sessions 56 and 57, Analytic Hours about 225

In this illustration, A is deaf to the transference meanings of P's behavior. He recognizes the resistance and that it is carried out by displacement. He tries to relate P's behavior to feelings about himself but he does not differentiate the various levels of meaning underlying P's provocativeness. Such a diagnostic step is a necessary preamble to making technical decisions on what to say to the patient. In this example, A's lack of understanding of the transference interactions led him to make a number of remarks to P which were out of tune with the dynamic line of the moment. They disturbed the equilibrium in the $A \leftrightarrows P$ system and intensified P's ambivalence and resistance.

Exchange 1

This period in the analysis occurred a few hours prior to the summer vacation. P had been coming late to his hours or had been cutting short business conferences with his boss in order to get to his analysis. In other words, he had been playing A off against his boss and trying to provoke each one to be angry at him. A interprets to himself the acting out with the boss as a displacement and related to frustration of P's wish to provoke A.

A says to P, "Look, this provocation of Watson is really the result of your inability to provoke me. If you can't provoke me you should talk about it and don't provoke Watson. You should stop leaving the conferences early. I will try to change your hours. You seem to be asking for punishment as though you are repeating something from the past." P felt reproached and thought A felt he was inadequate, but he tried to change his behavior with Watson. The latter praises P, whose work improves, but in the analysis anxiety and anger increase, manifested in coming late. P feels accepted by his boss, who is finally calling him by his first name.

Comments: A's interpretation is clearly too much. It presents current acting out and past conflict, hints at a superego reaction, and is probably poorly timed with respect to the coming vacation, since P is obviously in conflict over having to choose between A and the boss, and latently is probably feeling some conflict about the coming separation. This meaning is ignored by *A* altogether. Instead, he sees the displacement as primary. He intervenes and tries to prohibit the displacement. He tells *P* he should "analyze it," but he does not follow through with an interpretation which would help *P* to see that he feels he is being forced to make a choice. *A* adds to his first remarks an attempt to interpret the repetition of an infantile problem which, in *A*'s mind, is associated with guilt and a need for punishment. *P* feels accused and apparently punished. *A* lightens the load of conflict somewhat by offering to cooperate on the reality time problem and change *P*'s hours so they will not overlap the business conference. The message from *A* to *P* could be stated as, "You are not behaving correctly either here with me or with your boss. You should stop what you are doing with him." This sounds like a voice of childhood authority echoing in the present.

The transference, however, is not understood by *A*, who does not see the mother-father triangle in the problem of choice, nor does he see how his interpretation—at least the first part of it—reinforces *P*'s transference identification of *A* with mother, since it was mother who reproached him and found him inadequate.

Exchange 2

A—After vacation, *P* reports that he did very good work over the summer, that he received open and strong praise from Watson; he was conscientious and happy. He was taken by surprise, could hardly believe it and for a while he thought, "Maybe it's just like my father telling me that I'm great when I know I'm really not great." He has a vague feeling inside himself, thinks he's angry at his mother because she always fussed over small things that he considered unimportant and humiliated him in childhood over table manners, etc. He's angry at her because, on the one hand, she expected too much and, on the other, she did not believe in him. He's gaining confidence at work but mother never stood behind him like father did. I asked him if his anger had anything to do with me. He believes so. He felt deserted this summer but also angry at me for coming back because he feels I don't have any confidence in him.

The next time, he comes in jittery and excessively alert. He reports a dream: He is with me talking about his feelings for his parents and he tells me, in the dream, "My mother couldn't love me because she loved my father." He associates that it made sense when he woke up but not now. He realizes how angry he really is and how much he takes out on his environment.

Comments: Here, again, *A* tries to relate *P*'s feelings to himself but he does not follow through from *P*'s responses. It seems clear that *A* does not perceive how the wish for praise from mother is carried over to hoping for it from *A*, the result being anger when he does not get it. *S* was very silent for most of this hour. She did not challenge *A* to be more explicit to her about his understanding of the transference.

Exchange 3

A—He goes on to complain about his girlfriend who expects too much of his time. He finally tells her he can't see her every night. This is the first time in his life he has ever been able to say no to a woman's request. I got the feeling he was afraid of her, so I tell him, "You sound like you're afraid of her." He immediately begins to intellectualize. When I reviewed the whole hour, I could have bitten off my tongue for saying anything, because he responded by saying he's afraid she will get angry at him. He goes on and on trying to figure out a million reasons why I might be right. So I say, "Look, relax; drop it." He takes this as an insult, feels reprimanded, and wants to cry. He feels empty and is afraid he may get angry at me.

S—Why?

A—Why? Well, the manifest thing is that I told him to stop trying to please me.

S—That is what you meant, but not what he understood. You told him to "drop it." The word was wrong. It meant, "I can't help you because you are just that way." You should have told him, "We have to work this out because this is an important problem." And then followed with, "Your fear of submitting is the problem—to your mother, your girl friend." This is the line of interpretation.

A—Then he tells me he is having a fantasy at the moment and in the fantasy he is saying to me, "Look, if you didn't want to take a chance on my running your idea to the ground, you shouldn't have mentioned it." But he can't tell me this directly. He says, "I make it a fantasy of standing up to you." He realizes how afraid he is of his own anger.

Comments: The same problem presents itself. *A* does not understand the transference. Instead, he focuses on the manifest level of *P*'s behavior and reacts to it without helping *P* to see its defensive purpose or to bring out the affect by himself. By his behavior, *A* becomes so like mother that *P* is almost unable to differentiate them. He manages, however, to be less submissive to *A* and to assert himself a little if only in fantasy. *A* recognizes some of the dynamics of this interaction but not the transference meanings.

In these exchanges so far, the supervisor is confronted by the question, why is this so? Does *A* need to defend himself against being identified as the humilitating, critical mother? If so, his messages to *P* have the opposite meaning. Is *A* reluctant to be the target for the rage against the mother, transferred to all women, that shines through *P*'s various defensive maneuvers? From the next exchange this would seem to be the top level of an interpretation of *A*'s lack of understanding and his rather

clumsy interventions. On the other hand, A's remarks to P have a coun-
terphobic quality, since they seem almost calculated to provoke anger.

Exchange 4

The next supervisory session occurred about ten days later (Supervisory
Session 57).

A—He's very much on time these days compared to early in the analysis,
but he continues to be angry at the world. He overworks but wonders if he
should not work harder. I say to him, "If you are angry at me, why take
it out on yourself?" He says, "Because here, I can't get it off my chest.
But I'm beginning to be able to experience anger here in the analysis. I
act it out by putting things off like I always did with mother. It always
provoked her." He went on to say, "You pose an issue and then you stop
me, saying I'm working on it too much. Earlier, I would have felt like
crying. Now, I actually feel anger and I'm happy because this sounds like
improvement to me."

So at this point, I told him my choice of words had not been felicitous.
He says, O. K., but . . . .

S—Why did you need to be apologetic about it? You could have let him
be angry at you.

A—Well, I felt he has enough anger as a backlog from the past . . . .

S—But he needs to discharge it in a safe place.

A—I see. Because—he says, "Yesterday I felt reprimanded but it felt
good to be angry. Today, I'm almost sorry you explained."

Comments: The problem of diagnosing the learning needs here is very
complex. From this transcript, the supervisor's thinking is not clear on
this point except that in the earlier exchanges she seems to be responding
to A's inexperience and lack of skill by calling attention to mistakes in
interpretation and indicating what she would have said. She focuses more
on the form and choice of words than on the fundamental misunderstand-
ing and countertransference which blocks A.

In the last exchange, A's need to defend himself against P's anger becomes clearer. At the same time, his effort to help P express anger is also
clear. It is not possible from this evidence to evaluate all of the factors
that are playing back and forth in the $A \leftrightarrows P$ system here. Inexperience is
obvious in both the use of empathy and of technical responses. A's counterdefense against P's affect and transference identification seems clear
also. On the other hand, A's honesty and manifest good will toward P
have apparently established enough of a therapeutic alliance for him to be
able to depend on the reality of A as different from his transference images.
This situation enables P to ventilate some of his anger safely and to achieve
some insight.

Technique of Interpretation: So far in this chapter we have concentrated on the diagnostic phase of understanding the dynamics in P and in

the $A \leftrightarrows P$ system, with a focus on recognizing the many levels of transference meanings. The last illustration provides us with material relevant to another learning objective prevalent all through an analysis: the technique of interpretation. Having arrived at a diagnostic understanding, the analyst's next move is to communicate it to the patient. This involves a technical decision, a choice between several alternatives: to remain silent or to say something; and, if something should be said, what should the target be and what words should be used? Each step in this decision is based first on the analyst's understanding of hidden meanings and then on his estimation of how ready the patient is to understand the meaning of his associations on another level—that is, to realize that an unconscious determinant is influencing what he says and feels consciously. The analyst must decide how much of what he understands can be told to the patient. In other words, the technique of timing, dosing and phrasing his therapeutic responses in relation to the patient's resistance and degree of anxiety (Chart II, 4′) is an essential learning objective and teaching target.

In Example 13, taken from an elementary case but one with over 200 hours of therapy, A made a number of communications to P which were poorly chosen, poorly timed and dosed, and poorly phrased. Some of them were off the mark also. They were not tuned to the dynamic line of P at the moment. They disturbed the equilibrium in the $A \leftrightarrows P$ system and intensified P's ambivalence and resistance. The big dose and poor timing have already been commented on in reference to Exchange 1. P feels accused but also somewhat relieved. But what he is relieved of, and why, is not analyzed any more than what he feels guilty about. P experiences these affects in relation to the incomplete interpretation, but he does not understand his experience and A does not help him to develop his observing ego by communicating his interpretation to P in steps which can be followed by P's associations and gradually worked through until the whole conflict, its derivative motivations for present-day behavior, and its origins in the past can be perceived, understood, and integrated. Certainly this work cannot be accomplished in one hour or a few, nor will the first insight be stable enough to last. But the big dose of this interpretation permits P to react with old feelings. He is not given a chance to recognize them as inappropriate in the present, partly because A, too, accepts his behavior as uncalled for and therefore to be condemned rather than seen in relation to a deeper conflict which is influencing his present-day life inappropriately.

Calling attention to the displacement would probably have been enough to begin with, leading on to the provocative characteristics, and followed by a developing awareness of the conflict over choosing. The identification of analyst with mother and boss with father could come next in the unfolding process. How many analytic hours this would require is impossible to say, but in this analysis the stages of this process were condensed into a very short span of time, leaving the patient little opportunity to gain more self-knowledge. Instead, he simply reacted to the immediate experience as he had to similar experiences in the past (nagging of mother). There was a temporary change in behavior but no insight. It was as if, for the moment, he submitted to mother's demands that he obey father. This brought some real gratification in the present but did not relieve the fundamental conflict.

This exchange is a small segment of one supervisory hour which took place after the summer vacation, several weeks after the analytic incident. The supervisor chose to focus on later material, but the incident offers an illustration of a more general problem frequently encountered with beginners. The learning task is one of integrating a number of concepts regarding dynamics and the process of therapy with the behavioral manifestations of these concepts, and of following up this integration with learning the technical skills that facilitate, rather than interfere with, the analytic process. The supervisor, attempting to teach this integration, is assisted by the opportunity for a recapitulation of the analytic events examined under a high-power lens, so to speak. This second look at what did happen can be verbalized in conceptual terms and, step by step, P's responses on their several levels of meaning can be spelled out along their dynamic, economic, genetic, and structural dimensions. The process of the interaction can be reviewed by A with the help of S. This exercise adds perspective to A's understanding of P and the analytic experience. It also expands his cognitive understanding of psychoanalytic theory and its relation to technique. This kind of cognitive exercise is not feasible in the midst of an analytic situation, but one hopes that with practice on this level (Chart I, 3″, 4″) during supervision the pathways of association between specific behaviors and their more generalized meanings will be facilitated so that A's skill in making correct technical choices will become more habitual. Transfer of this learning should free A of anxieties by increasing his mastery of the interpretive process, and thus enable him to devote his attention to the inevitable incongruities (dissonances) in his patient and himself without conflict over not knowing everything.

A student's technique of interpretation is the overt manifestation of whether or not he has achieved this level of learning. In Example 13, A had gone a certain distance in understanding P's behavior but had not integrated this understanding with techniques of interpretation which would bring P to an awareness of the motivations of his own behavior of which he had been unconscious before. Some increase of self-observation and insight into deeper meanings was achieved by P, but not because of A's interpretations. For some reason A did not follow up the analytic work step by step.

The incident in Exchange 1 might be described as a manifestation of a beginner's tendency to "speak out" all he understands of the patient's associations at a given moment. Here it is clear that *A* understood more than *P* did. He assumed that *P* could see it, too. *A* was not able to put this knowledge about resistances and working through into practice. He had not acquired the skill to "spell it out" for the patient or to help the patient spell it out for himself. The sequences of interpretive process which are the essence of the interpretive work for both analyst and patient were disregarded here, and an end-point, the genetic interpretation, was lumped together with the initial focus, the displacement. In this exchange too much was attempted too fast. The gradualness which is an important ingredient of the patient's success in approaching the exposure of long-buried and painful problems was neglected.

Many beginners in psychoanalysis make such mistakes in dosing and timing, not allowing for observation of the patient's response to the first step. Ideally, the patient's response indicates to the analyst whether or not he has hit a target that calls up increased resistance or opens up channels to deeper levels of meaning. This initial response serves as a sign to the analyst regarding the correctness of his interpretation. It measures the equilibrium in the therapeutic alliance and indicates what the next step in the analytic work should be: whether to follow on to a deeper layer or to wait for the patient to catch up. The first dose of an interpretation prepares for those to follow, and the beginning analyst must learn to adjust the dosage and the pace according to the impact of the initial message.

The next example also illustrates problems in learning the technique of interpretation. It, too, reveals a need to recognize the effect of what the student says to the patient (and also what he does not say) on the shifts in resistance, on the facilitation of associative material, and on the speed and depth of the regression in the transference repetitions. The supervisor in working toward this learning objective proceeds as a good analyst does. He uses his own associative processes to empathize with the patient, to follow the patient's line of associations, to fill in gaps with his own associations, and simultaneously to register the effect of the student-analyst's interventions. By understanding his own "interpretive work," the supervisor estimates the learning needs of the student and proceeds to work as a teacher in helping the student arrive at the same position. This is often accomplished by a kind of reliving, in the supervisory hour, of the analytic experience with the patient. The supervisor stimulates the student's observing powers by questions that permit recall of forgotten observations of patient or of self. And by the steps of a process similar to the therapeutic process of interpretation, the supervisor provides a learning experience for the student that widens his span of understanding and opens the way for new skill.

EXAMPLE 14

HB (Case II), Supervisory Session 77, Analytic Hours 400

The event occurred in the third year of the analysis of the patient and in the third year of supervision. It illustrates a recurring learning problem of *A* which probably would be better termed a "habit of communication" with his patient. Although it created a technical problem, this habit could not be isolated from its matrix—that is, from *A*'s empathic understanding and responsiveness to *P*. These primary assets of *A* seduced him into assuming an implicit understanding that functioned mutually on the same level between himself and the patient. Such "empathic" understanding of *P*'s behavior allowed *A* to communicate to *P* his understanding of *P*'s behavior or what was going on between them in a metaphoric, shorthand manner, without following it up by an explicit interpretation of the interaction. It is often true that a more experienced analyst will communicate with his patient in this manner, but he will also assess the need to complete a metaphoric interpretation with more explicit elaboration. An inexperienced analyst, carried away, as in this instance, by the gratification of the psychoanalytic interaction, does not follow up his interventions with appropriate interpretation. The patient, left to his mobilized fantasies, then surprises the analyst by unexpected reactions.

Exchange 1

A—Some important action has occurred, frustrating and resolved, I hope. In the beginning of this session *P* was feeling disgusted with himself and talked with vague feeling about a college friend. I recalled an incident that had occurred two years ago in reference to this friend. *P* felt elated about my being able to remember and a few days later he told of responding with a vague feeling of love because if I could remember something that he had forgotten, it was a sign of real interest in him. The next hour he came in feeling very angry; he had overslept an important conference which was well under way by the time he arrived; the boss was angry because *P*'s report had been needed. I was angry also. At one point of this hour when *P* said, "I certainly have succeeded in impairing my relationship with the boss," my anger came out. I burst out, "Yes, sir." *P* got frightened and drifted off under the impetus of this fright into scattered associations, no doubt the result of anxiety.

The next hour *P* came in with diffuse anger; he did not know what he was angry about, just about everything. I said to him, "Can it be that something occurred in the previous session that you are reacting to with anger?" It clicked. He said, "I'm angry at you because you frightened me with your 'Yes, sir!'" His associations indicated that he felt criticized. So I said, "All right, I'll tell you exactly how I felt. I was very frustrated yesterday. You succeeded in frustrating me as you frustrated your boss, your parents, the women whom you string along . . . ." I added, "Now let's take a look at what is going on." P asked, "What were you frustrated about?" I replied, "I was frustrated by your repetitive self-destruction." P said, "Do you mean to say that by destroying myself I can really get at you?" I said, "Exactly." P said, "I had never given it any thought before." I said, " Well, let's reexamine today and the previous two days . . . ." P, by this reexamination, came to the conclusion, "It is a fact that you and I got too close Monday." "This was the hour in which I recalled the incident that P had forgotten. I said, "Well, therefore we have to examine what is anxiety-provoking in closing the gap between two people." He reexamined his actions of the past two days and realized that everything he did was aimed at "widening the gap."

S evaluated the $A \leftrightarrows P$ interaction during the two phases of this episode. She called A's attention to his gratification from his prompt recall and P's response to it. S pointed out that A could have anticipated P's defensive reactions to his "loving feelings" toward A, but had omitted considering them. Thus he was completely unprepared for P's negativistic, indeed self-destructive reactions, and became angry about them. S pointed out how, in the next hour, in order to regain his analytic stance he openly admitted to his sense of frustration, but at the same time did not make explicit to P the transference gratification afforded to P by the realization that A really "cared," that P could frustrate A like he has frustrated others. S connected the metaphor, "closing the gap," with P's vaguely loving feeling toward A when he recalled the incident, and explained why P might have responded to this metaphor differently from what A had expected. Since A did not give any definite expression of what he meant—the sublimated libidinal interaction between individuals—and did not explicitly differentiate it from P's fantasies, P seemed to have no other defense than to repress the positive feelings toward A and turn them into anger which motivated his negativistic, self-destructive behavior.

Comments: This incomplete interpretation and its consequences can be explained as the result of counterreactions compounded by inexperience. In this instance, A was satisfied with his own performance, first, by his recall and by P's reaction to it. On this basis he expected a positive therapeutic reaction from P. When the opposite was forthcoming, he did not have enough knowledge to understand P's reaction to defense against "homosexual" feelings toward A; he was simply frustrated.

A was also satisfied by the fact that he did not disguise his disappointment and frustration. A, indeed, felt justified in feeling so frustrated. An experienced analyst probably would have been able to predict the negative therapeutic reaction to the "loving feeling" and in this instance might have prevented it by some form of interpretation.

The following example presents another aspect of learning the technique of interpretation.

EXAMPLE 15

GF (Case IV), Excerpts From Three Transcripts: Supervisory Sessions 10, 12 and 17, Analytic Hours 80-175

In this example, the student learned to apply certain principles in the technique of interpretation. He was aware that in principle he should focus on the manifestation of resistance and clarify the defense mechanism before interpreting the content of the underlying anxiety or the layers of conflict and defenses under that. In other words, he understood intellectually that interpretation is a process of working step by step from the surface behavior, which at a given moment is ego-syntonic and relatively conscious, to more anxiety-laden levels where derivatives of persisting childhood conflicts remain unintegrated with present reality. His intellectual understanding of principles of technique, however, needed to be correlated with actual behavior in the analytic work. With supervisory help he could better objectify the phenomena of multiple levels of meaning, of resistance and defense, of transference as a form of resistance, and the significance of working through. Making this correlation of theory and behavior requires time and repeated experience in a situation where this kind of cognitive effort can take place and the work of synthesizing observation and diagnostic interpretation becomes more and more preconscious and intuitive.

In this example, resistance is expressed in a kind of playful erotization of speech and isolation of meaning and responsibility for what is thought, felt, or acted. *A* intuitively perceives the erotized game and erotized transference. He interprets that *P* feels with him as he did with his mother. This interpretation causes *P* to feel sexually stimulated and to shift to talk of homosexuality while at the same time he disclaims the erotic pleasure of the other "game" which is carried over from his earlier relationship with his mother.

Exchange 3

A—And then he goes back to my comment of the day before about the games of masturbation; he says somehow, in his mind, masturbation and homosexuality are confused: he keeps making slips, substituting one word for the other, and that perhaps his homosexuality was merely mutual masturbation, and that his intercourse with his wife is also like masturbation, that he is cold and unloving with her. And I said, " You mean like a cold fish," (referring to a recent dream). And he laughed. Then he says, "There's a pleasure in the analysis in being deviously hostile by not using my intellect." Then he tells me his masturbatory fantasies as a boy: very sadistic, all sorts of tortures of women, quite elaborate machines that he devised in his mind. But he wonders whether being a cold fish is the only safe alternative. Then he talked about his adolescence—how prudish he was but how curious about women. He starts to recriminate again that I don't help him any more than his parents did, and that I don't act the role of father; that, somehow, his helplessness that he displays so openly, as an identification with his father, who also acted very helpless much of the time, especially when the patient's mother was ill. The father had to put on an apron and sort of run around the house in an awkward and lost way. He was ineffectual, and the patient was able to manipulate his father by yelling and screaming disobedience. And that now, somehow, he deepens his feelings with his wife and this is somehow similar to the way his father acted.

He went right on with this the next day. He has never pursued a woman; his pattern has been to be very kind to some woman whom he considered inferior or defective, and then play on her guilt and obligate her to him. He says he behaves with me as he usually does with women, as he used to do with his mother; he's being very kind to me and he feels the right to be demanding, and says that before this hour he almost went into the wrong building where my office used to be—went in the wrong door. And he associates this to some kind of sexual crime. Then he starts to appeal to me that he is helpless and feeble and simple-minded the way he usually appeals to women. Then he says his father was this way, or he thought his father was this way. He also thinks that his professors are this way.

S—He says this with a degree of sincerity in his manner of speech?

A—Yes, I found this genuine; it struck me as some real insight, although he is still talking about it intellectually. There isn't a great deal of affect.

S—He has an accurate awareness as he looks back on himself in his earlier life?

A—Yes.

S—This is an objective observation of his own behavior?

A—Yes. I mean, there's no great anxiety in this as he's telling me about this, but, you know, this isn't his usual playacting.

S—No clear-cut feeling of conflict?

A—No. Then he says, "I abase myself to satisfy the woman." He suddenly gets very helpless, turns to me. "I want you to lead me," he says. "I want you to be my father, I guess." I told him that it seemed to me what he had been saying this hour was that he feels with me the way he does with women. He's sort of taken aback. He said he heard it but he's sort of isolated the idea. It seems unseemly, but he feels a stirring in his genitals like a dirty picture of a woman being tortured—stimulating.

S—Don't you find that rather amazing?

A—That he should get so stirred up?

S—In response to what you said, because he just said the same thing to you earlier.

A—Well, it's the kind of thing you talked about last time: that he says it but somehow doesn't listen to it.

S—He sounds as if he's really genuine? That's why I asked a few minutes ago, does he sound as if he's really genuine? And does he know what he's talking about? It's a common occurrence but it takes some special thought to figure out why it is that way and what to do about it. When you tell him that he's behaving with you as he behaves with women, you're more general than he was earlier when he talked about how he behaves with you as he used to with his mother—she's a more specific person—and then he acts surprised and shocked, but later he acts as if he has been stimulated sexually when you say this, not when he says it. He hasn't been telling you about the erotized sensations that he has when he tells you these things. So my point here would be to call his attention to this incongruity. This way, you can begin to focus on isolation as his defense, and on this particular tactic as a form of resistance against what's going on underneath.

If you take it that your remarks are stimulating him and simply call his attention to that without any playback of what happened before, then I think you permit him to shift his defense to what you just said. Then it's your responsibility what effect is produced by what you say!

A—Well, I didn't say very much because really he said it. He says, "I resist taking responsibility. It's an effort for me to see that you're just repeating what I just said."

S—Even though he says that, the incongruity needs to be focused on in an effort to explain it. Simply pointing it out is like saying, "There is something and there is something and there is something." But how those somethings got there and what the relationship is between them, etc., etc., is still unclear.

Comments: In this exchange, S is impressed with the bland, affectless remarks of P. He says things about himself that would ordinarily be accompanied by feelings of shame or guilt, but here they are reported seemingly without even a sense of conflict. S is further impressed by A's matter-of-fact tone in reporting, as if he too has no feeling of surprise or even question about what P is saying. She wonders to herself if he had any reaction, if he recognized the incongruity in P's behavior. If he did, his reaction was hidden and his explanation of it was not revealed. His interpretations to P, about being a cold fish and about behaving toward the analyst as he does with women, were mere reflections of the surface, at least in their content. They described P's behavior without calling attention to the incongruous lack of affect or the incongruous exaggerated response of what A said.

Clearly, a "game" is being acted out and P is able to continue his defenses of externalizing responsibility and isolation of meaning partly because A remains on the surface and does not "lead" him to a different level of self-awareness. P offers some insight achieved by himself when he says, "I resist taking responsibility." He is asking A to interfere with this old pattern and "be my father" who should have set limits on the games with mother. This transference expectation presents a dilemma for A. To respond as P wanted his father to behave would only continue the "game," albeit in a different arena with a different set of opponents. To fail to interpret the "game" in more than its surface aspects would not interfere with its continuance. The technical problem here involved a "reflection" of P's behavior with A, but it required several steps in this phase of the process of interpreting, leading gradually to a synthesis of affect and impulse and a change in the gratification P gets out of this sense of pseudovictory over both mother and father.

In this exchange, S focused on the recognition of dynamics, on whether A could see the game-playing quality of P's behavior. She played a little game with A herself in asking questions expressing her skepticism, her feeling of surprise and puzzlement—questions designed to test and to bring out his awareness of the problem. She met with some success in stirring A to think along a different line.

Exchange 2

(The following material is summarized from succeeding analytic hours but reported in the same Supervisory Session 10.)

In the next hour, P tells a dream (the content is condensed): He is in an analytic hour in a state of shock. A tries to bring him out of shock by amusing him. A jumps up and down making faces like a monkey. Later in the dream, A is washing dishes in the kitchen. P, in friendly fashion, says he understands that analysts have to wash dishes too, after hours. P thinks A did not understand what he was talking about.

After a number of associations, P reports that it was his mother, not his father, he was afraid would discover him in his childhood masturbation. A makes the interpretation that P is making fun of him and trying to undo the interpretation of the day before. P has the same squeamish but stimulated reaction.

In the next hour, P reports that he has been concealing a knowledge of A's "secret technique"—namely, to make interpretations at the end of the hour. He expresses some anxiety about destroying A, and then makes an exhibitionistic gesture with the remark, "I guess I want you to love me, and I defend against this by pretending you are an inquisitorial faultfinder." He condemns himself for being gawkish with women. A comments, "You behave gawkishly here, too."

Comments: In this exchange, the evidence for P's erotized power struggle becomes even clearer. A gives little evidence that he understands the dynamics of this level of the transference, although he apparently feels the depreciation. P expresses his marginal awareness of his oedipal guilt in relation to his father and his oedipal shame in relation to his mother by calling attention to the shift in his transference identification of A from a loving mother to an "inquisitorial" father. Then he punishes himself. A discharges some of his own reaction to being depreciated by interpreting, "You behave gawkishly here, too."

This interpretation again touches only the surface without any follow-through to clarify the stimuli for such a response or to reach a deeper level of meaning in terms of conflict and genetic roots. Also in this interpretation, A's feeling shows through and his own need to get back at P interferes with his technique, so that he lets his remark remain at this descriptive level with the emotional impact of a "slapping down." The only justification for such a remark lies in calling P's attention to his gawkish behavior in the present for the purpose of deepening his understanding of why it is necessary to behave this way now.

Such a move toward insight requires many small steps on the way and may take a number of hours of interpretive work timed and dosed according to A's estimation of P's tolerance for ego-dystonic awareness. A's system sensitivity (Chart II, 3') must be in tune with P's dynamic equilibrium. A's tuned-in empathy determines the timing of his statements so that they disturb the equilibrium at a moment which coincides with lessened resistance to becoming aware of less acceptable motivations, and the statements are worded in such a way that they hit a focused target without stirring up more emotion than P can handle. Too broad a target and words with stronger emotional connotations will touch off defensive maneuvers in P which block his capacity to perceive any part of what was warded off before the interpretation was made. P's ego is too busy protecting itself against an overloading with anxiety, depressive affect or other "dangerous" experience and so cannot use energy to observe itself and make new integrations of what it perceives. P's intrapsychic equilibrium can be disturbed only a little at a time if the ego's work of modification of childhood wishes in line with changing reality is to take place.

Developing skill in the use of interpretation to keep this process of modification and integration going is one of the most difficult things for a student-analyst to learn. Maintaining his own balance so that his energy is available for therapeutically empathic responses is the first requirement. Then in the same way as his patient, he must be able to tolerate confrontation with error and remain able to examine the causes and effects of his error (Chart I, a'', b''). Only then can he be free to make alternative technical decisions and grow in skillful use of his sensitivity and tact.

Helping a student learn this skill requires equal system sensitivity in the supervisor who must estimate the student's tolerance for not knowing and for awareness of error. With a patient, equilibrium in the therapeutic alliance is necessary for good progress toward insight for the patient, so in learning, equilibrium in the learning alliance promotes learning and a supervisor must take this factor into account in "timing and dosing" the teaching interventions. In this example, S decided not to disturb the learning alliance by a repetition of what had been said earlier or by confronting A with the evidence of his defensive counter-reaction expressed in the "gawkish" interpretation. She chose to rely on the other teaching focus in this session to orient A to the concept of interpretation as a process.[13]

In the next month, a good example of a "shotgun" interpretation offered S another opportunity to discuss the effect of "too big" and too unfocused interpretations.

Exchange 3 (Supervisory Session 12)

P is talking about being embarrassed that he "sneaked a look" at A's face and at the inside of his desk.

A—He wonders if there was anything I wanted to conceal. He has memories of searching through his parents' desk as a child, allegedly to see how much money his father had. With this point, an abrupt change of subject was begun. He starts talking about money, how much money he had for the analysis, and it comes down to the issue of next spring or summer sometime, he will have spent all the money he has available outside of his savings, and the issue is going to be, am I going to lower my fee at that time or am I going to ask him to take money out of his savings? He becomes frightened that I'm going to be angry now, like his father would be about the fact that he's trying to weasel off on our agreement.

This was very confusing to me. He didn't seem shy or frightened and it was kind of a lip service. I had the impression that he had no conflict at all about this, so I told him I had the feeling he had no conflict about this but that he was overtly trying to cheat; moreover, that he knew that I knew that he was inviting me to be corrupt with him in some way, like once his mother knew that he was stealing and did nothing about it. Well, he didn't respond immediately. As a matter of fact, this was very near the end of the hour and he was silent for the rest of the time, but this had a terrific impact on him, it subsequently turned out. He said, later, he felt overwhelmed by what I had said.

S—What was it that he felt overwhelmed by?

A—The phrase "invitation to corruption"; that this really had given him a jolt. It was penetrating; he felt naked. He compared it to his feelings when he had a homosexual experience.

S—He's still on the analytic beam, then, because he's responding with the derivative of much deeper libidinal impulses, which have to do with stealing from you, but not money.

A—You see, in his thoughts we would both be stealing from the Institute.

S—O.K. But it's not money that's really involved; money is only a representation. He responds that way because you give him four things at least that he could be overwhelmed by: (1) no conflict; (2) he's conscious of this as a deliberate kind of cheating; (3) he's inviting you to join him; (4) genetic—like when his mother knew he was stealing.

A—It was a large dose. But I thought he knew it, really—all except the inviting me . . . .

S—It isn't a matter of whether he knows it or not; it's a matter of dosing what you say in order to keep the analytic process going. I mean, you could have stopped with the fact of this being no conflict and see what happened, or you could have gone on to the business of his cheating and stopped there. Instead you went farther: that he was inviting you to be corrupt also. This is what he responds to, but he responds on the deeper level of his castration anxiety. However, he does not know what he is responding to or why.

Comments: In this excerpt from the twelfth supervisory hour, there is evidence that *A* has learned to recognize one aspect of the resistance: to externalize responsibility for disturbing impulses and to assume collusion with the other person. *A* also recognizes some of the genetic roots of this defense transference, especially since *P* does also. However, *A* becomes eager to get it all into one interpretation! He senses the "terrific impact," confirmed in subsequent hours although his interpretation is timed so that little opportunity remains in the same hour to follow out *P*'s immediate response of feeling overwhelmed.

S focuses on the "big dose" and spells out four different targets for interpretation. Objectified in this way, *A* can see the economics involved. What he has difficulty appreciating is the level of conflict on which *P*'s equilibrium finally comes to rest and how a more gradual technique of interpreting might have resulted in less energy spent on defense and more on insight. *S* emphasizes again the process nature of interpreting in small doses that permit a better integration of affective experience with understanding.

In the next excerpt, seven months later, the analysis has progressed. The patient is more deeply involved in a regressive transference neurosis. At the same time he is using his self-observing function and integrating his analytic experience to differentiate the present reality from the neurotic distortion of it. New insight permits a change in behavior with his wife and a new feeling about himself in the present.

The analyst, too, has progressed. His understanding of the transference and the process of the analytic interaction enable him to respond to the patient with much more skillful interpretations—in a way that facilitates the process of working through which is going on in the patient.

Exchange 4 (*Supervisory Session 17*)

P is struggling with the wish to be important to his mother, with the wish to give her a baby, and the simultaneous denial of this wish for fear he would be ridiculed by her.

A—Again he comments that he hasn't had intercourse for several days, and the thought comes to his mind maybe he—he's quoting me—he fears, maybe he fears he can't impregnate his wife. He has a thought that perhaps his feelings in his penis he gets on the couch have to do with paying me— this is the first of the month—that he has brought the check. I haven't billed him yet, but he's already ready to pay me. All of this very upset: he's sort of gagging, convulsions, while he's talking about this. He has the thought, "Maybe I'm paying you the price for wanting to take sexual liberties." I said, "Apparently you want to give me something." And he gets very angry with me. It turned out he's angry with me because when I talk like this, I turn him from achieving his wishes to understanding them; I jolt him into seeing me as a doctor. And that this is analogous with how he felt about his mother. I commented that apparently he's abstaining from intercourse at home as an act of loyalty to me then. Then he tells me that he is only able to feel sexually more or less free with his wife if he thinks that I do the same things too, that if I do these sexual things, then it's all right for him. And he remembers how in high school he couldn't even go out with a girl because he was so afraid of his mother's disapproval, that in this dream about the furnace, somewhere in the background his parents were hovering about and were forbidding him to try. He feels incapable—and then he stops. Ruminates about the check he has brought, that actually he feels it's excessively forward, that he would look funny, that he can't assert himself in that way—somehow, if he did, he would also lose the comforts of his neurosis. And he was talking as if, really, it were a terrible thing to be active and successful. And I said, "It seems to me that you are denying how you really feel about this which is 'that none but the brave . . . .' " I didn't finish it. He says, "That makes sense. Why don't I act brave? You didn't even have to say "deserve the fair." I choke on it, but you're not fair, you're dark." And then he talks about how fair, blond, lordly, poised woman is out of reach for him. He would be swept aside and not even be noticed by such a woman. He can only relate to a woman who has a flaw because then he has a chance, that he would like to make himself desirable to me but he feels doomed to failure. I said, "You mean you feel you can't stoke my furnace like in the dream." He said, "Yes, I have to sit on the sidelines while another man steps in. It's like the machine that my father had. I just couldn't handle it. I was embarrassed that I couldn't start or stop it."

And then later, he talks about how he cannot make it with whomever he's interested in, then he won't try at all; this is why he's not having intercourse. He says, "Though it seems ridiculous to struggle with these infantile feelings, that's not really why I feel so harrowed now." And that really this feeling of being so distressed is a repetition of how he felt as a child, and that he tries to throw an aura of unreality about it in order to deny. I commented that apparently he tries hard to compensate for this feeling of inadequacy by trying to give me something, but I wondered whether as a child he had had the wish to give his mother something but felt very incapable of giving her a baby.

Well, the next hour, two days later, was one of great resistance. He reported that he'd had a dream in which his wife was laughing at him in a friendly but scornful manner, and that after the last hour he had had intercourse with her successfully, but that in the intervening day, he didn't try. He tells me when I speak in the hour, he's afraid that he'll get an erection, that he's struggling for control. He feels incapable of something; he suppresses the thought he wants to crawl over me. Well, it went on like this but we really didn't come to anything.

S—I think that he's reacting to the work in the preceding hour where you told him that in compensation for his inadequacy, he wanted to give something to mother but felt incapable of giving her a baby. I'm not sure that's focused enough. It's true that he was incapable of giving mother a baby, but I'm not sure that he really felt so when he was a child. I think the fantasy that he could was more what he felt, but the fear was of trying, because she wouldn't accept him and would laugh at him, was what generated the conflict. Now, I made that note to myself several minutes ago, and then you tell me the next hour he had a dream of his wife laughing at him. I think the fear of ridicule for failing is a defense against recognizing the reality of his inadequacy.

You see, you skip the defense, his fear of ridicule—not trying because he's afraid of being laughed at. This is more a part of a child's experience than coming to a recognition of reality. You see, at this point, part of the working through of the developmental problem of learning how to test reality, how to accept the reality that he really is small. He doesn't want to do that; he wants to deny that.

A—Yes. Well, he didn't drop the theme, just because I didn't recognize what he was saying. Over the weekend he had been very, very angry with his wife because he felt that she was ridiculing him, and in a kind of hypnogogic state he saw faces of women, haughty women, laughing at him, sticking their tongues out at him. And in the hour he feels now as he did with his wife, in a funk, sour and balky. I asked him what I had done to him. His association is that I didn't come out immediately after the previous patient left—he had to wait. And then he is obviously in a rage and doesn't want to work; he wants to quit. He wants to protest that he's impotent; he says he has the feeling that concentric lines come out from me towards his penis, and then he tries to sabotage the free association process by straining very hard for some effect. And he recognizes that this is a kind of fake association. Then he has a kind of a half-erection. He says he knows that vaguely it has to do with me; he feels nauseated and harrowed, that somehow this is unthinkable, to feel free to have an erection, or anything at all except to be all tangled up, that somehow if he let go of his feelings, that he might do something. But I think the meaning of this was that he might do something constructive, that he wouldn't be taking revenge on me. Well, then when he came in the next day, he did something he has never done. Before he lay down on the couch, he walked to the window and looked down. He said this was a show of freedom, and then he felt afraid that I would rebuke him for being curious. He had hoped that I would admire him for his independence. And he pictures himself lying on the couch with his penis exposed, that somehow being in the room alone with me is like being on a desert island with a woman, and the question would be, would he be able to please her sexually. He imagines my saying something very scornful to him, indicating that I don't think that he could ever accomplish this.

S—I think what he's doing is that, without the interpretation of his fear of being ridiculed when he was a little boy, he is acting out the defense against being ridiculed, with a kind of mixture of counterphobia and dis-placement of the responsibility for the impotence. You see, he's saying you would reject him, you would laugh at him; therefore it isn't his failure. But he exposes himself to the fear in the situation with this kind of a de-fense: "It's not my fault, you see, you're the bad one in the case."

A—Essentially that's what I told him: he dares nothing because he is so afraid of being haughtily rejected and ridiculed by the woman.

S—But that doesn't go far enough. It is a description of his defense, but it isn't an interpretation of what makes him so afraid. You're telling him, you see, that he's afraid to do something because he's afraid of failing or afraid of being rejected or laughed at. He's telling you that. Now, you have to help him go farther than that, because otherwise you'd simply get a round and round repetition of this.

A—Well, what we ran into here was what we discussed in the last super-visory hour, which is the aggression, the anger that he's acting out by this too, that he fantasies himself very powerful, and he's going to hurt the woman, and I said, well—oh, that he's going to hurt the woman and him-self too in the same act, and that he does this by freezing or clamming up both in the analysis and at home with his wife, that although he defeats himself he also defeats me and his wife as he had defeated his mother, that he feels very powerful if he can balk the analysis, that even when he suc-ceeds with us, though he feels an intense distress while he's with me, that somehow he wants me to be equally distressed, and that he actually suc-ceeded in making his mother very distressed, and he can make his wife miserable with his funks. And then he expresses the fantasy that in their sexual relations he will drive his wife crazy by frustrating her, getting her so excited and then letting her down, so that this is a kind of torture that he subjects her to. And he remembers how one of the girls he had an affair with prior to marriage would express the distress of being left un-satisfied when he had a premature ejaculation. And that he gets very angry at the least little disappointment in the relationship, that if all his wishes are not fulfilled, then he gets sadistic.

S—Yes, you see what's happening here is that his impulse to get some sexual satisfaction through giving and getting recognition, etc., is blocked because he's afraid he will not succeed. He covers this with his fear of being laughed at. This is more painful to him; therefore it serves as a rein-forcement for his exhibition, but that's not quite enough so he goes through the motions of playing the game with the feeling that he's being rejected. Then he gets angry, because to be rejected is to be mistreated, and he has a right then to get angry, to get revenge, and he turns it around—an eye for an eye, in kind; what she does to him, he does to her . . . .

A—He recognizes, himself, there's more to it, because he says that it would be terrible to cooperate, and not to be involved in this eye for an eye spite-ful business, because if he were good and cooperative, I'd still not get ex-cited, then that would be terrible: he'd have no excuse to get revenge.

S—But that's true too, as far as it goes, and still avoids the fundamental reality conflict—the reality of the inadequacy. It's all a nice cover. There's a beautiful portrayal here of the shifting of the defenses and how one defense covers another, and all of them, you see, are the superstructure to succeed in avoiding the real perception of the reality of himself in relation to the outside world in childhood, something he can't tolerate even today.

Comments: In this exchange *P* is working through the same conflict about his sexual adequacy and acceptability. In this seventeenth supervisory session, however, the affect, both erotic and aggressive, is more freely expressed in relation to the analyst; the defenses are more clearly perceivable in relation to the fantasy which is being acted out in the transference. Obviously, a good deal of analytic work has been done and *A* has developed not only understanding of interpretation as a step-by-step process but also some skill in adapting his responses to the moment and dynamic level which will keep the analytic process moving. *P* repeats with *A* the childhood oedipal conflict he has been driven to repeat in many situations outside of therapy; he relieves his anxiety, fear of ridicule, sexual tensions, and defenses against a sense of inadequacy; he experiences again the alternatives of lowered self-esteem and guilt over his pleasure in revenge. Gradually, with the help of *A*, he recognizes that the present is not the same as the past, that what was feared in the past does not happen; and he can begin to recognize himself in the present as different from his childhood self.

In this supervisory hour, the teaching is less focused on orienting *A* to interpretation as a process and evaluating his activity; rather, it is more concerned with demonstrating the process by examining the steps in retrospect. Because the learning alliance at this point was good and the student had demonstrated in previous hours his understanding of the process nature of analytic work, *S* felt able to be more theoretical and try to correlate this patient's behavior with concepts of dynamic and childhood development.

One might criticize the teaching technique here as being too active in the sense that *S* frequently interrupted *A* and made comments without waiting for the material to reveal what was going on or for *A* to demonstrate his follow-through in the interpretive process. Her remarks were made in the form of statements, a kind of didactic instruction, compared to the catalytic questioning of earlier exchanges in this example. Her teaching technique here did not encourage *A* to do the associative work toward the broader understanding of dynamics and correlating theory with behavior that might have given more impact to the learning experience.

Self-Analysis: The tools of introspection and empathy, developed in his training analysis are further sharpened in the initial phase of the student's first case. Then, as his experience in the role of analyst expands, he learns to watch for out-of-context reactions in the patient, and when these occur he learns to look at his own behavior for a possible stimulus.

Sometimes these reactions will facilitate and sometimes interfere with analytic progress, and after he has learned this fundamental attitude of self-observation in interaction with his patient, he can comprehend better the dynamics of this interaction and turn his attention to his own motivations as well as the patient's. These learning experiences are steps on the way to knowing about himself as an analytic instrument and how he functions as such. The next step is to learn to use his instrument on himself and so acquire some confidence in understanding and managing his counterreactions (Chart II, 5, 5'). High-level system sensitivity and system responsiveness (Chart II, 3', 4') are insufficient by themselves to avoid interferences from countertransferences, so that when crises occur, self-analytic skill is needed to find the cause and to repair the damage. When the student understands this, a significant piece of psychoanalytic learning will have been achieved, although he may be unable to analyze fully the roots of his own motivations.

There have been many references throughout the book to self-analysis as a learning objective and as a pedagogic problem for the supervisor. The examples already given illustrate in how many ways "flaws" in the analytic instrument show themselves and on how many occasions a supervisor is faced with the task of evaluating the situation from several angles before deciding what to do about it. In Chapter IV and in Chart I (below the line) we have pointed out the areas of information to which a supervisor pays attention in evaluating how well the student's self-analytic functions are operating. Of special interest is his alertness to the reciprocity between the patient's reactions to interpretations and his own responses (Chart I, a', a''). Measures of the success of his self-observation and empathy (Chart I, b', b'') are reflected in the degree of insight into his motives for a given communication to his patient and the effect of his action on the patient.

We found three principal means by which a supervisor teaches about self-analysis: (1) confrontation with the need for self-analytic work; (2) motivating the student for carrying it on; (3) assistance in exercising the functions active in self-analysis. All three ways have developmental and corrective aims, and we wish to stress their additional value in teaching about the analytic process and the analyst's instrumental role in that process. In other words, this supervisory activity is directed toward pointing out mistakes and removing the "flaws" in the instrument. But, in addition, and perhaps even more important, the supervisor teaches his student that, whatever his responses are, they have significance and meaning in the flow of communication with the patient. These responses may not coincide with the "model" of an analyst which he has been taught, and he may try to deny their existence, repress them, or avoid revealing them to the supervisor. Moreover, this behavior is especially true when the student-analyst gets angry at the patient or responds with some erratic fantasy. The beginner may understand the inappropriateness of such reactions, but often he does not realize that they can be useful in understanding some obscure behavior in the patient. The supervisor can help a student learn how to use his countertransferences constructively.

These teaching activities are not limited to any one phase of supervision or to elementary or advanced levels of learning; nor are they easily separated from each other in the process of teaching. The primary objective is for the student to acquire an attitude toward himself as an instrument that recognizes that constant vigilance is necessary to keep it in good operating condition and that constant exercise is essential to increase its skillfulness. This attitude forms the background for all psychoanalytic learning and teaching. It is inherent in the training analysis where the combination of curiosity and honesty begin the process of self-examination, where the wish to know and the courage to face painful discoveries are harnessed for efforts at self-mastery. The supervisory experience continues to reinforce this attitude through identification with the supervisor for instrumental learning, just as identification with his training analyst promoted the student's learning how to listen. In the supervisory process, teaching directs this listening toward himself as well as the patient in order to differentiate what belongs to himself and what belongs to the patient.

The countertransferences, like transferences, are motivated by unconscious forces which establish barriers to insight more or less difficult to penetrate. Consequently, in his efforts to activate a student's self-analytic functions, a supervisor needs to use the same empathy and interpretive skill he would use with a patient. The timing and directness of his supervisory interventions depends on his understanding of the student's problems as well as the patient's (see Chapter IV). Strategic waiting (see Example 2) is as important for avoiding interference with the learning process as it is in therapy. This is sometimes more difficult for a supervisor in his teaching role than in his work as a therapist, since his expectations of his student are higher than for a patient and his sense of responsibility for the supervised patient is more easily frustrated by the student's mistakes. Such an attitude is important in all phases of supervision, but especially so in the middle phase where the resistance offered by blind spots and other forms of countertransference often becomes more intense (see the section on Transference in this chapter).

Supported by knowledge of resistances and the length of time required for working them through, a supervisor's unbiased openness and patience presents an attitude for his student to emulate in his self-analysis as well as his activity with a patient. All of this is part of what a student needs to learn about the concept as well as the practice of self-analysis. We discussed in Chapter II the futility of trying to force insight, since premature interpretations given to oneself may disturb the preconscious auto-analysis just as they may disturb a patient. The first and primary lesson for a student is to accept the need for continued listening to himself as essential for the therapeutic process.

The pedagogic problem for the supervisor is to decide how far he can assist his student in self-analysis. Since insight is not something that is conveyed from one person to another, it is clear that the process of integrating insights is ultimately achievable only by the student himself. When formal supervision is over, the student analyzes himself by himself. As long as he is in supervision, however, and until the necessity for continuing self-analytic work is thoroughly understood, there is much that a supervisor can do to catalyze the process.

To serve as a catalyst is to act as an intermediary, separating and bringing together parts that would not otherwise be connected, but without becoming substantially involved in the ultimate change of the catalyzed parts. We apply this term to a supervisor's teaching about self-analysis because his principal task is to point out discrepancies between stimulus and response and gaps in empathic understanding. This analyzing-synthesizing activity is comparable to the steps toward insight in the psychoanalytic process,[63] and the supervisor's task is comparable to the training analyst's in these preliminary stages of working through resistances. But it is different in the degree and the nature of the supervisor's involvement in the process within the student. The supervisor does not offer himself as an object for transference repetitions as the training analyst does; he does not facilitate a regressive reproduction of childhood conflicts, nor is he in a position to make genetic interpretations. This work should have been well under way before a student begins his clinical training. When such is the case, a supervisor's task is easier and only a word or two is needed to bridge a gap in a student's awareness or to open his eyes to something he has been defending himself against.

The many manifestations of countertransference (used very generally here) demonstrate different degrees and forms of resistance to understanding the patient and to responding appropriately in the analytic process. Inadequate empathy or distorted use of it[53] may be easily diagnosable as a result of inexperience or a defense against some more deeply rooted anxiety stirred up by the patient, by the supervisory situation, or even by a concurrent event in the analyst's private life which drains energy and attention away from the patient's concerns. Such defensive maneuvers include (1) various distancing devices, such as changing the subject or talking about the past instead of the present; (2) permitting inappropriate affect, such as irritation, sarcasm, or anger to appear in voice or words; (3) committing acts such as slips of the tongue, or forgetting, or teasing with rejecting or seductive implications; (4) day or night dreaming about the patient. Any of these defensive behaviors can serve to protect the analyst against something which threatens his impulse control or his self-esteem, probably the two most vulnerable areas. At the same time such defensiveness prevents empathic understanding of the patient's needs.

Often a student can become aware of this behavior spontaneously as he studies his material or talks with his supervisor. He may be able to recognize its inappropriateness and even its defensive purpose with only a question to prod him. Acts of rejection or dreams about the patient are probably indications of more serious disturbances in the analyst's empathic functioning and may require more rigorous and persistent confrontation or partial interpretation by the supervisor.

In every supervisory session there is material relevant in some degree to the various aspects of self-analysis. Consequently, reference will be made to examples in other parts of this book partly to avoid adding to the already large amount of clinical data and partly because certain examples highlight self-analysis problems as well as other things. A common denominator for the illustrations in this section is the student's capacity for self-observation, since it is disturbance in this area which influences the supervisor's efforts to catalyze his self-analytic functions (Chart I, below the line). A range of degrees of self-observation and resistances against it will be presented with the correlated range of supervisory teaching tactics. It may appear to some of our readers that we include more supervisory activity under the heading of catalyzing the student's self-analysis than belongs there. We feel, however, that the following examples represent the many small steps along the way to the integration of the analyst's self-analytic capacities with his instrumental therapeutic work. These steps can be viewed as a sequence progressing from the most fundamental and elementary insights to the more complex and intricate levels of countertransference involvements.

The first steps include teaching A to observe himself in relation to his effect on the patient, as illustrated in Example 11 and Example 12 in this chapter. It may seem naive to give such emphasis to this aspect of the instrumental role of the therapist in relation to his patient. Yet, in spite of the importance given to the doctor-patient relationship in most medical education today, and in spite of talented students who were intellectually conscious of its significance, we found evidence for failure to perceive these unexpected responses from the patient and to understand their message. In many cases, the cause seemed to be inexperience, which is why we put this learning problem at the beginning of this continuum. Example 11 also demonstrates how S explored A's sense of dissatisfaction with his response to P. The discussion between A and S relieved some of A's tension over his inadequacy and helped him to recognize his feelings more explicitly. The teaching procedure was to outline technical alternatives without emphasizing mistakes and making him feel more ashamed. By this kind of teaching S reinforced the compensatory value of increased self-awareness and correlated it with A's professional goals.

The following example takes the process of catalyzing A's self-awareness one step further. In this instance, instead of the aim being recognition of the unanticipated effect of his behavior on P, it became recognizing the effect of P's behavior on A himself. In Example 9, A was aware of his own response and felt it to be inappropriate. In the next example A was not aware of his "slip" of behavior in letting the patient go early; and he was even less aware of his tension and its cause in a counterreaction to P's affects and to his own frustration over not-knowing.

EXAMPLE 16
JB (Case IV), Supervisory Sessions 1-7, Analytic Hours 0-30

This was the student's fourth (last) case of supervised analysis. The analyst was a talented, capable student who, in presenting the case and his diagnostic evaluation of it, made an excellent impression. His response to the clinical material was good on a theoretical level and he was in empathic communication with the patient and the supervisor. His reporting was verbally good, although the content tended to be understated. A certain lackadaisical attitude seemed to cover up anxiety . The patient was an intelligent, well-trained, professional man; his work required psychologic aptitude and self-discipline. His personality was well-fitted to his chosen profession. A typical compulsive character, he was aware of his aggressive tendencies and the self-control that he exerted against his impulses.

In the second supervisory session A reported the first dream of P, an anxiety dream of falling. P interpreted his own dream as an expression of his fear of losing himself in the analysis. A reported that P had many ideas about this and wanted to find his way without the help of the analyst. A described how P was critical of himself and could not admit that he did not know something.

In the third supervisory session, A began by reporting about the general defensiveness of P, especially about his flow of constant talk.

Exchange 1

S—Against what is this a defense?

A—Against anal giving. [This was in reference to the content; P blamed himself for being unable to give, even to himself.]

S—Such a general defensive attitude is usually against anxiety, against apprehension. In this early phase of the analysis, it is probably an expression of his fear in the analytic situation. What do you think he is afraid of?

[Since *A* did not reply, *S* went on.] He is afraid of being "surprised," surprised by the unknown. The surprise might come from you or from himself. [*A* was tensely attentive but did not say anything.] *S* continued, "You said several times that his talk impresses you, its high pressure, its continuous flow; you also mentioned his own intepretations. It seems to me that all this is really a defense against surprise, against the unexpected."

A—Yes, I see.

S—What would create the anxiety more specifically?

A—Not being able to control the object. It is the anal wish to control the object relationship.

S—It seems that you have a need to interpret in terms of theories; these statements sound like cold cliches.

A—(Defensively) I didn't say it to the patient.

S—I know, and that is fine. Of course, such statements would not mean anything to him in this early phase of the analysis or maybe ever. [*A* was tensely attentive and silent.] Your readiness to interpret with a theory is like a wall or a screen between yourself and him. It also serves you as a defense. [*S* mentioned Theodore Reik's book about the function of surprise in analysis and went on to explain the necessity for *A*'s bearing up under the frustration of not knowing in order to give the patient time to perceive his feelings and come to some degree of insight through intrapsychic processes.] Your knowing theory and using it so readily in your thinking instead of exposing yourself to your perception of his feelings interferes with those processes which would lead to insight in him and also in you. [This explanation took a few minutes during which *A* had become obviously distracted.]

A—You said, "standing the not-knowing," something I obviously could not stand because I interrupted the session and let him go twenty minutes before the hour should have ended. I was unaware of my slip. I stood up, he looked at his watch, stood up and left. I did not realize what had happened until he brought it up in the next analytic session.

S—This was indeed an intense reaction to your patient. It is necessary to find out what makes your reaction to him so strong.

A—In a general way I know; there is a great deal of similarity between us.

S—So you have an opportunity to work something through for yourself. By analyzing your patient, you can add to your own insight.

Comments: This is a good illustration of how the supervisory process runs into snags that can be removed by the supervisor's use of analytic perceptiveness integrated with teaching technique. The flow of communication between *S* and *A* demonstrated tension and *S* detected an intellectualizing defense against *A*'s intolerance for not-knowing. She was also aware of this defense in *P* and that *A* saw it in *P* but not in himself. When *S* confronted *A* with his own intolerance for not knowing and demonstrated his intellectualizing responses, *A*'s introspective associations were mobilized. He recalled the "slip" and reported it, recognizing his identification with P, his tendency to compete, and some of his defensive behavior.

A good learning alliance had been established so that the learning problem of this student did not consist of hypersensitivity toward "being taught." Instead it was rooted in defensiveness against affects and was increased by his frustration over "not knowing." As a consequence, he grasped at stereotyped theoretical interpretations which gave the appearance of "knowing" and at the same time maintained a distance from the immediate experience of affects in P and in himself. S chose to confront A with this problem. She did more than a simple confrontation, however, since she identified his behavior as a defense and explained how it blocked insight in himself and P. A's response was in no sense resistive to the confrontation. His admission of the similarities between the patient and himself indicated that he was capable of insight, albeit with some effort. A's self-analysis, however, was allowed to rest at this point. No attempts were made to trace further the explanations for his behavior.

In this episode of JB, his self-observation had to be encouraged by direct confrontation from the supervisor. This was in contrast to HB (Example 9) who also let his patient go early, but who realized it immediately and deliberately used the available minutes to do a piece of self-analysis. In that instance, the supervisor was not necessary as a catalyzer and the supervisory problem revolved around how to handle the "slip" with the patient.

The next example illustrates good perception of process and good awareness of himself as a part of it, but only on the surface, since A's empathy for understanding P was blurred by his ambition to find an answer. This situation resulted in a loss of control of his empathic responsiveness, to use Greenson's category.[53] In the following example, the supervisory teaching in the three exchanges proceeded in three steps: (1) calling attention to A's failure to maintain an analytic posture, (2) recommending some questioning of himself, and (3) finally to a partial interpretation of A's motivation.

EXAMPLE 17

HF (Case IV), Supervisory Session 15, Analytic Hours about 200

The patient is the student's fourth case, a graduate student who entered analysis at 31 years of age on the recommendation of a teacher. He realized that her immature, childish demandingness would be a severe professional handicap. The patient had lost her father when she was very young and her mother in adolescence. Fears of abandonment and rejection coupled with intense ambivalence and low self-esteem stimulated much impulsive anger, little-girl flirtatiousness with men, and homosexual fantasies about women. At 31 her object relationships were primitive, need-fulfilling, and tenuous. For many months she had tested the analyst's patience and dependability in many ways. A woman physician, Dr. K., served variously as a good object in a split ambivalent maternal transference and a maternal object in a complicated oedipal triangle where brother (ten years older) equaled father equaled analyst. The following example is taken from the second year of her analysis.

Exchange 1

A—These sixteen hours, I think, give us a good chance to study the fluctuations in her feelings towards me, in terms of affection and hostility. She comes in and states that she felt a real change since the last session, in something that had tortured her for 21 years—that is, the urinary urgency. She had a partial insight as a result of the previous session, and she hopes that things are going to be different now. She feels more confident. She wonders if she's taking too much credit for her understanding. She knows now, or has a pretty strong suspicion, that the urinary panic is more related to men than women. For instance, she says, if she's on an intercity bus, she figures that the driver might not stop even if she asked to go to a gasoline station comfort room, because he would figure she's just a woman and why should he satisfy a woman's needs. Men are mean that way. She goes on to elaborate, however, saying, "Well, since the panic is with men, is it related to something else besides urinary urgency? Is this a coverup?" So she has a good idea of the screen functions of this issue. She tells me that in childhood her urinary panic was related with her brother. Once she urinated in her pants at the house and wondered, "Where is brother? Will he know?"

Then she tells me what has been bothering her since the end of last week. Something disappointed her. She asked me a question and the question was, did I know what she was trying to get away from when she had to leave that session to go to the bathroom? And I said, "No, I didn't. I just had a hunch you were trying to get away from something and it was our therapeutic task to find out what it was." This produced great disappointment in her. She then goes on to discuss curiosity about me, my life outside the office, and how can I think of so many people all day long. The hour ends with her commenting that maybe she doesn't let herself go here because when treatment is all over she'll never see me again, so why should she attach herself to someone that she'll never see again. She feels like crying over her disappointment because I don't know it all.

Two hours later she attacks me for my intellectual failure at not knowing exactly what she was running from when she had to leave the office for the bathroom.

S—She calls it intellectual failure?

A—Yes, she does, and she qualifies it by saying, in her words, that I have empathy, but that's not enough for her. She says I'm O.K. with feelings but I'm a dunce intellectually.

S—I would put it just the other way! Your answer to her question was a very intellectual, therapeutically oriented one, not in terms of the response that keeps the associations going, but that shuts off the affect.

A—You mean my response, if it had been, "What do you really expect from me?" would have kept the ball rolling, rather than to say, "I don't know what it is; it's something we have to find out"?

S—Yes. You certainly did not give her what her transference expectation was hoping for.

Comments: *A* reports his understanding of the oscillations of *P*'s associations and his diagnostic inferences. *P* moves back and forth from present to past and back again, from insight to renewal of conflict, from self-observation to symptomatic action on a regressed level, from positive to negative transference. *A*'s answer to *P*'s question, however, reveals lack of understanding blurred by his concentration on the effort to explain the symptom dynamically. He admits not knowing the answer but does not empathize with the affect and dynamics of the transference. This is a complex problem and the mistake is not his ignorance nor even his admitting it, but his responding in the way he did. The responses in this exchange and in the next one serve to satisfy his own image of himself as a kind therapist, not frustrating and eager to "analyze." He assumes that *P* sees him in this way too.

Exchange 2

A—In the next hour, she tells me she's mad at herself for trusting me, for thinking that I was intelligent. She says, "In this treatment with you, the patient has to interpret and then interpret her interpretations. The analyst doesn't know what's going on. I look for strength in men and I don't find it; that's what's disappointing. No man really cares about a woman. My brother didn't; he was brilliant. (Pause) I feel alone because my doctor doesn't know what's going on." She felt she had to go to the bathroom and after a few minutes she left the hour ten minutes early.

Next time she tells me that she went to the bathroom and cried and cried, and then she went to see Dr. K. with some questions about hemorrhoids. She talked to Dr. K. for about an hour and tells me what the conversation was. She told her that she was plenty mad at me. "Dr. K. said that she had met you in the hall. Did she ask you about me?" Once again, I respond directly here instead of asking her what the fantasy was. i said, "She did ask me how you were, and I said that you seemed over the effects of the surgery." Patient then became very suspicious and feels suspicious in terms of my not telling specifically what was said.

S—Why did you answer at all?

A—I don't know. I guess the only reason I can give you at this moment is that I don't know what went on in my mind then. The only thing I can say, as I look back over this data, is that I wasn't really with it in terms of the brother transference becoming more intense.

S—I don't think it's only that, because to answer any patient's question like that without exploring it further is contraindicated, whatever the state of affairs is, unless you have a specific conscious reason for answering. This is a loaded situation which you're well aware of, whether you're brother or somebody else. I think you ought to do a little questioning of yourself as to why you answered her, because your gratuitous remark about the surgery was a loaded statement too.

A—Yes, in terms of what we think about what the appendix means to her.

S—Not just the appendix but any kind of surgery, and surgery done by a woman and the subject being the urinary problem here, etc. I'm very curious as to why you answered her at all.

A—I can't give you a dynamic reason at this moment. I can give you something that smacks of my being defensive, but . . . .

S—Well, think about it, because I really think there must be something here that belongs to you, and it's contaminating with the patient. It's more important that you discover what this is than that you and I talk about it.

Exchange 3

Several hours later the same problem came up regarding *A's* answering questions which the patient asks, without thinking first.

A—She reports that she met a young man and had a conversation with him in the restaurant downstairs. She was flattered when he told her that he broke away from her because he was getting too involved. She had thought that he hated her, and she told him that she hated men and therefore couldn't marry. He said, "Oh, I don't get that impression about you." She then has more curiosity about what Dr. K. and I said to each other when we met in the hall. She's suspicious that all has not been told to her. After meeting this young man she realizes that not all men are so bad. So she asks me, "Do you think from what you know about the relationship with him, that he cared?" And I said, "Well, I couldn't say; I don't know." And she feels that I don't like her.

S—Wait a minute. Why did you answer that at all?

A—For the same reason that I don't really know why I answered the others. There are three or four questions in all this time that I have answered without realizing why. I guess I have begun to fall into a pattern in which she is setting up something for me to fall into, like saying, "I am a poor, deprived, helpless, needy someone or other and please pour it into me." I respond to this without analyzing it.

S—This must satisfy some need in you to be looked upon by her as somebody who knows all the answers, who even might know whether Joe loves her or not. What you said implies that you can't say because you don't know, but that the possibility of knowing is there, and actually you don't even have the possibility of knowing that.

A—I wonder if she's getting to me in some kind of flattery?

S—Flattering you on this question of knowing it all? Her brother was brilliant! (See Exchange 2.)

A—She lets me know that over and over again. (Chuckles) She goes on about her brother and then comes back to the problem of the conversation between me and Dr. K. She is very sarcastic and bitter.

S—Why don't you ask her what her fantasies are about that conversation? She is still operating on the level of her fantasies here. When you continue to act as if there is something that you're not telling her, she feels you could if you would, but you won't. One can say, "wait," but wait for what?

A—No, I'm not waiting. I think that I want to get more understanding of what's going on. But somehow or other here I have a formulation which is blocking me from going on to really get what the formulation is. The formulation is, Dr. K. and myself—Mommy and Daddy, with transference and all that stuff. But this is the little bit of knowledge which is far from being the whole truth, and yet I realize now as you ask me that I have an intellectual formulation about it and that this has somehow or other satisfied me and made me unaware of the fact that we really don't know what the truth is about this.

S—This intellectual formulation satisfied you, but it doesn't help her analysis if both of you get stuck there with acting out the fact that Dr. K. is her mother and you're her father, etc., etc.

A—That's right. And she goes on to say, "I don't suppose an analyst always likes his patients." She's crying. "I think the best I can get from you is a scientific attitude. If I shot myself you would probably say, 'good-bye.' "

S—She's got your number!

A—That's right, but it won't be for long, because I think I've finally got it myself. (Chuckles)

The next example illustrates the analyst's self-questioning as he becomes aware of an impasse in the analysis. This excerpt, from Supervisory Session 35 on his fourth case, demonstrates the progress HF has made in exploring his own reactions to analytic events. He goes farther here in arriving at an explanation of his counterreaction than he was able to do on his second case when he let the patient go early (see Example 9). With his fourth patient, a subtle countertransference problem comes into clear focus. The resistance in the analyst shows itself as a failure to empathize with his patient who perceives him as being a transference object of the opposite sex.* This happens in spite of good theoretical knowledge of transference. The patient's sexual misidentification seems to threaten the analyst's sense of sexual identity, creating defensive resistance which blocks understanding of what conflict the patient is reliving. Experience

---

* This problem was mentioned in the section on transference and resistance and in Chart III under B, 2, d. In Example 18, a male analyst has difficulty understanding the competitive mother transference of a female patient. Not illustrated here, but frequently encountered in supervision, is a female analyst's failure to recognize the competitive father transference of a male patient or the genital father transference of a female patient.

with this degree of regression of perceptual functioning in the patient is rare outside of the psychoanalytic situation and even there it occurs in the transference neurosis. Insight into this problem is often very difficult for a beginner and even an advanced student has trouble.

EXAMPLE 18

HF ¡Case IV), Supervisory Session 35, Analytic Hours about 450

(For data on the patient see Example 17.) The patient reported that, over the period of the analyst's and her own vacations, she had been carrying on a number of flirtations with various men, including an "older man (who could very well be the age her father was when he died). The material alternates between feeling toward A as toward her mother who would have disapproved of any sexual adventures, and a flirtatious, provocative teasing of A as if she wanted him to respond as these various men did. Her cry is that she is either prohibited unfairly from growing up and becoming a woman, or she is rejected by men who are mean, unkind, and think only of themselves. There are moments of competition with mother and wish to be free of mother, about which she also seems to feel guilty. Much of this is touched on without elaboration, followed by a regressive wish to sit on the analyst's lap and be taken care of as a little girl is cared for and admired. As this is gone over in the supervisory session, the following exchange takes place.

Exchange 1

A—Something has been troubling me that I haven't been able to formulate. It seems to be connected with my emphasis on helping her and on my formulating the transference resistance as her wishing to reexperience me as mother. I told her she repeats with me something that went on with her mother, but she keeps repeating it without insight. Have I gotten hung up on this somehow?

S—No, I think you developed this point so that she can see clearly that there are many longings for you that are the same longings she had for her mother at various times. But this wanting to sit on your lap has reference to more than one conflict. The same wish or impulse can have different meanings at different phases of the analysis. For example, she might want to sit on your lap because she feels helpless and frightened; or as a reassurance that you still love her even if she has been a bad girl; or as a reassurance that you are not interested in leaving her for someone; or, you are not interested in punishing her for her rivalrous "death wishes," or for her wish to leave you and grow up to be better than you are with men.

A—What I've been thinking is that while I think I understand the mother transference, I am not used to thinking of myself as a mother, and that makes me sluggish when it comes to interpreting the oedipal triangle in terms of my being the mother in it. I know about this very well, but have difficulty seeing it in action. It seems, at least in my working with patients in analysis, easier for me to deal with the mother transference in terms of oral fixation. When I am the mother in the oedipal situation, I begin to slow down in my understanding and my interpretations.

S—This is a common kind of counterreaction in an inexperienced analyst when the analyst is a man and the transference is such that he is being reacted to as a mother on a genital level. If the patient is a woman, the analyst often makes interpretations on an oral level. If the patient is a man, the analyst interprets it as homosexual; in other words, he fails to accept the transference identification as a female object on the genital level, but responds as if the reality of his identity as a man makes the transference that of father, and the aim as homosexual. It seems you're much more comfortable in accepting the patient's orality toward you as a mother than you are in accepting the patient's genitality. You see, if the patient is a man this requires some appreciation of female genital functioning and what it means to the patient. If the patient is a female and you are the rival for the father, then you must be able to understand her competition with you as a woman. This also rests upon your ability to empathize with the problem of the little girl in relation to her big mother without resistance or anxiety on your part.

A—You know, this is interesting because I know the words about these things and I listen to you talk and realize that I've heard the same thing many times before, but I seem to understand only disconnected segments. I can't put it altogether. I can accept orality with my being the maternal object, but when it comes to accepting the genitality of the patient, regardless of the patient's sex, as the mother, then I become numb.

S—It is sometimes a difficult thing to understand positively, but also negatively. You see, with this patient in the mother transference, within the oedipal triangle, you are the rival. You are the person that she has strong negative feelings for and wants to get rid of, while at the same time the more positive genitality goes towards somebody else. Now, in a male analyst, that very often produces a complicated countertransference situation.

A—I understand now what she meant before she left on vacation, when she said, "Be careful; don't get killed." I realized it was negative feeling at the time but felt it was a reaction to being abandoned. Now I would formulate it in terms of "you are my mother rival and I wish you would die, but I need you too." This accounts for some of the guilt and for some of her preoccupation with regression to wanting to sit on my lap and with the insistence about feeling rejected.

S—Of course, if you fall in with her business about being rejected it's not quite as bad a developmental experience as if you fall in with her demands to be petted and treated as a heterosexual object. But it keeps everything on the defensive fixated level. She doesn't really begin to differentiate herself as an adult from the little girl that she was once upon a time. Neither does she differentiate you as an adult in relation to herself as an adult from you as an adult in relation to herself as a child.

A—I see. I really have the experience now of a load having lifted off my chest, because there was something really bothering me, and I think the essence of it was that I was not really appreciating my role as a mother object in the rivalry for a man. I can begin to see how, with a woman patient, I defended myself as seeing the situation as oral, and with a male patient as homosexual.

S—I think your work here is achieving an integration in yourself. Many an analyst achieves integration through the gradual empathic analysis of his patient's problems. I mean the analyst is forced, empathically, to live through what the patient is struggling with, and little by little you understand it more if your countertransference isn't too strong. As you begin to understand it more, you understand the patient better, and you're different within yourself too.

Example 3 presented in Chapter IV to illustrate the supervisory process also demonstrates several points regarding teaching about self-analysis. AF's resistance to learning was composed of a mixture of a block in understanding his patient and a transference repetition of a childhood conflict with the supervisor. This example shows clearly how a countertransference which produces a blind spot in therapeutic work also interferes with the learning process. The interference in this instance brought into clear focus the need for self-analytic work. In comparison with HF in the example just discussed in this chapter, AF had not achieved enough insight into himself to be able to recognize the gap in his understanding and the stalemate in the analysis to which his identification with his patient was contributing. He was aware of feelings of resentment toward *S* but not clear as to how they showed themselves or where they came from. Confrontation by *S* partially broke through the resistance against learning and freed AF's function of self-observation enough to permit him to look at his part in perpetuating the analytic stalemate. *S* also attempted to mobilize his intellectual curiosity in relation to his professional work-ego, his instrumental equipment. No attempt was made to interpret to AF his motivations on a deeper level although *S* formulated some for herself. No recommendation was made regarding the necessity for more formal analysis. (He had terminated his training analysis sometime before this episode.) AF was able to use his self-analytic functions in the course of the next month so that some insight was achieved and he reported it to *S*.

Some of the results of AF's self-analytic work were made explicit to *S* in this example. This does not always happen, and frequently the supervisor is aware of results only as they are reflected in changes in the learning alliance. The most usual response to confrontations of the sort in Example 3 is an immediate but temporary increase in tension. Then, the tension diminishes and the student's analytic work improves. Often nothing further is said regarding the specific countertransference. Such a fortunate outcome is not always the case, however; tension remains in the learning alliance, and the therapeutic problem persists.

Since a good prognosis for professional development is contingent on the student's ability to utilize his self-analytic functions, it has been our experience that return to formal analysis becomes necessary when confrontation with the need for self-analysis does not eventually produce positive results. The supervisory process in this area of learning reinforces the continuing "processes of ego transformation" which Freud stated "makes the analyzed subject qualified to be an analyst himself."[47, p. 249]

— VII —

The Supervisory Process: End Phase

IN THE INITIAL AND MIDDLE PHASES OF AN ANALYSIS, THE SHORT-term transactions claim the bulk of the analyst's effort as he follows the patient's responses to his interpretative work. Yet this concentration on the day-to-day cycles of changing resistances and the regressive behavior of the transference neurosis may cause him to lose sight of the subtle signs of progressive movement toward the end-point of therapy. It is this long-range movement which serves as a kind of obligato to the dynamic themes as they vary from moment to moment, and it is in the end phase that the underlying curve of progression becomes traceable through the whole of an analysis. In this chapter we intend to discuss the learning objectives and problems correlated with the phenomena of this terminating phase of the analytic process. The main emphasis will be on the practical aspects of recognizing the behavioral signs of progress in the patient and the technical problems of bringing an analytic relationship to an end.

The phenomena of working through the conflicts of a regressive transference neurosis provide the material for this learning experience and stimulate various learning difficulties specific to the end phase. Sometimes both patient and analyst forget that an analysis does end and that very often during the terminating phase, the subtlest and most persistent forms of resistance are in operation. After a period of regressive reliving in the transference, when the patient has achieved some integration of current reality and childhood experience with some degree of insight, retrogression appears and the whole conflict is "reworked." Kris, in his paper "On Vicissitudes of Insight"[63] describes this process vividly. He also highlights the result of persevering work by the analyst who realizes that one hour of insight does not finish on analysis, but who realizes that the realignment of integrative forces takes a long time; that it is possible only as a result of gradual differentiation of current reality from elements of childhood experiences persistently carried over into the present. Gradually, after many repetitions of experiences examined at all levels in the analytic relationship, the anachronistic elements from childhood encounters can be differentiated from the current reality in the patient's analytic and nonanalytic world and adaptations to the present can be changed.

172

To accomplish this goal requires time and patience from both analyst and analysand. Working through these resistances is often stressful for both. To avoid this pain the patient will sometimes argue for a quick ending or will call up his old defenses and behind a barricade of transference resistances settle for an interminable analysis.

The student-analyst has his own problems in this phase. Anxious to terminate an analysis, if only to satisfy a graduation requirement, he becomes impatient with the length of time the patient needs to achieve a new solution to old conflicts, or impatient with the need to remain steadfast in order to help the patient overcome the remaining bastions devoted to guarding infantile illusions. Growth is a slow process, a fact often ignored by the student eager to achieve a "completed case."

Moreover, this fact is often ignored by those persons who are critical of the length of psychoanalytic training. Yet the process of reworking that makes an analytic treatment so long is also essential for consolidation of gains in analytic training since working through is a factor in learning as well as in therapy. In our opinion, what can be learned by careful supervision of the terminating phase of an analysis is of the utmost value for a student-analyst. Without the learning that belongs to this phase, many patients are permitted to stop with only a "transference cure," or in a negative transference camouflaged by various rationalizations, and many students are deprived of a most important experience for his development.

It is not our intention to discuss the theory of the curative factors in psychoanalytic treatment nor to review the many interesting papers contributing to this subject. It is necessary to call attention, however, to the most common formulation of the criterion for considering an analysis well terminated: the "resolution of the transference neurosis." This formulation stimulates many questions concerned with both theory and technique, as the paper by Zetzel on "The Theory of Therapy in Relation to a Developmental Model of the Psychic Apparatus"[96] testifies. The concept of resolution of the transference neurosis implies intrapsychic changes in economic and dynamic forces that lead to structural modifications which permit a new solution for an old conflict. Reworking the infantile conflict

---

* The hyphen in this word and the long ē give a different twist to its meaning. Resolution can be pronounced in such a way that the meaning is indistinguishable from what happens on New Year's Day—that is, a promise to someone to change one's habits. We refer the reader to Schlesinger's paper on promising for a discussion of the frailties and defensive loading of such promises.[84] To pronounce the word, *resolution*, may refer to the meaning useful in physics and somewhat appropriate to psychoanalysis—that is, resolution of forces, meaning some separation

in the transference neurosis to a *re*-solution* makes it more possible for ego to take the place of id,[46] Freud's succinct phrase for this process.

Not all analyses terminate in this way. Many external situations necessitate interruption which can be called only partially "terminated" even if conditions permit a working-through of the motivations and reactions to the separation from the analyst. There are also many internal, psychological reasons for interruption of an analysis. It may be abruptly ended by the patient in a state of intense resistance, either positive or negative, that drives him into a "flight into health." It may be prolonged forever by the patient who sinks into the couch and enjoys the game of emoting or sparring with the analyst. It may be abruptly ended by the analyst in a moment of intense irritation and frustration at what seems to be the patient's unnecessary clinging to an infantile position, or similar form of resistance. And, it may be prolonged by the analyst whose therapeutic ambition expects more from the patient than is reasonable—or who gets gratification from him and cannot let him go. The first two are motivated by transference resistances, the last two by countertransference resistances. Such resistances on both sides of the relationship often repeat the parent-child situation in adolescence where the child's moves toward separation and independence are experienced as threatening to the parent (analyst) as well as the child (patient). Weigert, in her paper "Contribution to the Problem of Terminating Psychoanalysis,"[93] points out that it is not re-solution of the transference neurosis, but the re-solution of the counter-transference which is an important measure of approaching termination of an analysis. Actually, of course, it takes new solutions of both to accomplish the goal.

The problems crucial for the end phase are associated with terminating a relationship which has been a unique experience. To terminate means that the patient is able to separate from a person who has become a confidant of things unknown and thought to be unknowable, and who has assisted the patient to achieve a new state of emotional freedom

---

of conflicting forces and the striking of a new balance. We prefer, however, the use of a hyphen and a pronunciation that emphasizes the syllable *re*, which stresses that a problem is being solved in a new way. "Dissolution," sometimes applied, here is equally inappropriate, although it carries the meaning of separation from, or dissolving of, something. That is, the transferred patterns of behavior have disappeared. This may seem true manifestly but not in the sense of no longer existing. The old problems still exist but are integrated into the total personality structure in such a way that they become subordinated and under more effective ego control. Since the concept of re-solution of the transference neurosis belongs to the theory of therapy, we limit our discussion to the phenomena as they frequently appear in supervision.

and maturity. It is hard to let go of such a relationship and permit the analyst and the experience with him to become a memory. This integrative task has been compared to mourning work by several authors[16, 28, 71, 88] who emphasize the similarity between separations caused by death and those brought about by normal psychological growth. Both events stimulate a sense of loss which activates processes of mourning. Mourning work and healthy growth are accomplished when a relationship is given up which is realistically over and when giving it up can be differentiated from a sense of being deprived or rejected. The problem of termination is similar to mourning and psychosocial development in that a current experience should be "metabolized" into a memory and energy freed to be directed toward new objects and new levels of relationship.

In a good termination the working through of the middle phase brings the patient to a beginning recognition of change and the stirrings of a wish to separate and go on to new experiences. Associations to this effect initiate the end phase. Analyst and patient then proceed to the task of setting a date and working through the actual separation. In other words, material in the beginning of the end phase takes on a different quality that forecasts the possibility of termination and turns the patient's thoughts to present reality and the future rather than the past. The duration of the onset of termination may be long and very gradual and the analyst may be aware of the changes long before the patient is.

Much more could be said on this topic, but our chief concern is to study the teaching-learning process as it was demonstrated in our students. We found that it was useful to divide the end phase into three steps which the analyst and patient make together although at a different pace: (1) recognizing changes in the patient which indicate that termination should be thought about; (2) deciding on a date; and (3) terminating. The duration of each of these steps will differ, depending on the individual patient and analyst. Each step requires a different level of adaptation to present reality, which is influenced by past experiences with similar problems and by the knowledge and skill of the analyst.

Learning objectives in this phase of the supervisory process are a natural outgrowth of the effort already spent by teacher and student on developing system sensitivity and system responsiveness. As working through proceeds, it becomes easier for a student to organize what initially appeared as isolated events, into dynamic lines of recurring themes and trends of behavior. He can identify the manifestations of transference and countertransference reactions in terms of increasing or decreasing resistances in response to stimuli inside and outside the analytic situation (Chart II, 5′, 6′); and he reports his observations as such to his supervisor (Chart II, 5, 6).

An experienced analyst or a very talented student understands preconsciously the relationship between these short-term transactions and the
goal of therapeutic change. A beginner, however, needs help in seeing the
evidence of working through. Recognizing evidence of growth should,
therefore, become a deliberately sought learning objective in the end phase;
otherwise, these aspects of analysis as a process and the cues that indicate
structural change can become lost in a series of interlocking repetitions
that keep the analysis in an interminable stalemate. To perceive these
cues and understand their meaning is a complicated task, and a student's
success in learning this objective can be measured by his pattern of reporting the evidence for insight and growth (Chart II, 7).

The pedagogical task (Chart II, 7′) is to teach the student to recognize
the patient's resistances associated with ending and to be alert to the possibility that some resistance in himself may be blocking a good termination. The student clings to the old without being aware of it, or aware
of how easily the evidence of maturation can be missed. Signs of a patient's growth are often difficult to recognize because they commonly
appear clad in the same language he has used to express other things and
are often accompanied by old forms of defense. But what appears to be
the same material on the surface can be perceived as qualitatively different by an ear tuned to listen for these, at first, small evidences of change.
Such sensitive perceptiveness may be part of a high level of endowment,
but more often it is developed only by the kind of listening taught by a
supervisor whose "instrument" can hear these signs of growth and can
help the student sharpen his own acuity.

The following example is taken from the beginning of an end phase of
an analysis. It illustrates some of the problems connected with learning
what is meant by the process of an analysis as well as the need to listen
for and recognize clues pointing toward termination. Other learning problems, such as understanding dynamic lines and the technique of making
transference interpretations, were an important part of the supervisory
teaching in this instance and were related to the technical work of facilitating an analyzable transference neurosis. The patient was most un-
willing to "give up" her childhood fantasies and the hope of their being
realized today. Separation from the analyst was experienced over and
over as a "traumatic rejection" for which he was supposed to feel guilty.
The idea that separation could have a positive developmental and adaptive function seemed new to both patient and analyst. It is understandable
that a patient frequently clings to his infantile defensive interpretation of
separation as being a rejection or abandonment, but the analyst only per-
petuates a developmental fixation if he too sees it only in such traumatic
terms. In this instance, progress toward a re-solution had been slowed
down by technical mistakes.

EXAMPLE 19

KF (Case V), Supervisory Sessions 6-14,* Analytic Hours about 1000

The patient was a married woman in her late forties with two adolescent children. Her husband was a successful businessman who traveled frequently. She complained of social anxiety, irritability with her children and husband, a chronic feeling of inferiority, and sexual frigidity.

Circumstances necessitated a change of supervisors after the analysis was well advanced. The supervision was arranged for once a month and was not recorded. Hence, the following material is an elaboration of notes made immediately following the sixth supervisory hour and the next eight. Our usual format for illustrations of exchange and comments could not be employed. Instead, the material is organized around three learning problems. This example also illustrates some of the problems that were discussed in the middle phase of the supervisory process.

The analyst's learning difficulties could be grouped under three headings: (1) technique of transference interpretations, (2) a defensive countertransference, and (3) understanding of certain phenomena of working through. Overcoming these three difficulties opened the way to a comprehension of psychoanalysis as a process which this student-analyst had not integrated before (Chart II, 6), and provided him with a new perception of the movements of the process toward a transference neurosis, working through and termination (Chart II, 7'). Awareness of insight and growth in the patient and himself was a gratifying step forward in his learning (Chart II, 7).

When supervision with the new supervisor began, A had been accustomed to phrase almost all of his transference interventions so as to focus on the repetitions of childhood experiences, emphasizing simultaneously the similarity between what P was experiencing now toward him and what P had experienced toward her father, mother, or someone else in the past. Usually this interpretation was given in one dose. He paid less attention to other forms of transference interpretations. This technical habit had served a useful purpose in the therapy by helping P to recognize that the past was being repeated in the present. The resulting intellectual insight enlarged the field of her observing ego and cemented the therapeutic alliance. It also relieved some of her sense of inadequacy and helplessness in spite of the guilt and shame stirred up by the increasing pressure of childhood longings which had never been well repressed or otherwise defended against.

This type of transference interpretation, however, had the effect of intensifying infantile longings and bringing childhood fantasies closer to the surface. The effect was positive in this direction but it also had a negative influence. P's ego was flooded with regressive affect that, so to speak, had no place to go. Continued genetic interpretations such as "You are repeating with me what you felt toward your father when you were a little girl,"

---

* Much of the supervision in this instance had been conducted under another supervisor.

were experienced by her as a rebuff and a pushing away. She responded with frustration, humiliation, shame, and anger, defending herself by repression and masochistic preoccupations. The constant request "to recall the past," kept the childhood fantasies alive and active, but without gradual insight into their inappropriateness or opportunity to discharge regressive affect. The patient became involved in an erotized defense transference where the secret pleasure afforded by her masochistic adaptation in childhood was reenacted in the current analytic experience. The transference resistance was facilitated by A's failure to bring into clearer focus the here-and-now experiences of reactive humiliation and shame and the increasing sense of failure concerning her hopes of (oedipal) "recognition" from A. Her childhood hopes had been frustrated by her father. The latter had behaved as A seemed to be behaving—that is, alternately leading her on and brushing her off. In this respect A could not be differentiated from him. She had reacted in childhood with a deep sense of failure relieved by compensatory fantasies of someday being successful, and a guilty feeling of secret superiority to her mother. Her rage at teasing frustration and her sense of humiliation had been solved in the past by masochism, physical symptoms, sexual inhibition, and social withdrawal. All these phenomena appeared again as a result of her analytic experience under the conditions induced by A's technical behavior. Their recurrence, however, threatened to set up an unanalyzable transference resistance.

As S saw the problem, several factors seemed to be contributing. The chief obstacle was a countertransference which interfered with the analysis in a special way and which also blocked A's ability to learn from supervisory help. It became clear to S that P was perceiving the present behavior of A as being identical with that of her father in childhood. A knew intellectually that regressive reliving in an analysis is not therapeutic unless there are elements of the current experience which can be differentiated from the past, but a counterreaction to P's intense affect and erotic fantasies prevented him from helping her to verbalize them directly and so permit her to see the incongruities in the past as well as in the present. Doggedly, he continued to make interpretations and to urge her to remember, ignoring her responses with angry frustration and sense of hopelessness alternating with attempts to adjust to A's expectations by pseudoconfessions of guilt and self-condemnation for frigidity, jealousy, and sexual competition. There seemed to be a stalemate contributed to by A's rigid adherence to what he felt he had been taught to do and by P's ability to erotize her transference neurosis masochistically. The complex mixture of childhood wishes, hopes, frustrations, anxieties, conflicts, and defenses was being reenacted in all its many-layered forms which, however, were not within range of the observing egos of either A or P so that working through to insight could occur.

Evaluating the situation, S decide that the chief cause was not lack of knowledge or experience. Something was interfering with A's ability to learn from his experience. His motivation for learning was strong and sincere, but he seemed to labor under a heavy inhibition of free expression of affect and of fantasy. His inhibition interfered with his empathic understanding of P's associations. He could not allow himself to perceive their meanings and deal with them directly any more than she could. Consequently, he could not help her. The severity of his inhibition and the professional blind spot it produced created a difficult teaching problem for S to solve. Fortunately, A was in a position to get analytic help for himself. This fact made it easier for S and permitted her to limit herself to confronting him with the evidence of his blind spot and simply to suggest that the cause might be within himself. The rest was left to A and his analyst, resulting in gradual improvement.

A second learning problem was associated with the first and had to do with the perception of dynamic lines running through P's associations. Since A's inhibition involved both affect and imagination, it interfered with the analytic process by causing him to put distance between himself and the patient. Inhibition of imagination, however, also blocked his ability to understand her communications. He could not put himself in her place and empathically "taste" her experience. Thus, he could not translate into his own words his introspected understanding. It is by such translation that the meaning of a patient's words, feelings, gestures, and sensations gradually come together in an analyst's mind and form the recurrent themes that underlie the manifold expression of conflicts and resistances. These condensations represent the dynamic lines of the analytic process. In this case, the student-analyst found such a translation into dynamic lines very difficult to do. Without this ability, however, he could not follow the vicissitudes of the analytic process.

Confronted with this second learning problem, S found herself making use of several teaching techniques. At intervals she stated her formulation of the immediate dynamic line herself with the hope that A could understand it in the supervisory situation distanced from the patient and could then permit his interpretive functions freer play when with the patient. Occasionally, this technique was successful but more often it served to reinforce A's dependence on S's "fantasy" and did not bring his own into action. S tried this teaching technique more often in the beginning of the supervisory work, soon recognizing, however, that it was usually ineffective. More successful was another teaching technique which involved active fantasying on the part of S in language which expressed the patient's feelings, fantasies, and conflicts as S understood them. This dramatization had the effect of breaking through A's inhibition to some extent. It involved him in a way which he could tolerate since he did not need to worry that a mistaken response from him would do the patient harm. This dramatization painted for him a picture of P's psyche in action but as if seen on a stage rather than in intimate interaction. S went beyond P's manifest content to the latent levels. This forced A to participate on a level he had tended to avoid. It permitted him to exercise his associative functions safely and to rehearse possible interpretations to the patient. S occasionally responded as P might have done in order to keep A involved and to highlight the interaction. This supervisory "play acting" usually occupied very few minutes and was followed by discussion of the event.

As time went on, *A* gradually became freed of his private inhibitions and demonstrated that he had learned to follow the oscillations of *P*'s transference reactions. He stopped making genetic interpretations only, did not ask for memories, and refrained from "dissecting" a symbol or a symptom. These techniques, although indicated in earlier phases of an analysis, were handicapping at this point. When he fell into his old habit of interpreting, he was quicker to recognize his error and to correctly understand *P*'s response. His interpretations were more often on the beam of the analytic process and served to carry *P* farther in the analytic work instead of reinforcing a resistance or raising her tension beyond an analyzable level.

As progress was made by both *A* and *P*, a third learning problem appeared, which belongs to a broad objective of understanding the process of change over time in the course of analytic work. One aspect of this objective was illustrated when *A* learned that with analytic progress the changing equilibria within *P* caused the state of the transference to change, necessitating a shift of technique in order to promote the process of regression. As *A* was able to refrain from distancing himself by means of genetic interpretations, *P* was able to verbalize her transference expectations more directly and *A* was able to assist her to express her affects and to realize what stimulated them in the present. He did not need to back away from either her erotic fantasies or her rage at being frustrated. He was able to interpret her sense of humiliation for exposing her longings. As *A* made progress, so did *P*. She experienced acceptance for herself in spite of frustration; the affect was less painful; the inappropriateness of childhood hopes came more fully into consciousness. She began to return from the regressed level of her transference neurosis and to bring her reality testing functions back into more efficient operation. She began to recognize the fantastic nature of her current expectations of *A* and her childhood expectations of her father. She began to differentiate *A* from her father as well as herself today from herself then. *A* was able to help her accomplish this with well-phrased interpretations.

P became aware of a need to give up past fantasies and hopes. This made her sad and depressed since it meant to her giving up her relationship with *A*. To "wean herself" she suggested a decrease in hours. *A*'s first response was to interpret this suggestion as resistance and running away. *P* protested and felt depreciated. *A* recognized her reaction and recovered from his mistake by admitting it was a question which could be discussed. He failed, however, to understand the dynamics of the sadness and renunciation as evidence of progress. He perceived her willingness to "separate" more as flight than, at least partially, as an adaptation indicative of new integration. It was not difficult to orient him to this different level, yet the supervisor's interpretations of it came as a surprise since *A* clung to the feeling that separation could be nothing but traumatic.

At this point in the analysis, *P*'s new-found position was insecure and vacillating. She regressed again but not so deeply this time, and *A* was able to follow the shifting levels with greater skill. Much working through was required, but during this experience *A* gained an appreciation of what is involved in the total process of analysis.

The following example from the recorded supervision of GB will give another illustration of the phenomena of the onset of termination. In this example from a transcript it is easy to follow the shifting dynamics in the patient and between analyst and patient. Impulses and fantasies long repressed break through in words and *P* moves from one regressed level to another and back into the present. The process of realignment is observable, although the changes at this point are very unstable. *A* remains tuned in and keeps the process going with timely interpretations. He recognizes the progress but is not aware that it forecasts termination.

EXAMPLE 20

GB (Case I), Supervisory Sessions 71 and 72, Analytic Hours about 450

The material of this period of the analysis occurred at the end of about two and a half years and was associated with the analyst's third summer vacation. Up to this time, the transference neurosis had oscillated between the oedipal fixation to the idealized dead father and the oedipal and preoedipal identifications and conflicts with the mother. The patient gained fleeting and fragmented insight into her unconscious conflict over the wish to fulfill the fantasy of being pregnant by her father, and also into the rejection of her babies (see Example 2, Chapter IV) associated with the belief that her father was alive in her belly. Live babies contradicted this second fantasy; hence, she must give them up. Her guilt toward her mother as well as her dependence on her maintained a sense of worthlessness and helplessness which was overcompensated by a sense of specialness that was most prominent in relation to men. She used her overconfidence to cover up her masochistic needs which led to the rupture of every close relationship with a man. There could be no commitment to a realistic and adult relationship, since the defenses supported by her fantasies would be threatened and she would have to face her feelings of loss in separation.

On the basis of having worked through these conflicts to some extent, the reality of separation from the analyst, confirmed by his vacation, intensified the fantasies about her idealized father. The analytic work in this period before and after the vacation gave evidence of a beginning shift in the patient's orientation to reality.

Exchange 1

A—Last time you emphasized her fear of physical hurt in close relationships in childhood, at least in her fantasies. This is how the material came out. She several times experienced epigastric pains to which her association was, as she put it, "The living God is inside my belly." Apparently this has been a theme with her all her life. The line I quoted is from a poem she had written when she was an adolescent and now her associations to this are having missed me over the weekend, and then her father's death. And then she talked at some length about how adults in the family had not supported her at the time of her father's death. They made her into an object of pity, cried over her, "The poor little thing," instead of asking her how she felt. [*P* was six years old.]

S—Would she have been able to tell?

A—I don't know. She says that one of her teachers in school was the only one who dealt with her as if she were a human being. I think the point she is trying to make is that nobody took her seriously enough to consider that she might have known what had happened to her father and that she might have had some feelings about it, and as she felt this, she suddenly said, "I have no baby to hold." This was so out of context that I asked her what she was talking about. She repeated, "I never had a baby to hold. My mother had children from my father. I didn't have any."

She talks of being angry at her mother for treating her like a baby. Then she says she cannot stand her boyfriend who is so kind and affectionate. She likes him; she wants him to leave but she cannot send him away. She wonders if she felt as a child she had sent her father away. She has tried to provoke me into sending her away. She feels that anyone else would have done so by now out of irritation with her. I told her that apparently she's very much afraid of being hurt in any close relationship. She agreed.

There was some construction work going on in the building and everytime they hit something with a hammer, she felt as if she were being hammered on. She remembers how her mother was unpredictable, especially when punishing her. She recalls lying awake while her father was alive, listening to them argue and fight.

The next day she says she keeps forgetting when I am going on vacation. She wants to ask me to change an hour, but she's afraid to because I am so unpredictable and might punish her. I told her she needed to see me as a monster. And then she began to fight. "It's a hopeless battle. I am just an insect on a pin." I told her she needs to provoke an attack so she can feel hurt. She says she knows this but she does not believe anyone loves her; hence, she is hostile and therefore not obligated.

She was talking with her finger in her mouth and I said I could not hear. At first she felt defiant and said she would not talk. So I told her she can do it if she wishes but the consequence is I cannot hear and it's up to her whether she wants me to hear or not. She said, "That's nice. I resent you and provoke you, but it's a hollow triumph. I have the novel idea that I might get more from you if I see you as a doctor."

She talks about her boyfriend and of mixing him up with me. She feels ashamed because she goes into a dangerous situation without knowing it's dangerous. She guesses with me she feels like a little girl with her father and what she wants is a permanent relationship like mother had, but this is forbidden and unavailable.

She has a dream about looking in a file for something which she can't find. It belonged to a man whose name was like mine. Well, I took up the dream and she had given some associations connecting it with me, and so I pointed out that this must be her reaction to my going away and that she's angry with me for leaving her, and she says she knows she has no right to be angry. She wonders whether her father died to punish her for something, and then she talks of mother having deprived her of a father—she means by never remarrying—and she starts to cry. She was very upset and she said she wonders if this is why she had children without a father, somehow to recreate the situation, except she's the mother now. She's afraid to be angry with me because she might lose me and the implication was that I would never come back. And I asked her if she felt that somehow her anger would magically destroy me. She didn't answer this but indicated that she is always acting the role of the compliant child who hides her anger, at least superficially.

I told her then that I thought she was reexperiencing with me the disappointment and hatred that she had felt towards her father *before* he died. This was a very shocking statement for her. How shocking she didn't indicate then, although she was crying at the time, and she said vehemently, "No, not before—only after he died, not before he died!" And then she said in a sort of petulant way, it's not true, she's not afraid of giving me up; she's more afraid of a continued relationship than of losing me. I told her I thought that might be true, but that since I am going on vacation, I thought the other one was currently more important.

The next day she tries to fight with me but finally admits that she is fighting so as not to confess that my interpretation about her hatred and disappointment before her father died was correct. I repeated it and tied it in with when I'm not a loving father she repeats with me the childhood rages she must have felt when her father wasn't what she wanted him to be. She says after that last hour she felt shaken up like an earthquake had happened. I told her I thought she could no longer maintain the fiction that all her trouble came from losing her father. She said she knew her father had not been perfect, yet she denied it; "'I wanted too much from my father.'"

Comments: In this supervisory session there was little need for teaching activity. This exchange confirms definite progress in the analytic process and also in the development of the student. *P* continued to be free in expressing her affects but was also more able to return to a level that permitted cooperation and insight. Her observing ego functioned well in the analytic situation. *A* was well aware that *P*'s concentration on losing her father and on the magic wish to undo the separation, as well as guilt for having caused it, was an expression of *P*'s transference neurosis. He was able to wait through the resistances and emotional turmoil, responding calmly, directing *P* toward new and significant insights, focusing primarily on the ambivalent feelings.

The manifestations of the changes in P which indicate some intrapsychic modifications, and therefore the beginning of the end phase of the analysis, can be summarized as follows: (1) P remembered the quarrels between her parents and the inadequacies of her father, thus indicating a lifting of repression permitting recall of the reality of childhood. The need to distort the past was diminishing so that she could begin to see her father in a less idealized form. The reality of childhood could be tolerated with less conflict between childhood wishes and childhood frustration. Idealizing her image of her father accompanied her secret fantasy of being especially attractive to him and so maintained the fiction of oedipal success and her narcissistic illusions of omnipotence. At this stage in the analysis, the guilt and shame of oedipal rivalry were less intense and could be seen as belonging to the past, indicating a better perception of present reality and better mastery of the pressures of primitive needs. (2) P began to recognize that she had actually wanted too much from her father when he was alive. One can infer from this some objectification of her childhood self, seeing her expectations then as being unrealistic, a sign of regulatory mechanisms more adapted to reality and less under the control of childhood anxieties. She could also recognize the inappropriateness of repeating these anachronistic demands with A. Insight and structural change were on the way.

Five weeks later (Supervisory Session 72), after A's three-week vacation, the process of working through toward insight continued. New memories of childhood were recalled and gained new meaning for her. Anxiety and defensiveness diminished further and she could perceive A more as an ally and a real object in the present. (Details of this material will be presented in Example 25 in Chapter VIII with emphasis on the student's progress in learning.)

Characteristically, retrogression set in, and as if startled by her progress P began to repeat her old defensive patterns in the few months that followed Session 72. During this period A had learned to anticipate the end but was not prepared for the problems of the next stage of the terminating process.

In the next illustration, the events concerned with setting a date for this patient's termination are demonstrated. The period of time necessary for this integrative work included some 84 analytic hours over 5½ months and 12 supervisory sessions. Interesting and instructive as the material is, it cannot be reproduced in its entirety. Consequently, we have severely condensed and extracted the episodes most pertinent to the end-phase problems, trying at the same time to preserve the thread of forward movement showing through the patient's struggle with herself and with the analyst. This example covers Supervisory Sessions 74-85 and will be divided into episodes in which the supervisory activity will be presented mainly in summarized form rather than quoted from the transcripts.

EXAMPLE 21

GB (Case I), Supervisory Sessions 74-85, Analytic Hours 500-584

Episode 1

In early October, about two and a half months after Session 72, *A* reports a feeling that the material is very repetitious and the analysis has reached a stalemate. Following the spurt around *A*'s vacation, *P* seemed to be settling down to her old ways of beginning a relationship with a young man and then doing something to interrupt it. When *A* pointed out that she seems to prefer to live out her fantasies rather than analyze them, *P* protested that was not so and that she had changed in many respects, but "I prefer the irresponsibility of being in analysis where you can say or do anything."

At this point, *A* said, "You are making analysis into a way of life and using it to prevent change." *P* offered resistance by talking about her old boy friend, Peter, about whom she continues to have fantasies. In the next hour, she agreed the analysis had come to a standstill. "I want to derive all of my satisfaction from the analysis and am willing to settle for things as they stand now. At least I don't have asthma anymore." (Here we see a common phenomenon in this stage of analysis. Symptomatic improvement and a little insight relieve enough suffering so that the pressure to work toward further change and more insight is lessened. When this decrease in motivation is accompanied by the gratification of being able to substitute the analytic relationship for the defensive fantasy transferred from childhood, then resistance to further analytic work becomes pleasurized with the secondary gain of "acting out" the fantasy. To continue the transference relationship becomes more important than getting well. Interpretations of this transference resistance are felt as threats to a very cherished and often sucessful denial of reality. In this analysis, this patient was able, however, to struggle with her conflicts and *A* was able to help her. He was very permissive in letting *P* bring up on her own the reality of ending. This step took another four weeks. However, an actual date was not mutually agreed upon for another four and a half months. Thus, we see the slow process of working through again and again the pathogenic conflicts that began to show some evidence of erosion at the early part of the summer.)

In the next hour *P* agreed that *A* was correct and that she "had assimilated the analysis into a life pattern and was not using it for change but to maintain the status quo." She talked of her inadequacy in intercourse, and *A* focused on her envy of other people who have a sexual life which she can avoid by claiming she is satisfied with what she has. It came out that *P* envied *A* his education and consequently had started back to school. This fact she had kept secret and *A* interpreted some feeling of guilt back of the secrecy. A dream followed in which *P*, after a series of acrimonius fights with a fellow in the office, apologized and offered to cooperate from now on. She associated her antagonist with *A* and then added a second dream about cockroaches. (See Example 2 at the beginning of this analysis.) This time there was only one cockroach, a great big one, which she wanted to kill, but it escaped. In the dream, she thought, "Why do I want to kill it? Maybe I ought to look at it." Then she realized it was a beautiful gold color, irridescent like a peacock. She associated that this cockroach was really what she would like to be. It was not a bad insect but a beautiful bug. *A* tells *S,* "It was clear she understood this dream about wanting to cooperate as an attempt to avoid the theme of hostility."

Over the weekend *P* felt angry and upset but reported that it was not disintegrating as before. She becomes aware of how she gets angry outside to avoid anger at *A.* She enumerates the changes in her life, but protests she is still afraid of an intimate, on-going, real sexual relationship, and then she think's of *A*'s wife. In a dream she accepted a nice young man sexually, although she tried not to. She associates *A* to this young man. At this point *S* remarked that to permit her to think of *A* in the role of a love object, albeit in the future, would not break up the analytic stalemate. It would only permit the perpetuation of the fantasy of a sexual relationship with an idealized, detached, and inaccessible man. *S* emphasized how *P* desexualizes everybody in reality, including herself, as long as she can "dream" about sexuality in the analytic relationship.

A reports that *P* associates to seeing another patient who is pregnant. He tells her she prefers to have him "four times a week in this limited way than to take a chance on losing someone else in a different relationship."

P thinks of calling her old boyfriend, Peter.

S emphasizes the basic narcissistic problems here and how much *P* lives in unrealistic fantasy. Men are important only as their interest in her signifies her attractiveness. *S* says that confronting a patient with the reality of her situation is only a starting point. It is never enough. *A* feels that he and *P* do not know how to deal with this problem. *S* reviews the impasse which has developed, starting months ago with the mourning for her father and beginning to see him realistically, but since then making *A* a love object and so stabilizing the transference, which *S* feels *A* accepts without questioning it enough.

Comments: This material underlines many of the problems met by both analyst and supervisor at this stage in an analysis. Changes have occurred, gratifying to everyone, but change also means losing *A.* *P* keeps her progress secret and retrogresses to a repetition of a transference resistance which is difficult for *A* to understand and to deal with. Confrontation with reality and exhortation to change is clearly not enough; *A,* who has never terminated an analysis, needs help. The pedagogical diagnosis of the difficulty is inexperience with these transference dynamics mixed with some form of counterreaction in *A* which *S* perceives as vaguely similar to *P*'s special manifestation of narcissism. She confronts him only peripherally at this point.

These difficulties presented by *P* and *A* are not uncommon and are often responsible for a premature ending of an analysis, both parties being willing to settle for the changes that have been made and to end on a positive note. In this case, however, *A* understood that *P*'s "cooperation" was a cover for hostile feelings and a defense against the fear and pain of separation, which to her meant total loss. The following excerpts will bring this out.

Episode 2 (Supervisory Session 75, Analytic Hour 508)

This session begins with the report of a dream in which *P* is changing from a woman to a man gynecologist. He wanted to rape her but she wouldn't let him because she gave herself to him. Reluctant to tell the dream, *P* followed it with the repetitive resistance that she did not know if she wanted to change. To get well means to compromise, to admit losses. *A* tells her she is living to prove she is unique and lovable and that relationships to other people are unimportant. She responds by saying she is afraid of *A*, that she is fighting to hold on to the only self she knows, that analysis is taking away one characteristic after another. *A* focused her lack of real satisfaction. *P* accused him of talking like her mother. It comes out that *P* feels she must be faithful to father just as mother was, since she never married again.

The triangular conflict is further elaborated. *P* has a fantasy that the wife of a man whom she recently met, dies. She reports, "I realize that I have the same feelings about you and your wife and that's why I'm so concerned about something happening to you." *A* interprets that as a child she felt her father died to punish her because she really wanted something to happen to her mother. *P* responds "How inconvenient it would be if you died. Without you I wouldn't qualify to replace not just your wife but any wife."

S reemphasizes the narcissistic defense and the fixation on a childhood level where sex is only play and fantasy. She stresses the defect in *P*'s sense of reality in that the playful sexuality is not only with *A* but with all men, and unlike a fantasy it has resulted in two pregnancies.

In the next hour *P* takes an important step, which on the surface looks like the acting out of defiant resistance. She confesses that she has been secretly planning to go to a ball game on a day which means canceling an hour. She was afraid to tell *A* and half hoped the game would not be played. *A* thought this was a loyalty problem; *S* thought that *P* felt *A* would be hurt and is trying to make him feel important to her. *S* felt that *P* wanted *A* to feel the same pain she was feeling.

A finally interprets, "I think you expect me to envy you if you go to the ball game just as you were unable to go to Mexico because your brother would envy you." She protests she can't stand to have anyone envy her; she's never competed with anyone. At the end of the hour, she hesitated, said, "All right, I won't be in tomorrow," left very scared, and did not come to her hour.

The weekend intervened. She had been sick with a severe cold and asthma, the first in over a year. Also she overslept so she couldn't go to the game, but she watched it on television. She knows this is emotional. It is related to envying and being envied, especially by *A*. "It would be terrible if you became so human." She reveals the fantasy that *A* envied her old boyfriend, which is why she gave him up. She feels glad she canceled the hour, excited about thinking of calling Peter.

P then becomes depressed and angry and talks about refurnishing her apartment with things which remind her of *A*'s office. After much beating around the bush, *P* tells *A* that she wants his opinion and hopes he will come and see her apartment. *A* compares this with *P*'s wanting approval from her mother or sister. *S* feels a historical interpretation is not the point, but that *P*'s behavior is associated with her sadness over thoughts of separating and she wants *A* to be sad too.

Comments: Somewhat confused by *P*'s anxiety and *A*'s tangential interpretations, the material seems to be basically a struggle with the theme of separation and progression. *P* clings to her resistance but simultaneously makes little moves toward independence. She tests *A*'s tolerance to this, hoping that he will demonstrate some envy or jealousy. He remains detached and fails to understand her identification with him as a sign of progress. Progress brings a growing sense of separation, which to her means loss and which provokes anger and depression.

Episode 3 (*Supervisory Session 76, Analytic Hours 516-524*)

Since the interpretation reported in Session 74 that analysis is becoming a way of life for *P,* no mention of terminating has been made. *A* let matters take their course. In this session, however, he reports, "Her process of changing has taken hold now. In a very timid way, she brought up the question of when the analysis might come to an end. She feels it is dragging on, that she is useless and I am bored." So *A* told her that he thought she had felt rejected by his interpretation that it was all right to form an attachment to someone else. She said her original reaction had been excitement, pleasure, and hope. It was the first time anybody had told her she could make her own decisions about important things, but she felt afraid and not ready. She felt she was walking on water and suddenly she looked down, saw it was water, and sank.

The next hour she felt better and began the same themes again, so *A* interpreted her avoidance of talking about her independent decisions and choices. She continued to do little things to be a good patient, like closing the office door by herself. She realized that maybe she was exaggerating her helplessness but she preferred to think that *A* let her go to the game to prove she was not ready to leave him. Now she knows this is not true. "I do need you but not permanently." *A* reports this is the first time she has seen the analytic relationship as temporary. This is followed by an affair in which for the first time she admits she needs a man. *P* recognizes this change.

After the weekend, she spoke of plans to change her job around January 1. *A* reports that he "did not catch on at first that this is the beginning of thinking about stopping the analysis then." She talks of fantasies about her new boyfriend, of how *A*'s little boy must be no longer a three-year-old as he was at the beginning of the analysis, and of envying *A*'s patient who is pregnant. *A* told her he thought she was trying to reassure him that she is loyal to him. *P* says, "No, I'm saying the opposite."

The next hour, she says she's in conflict between wanting to show that she doesn't need *A* and not wanting to fall into the old trap of saying she doesn't need anyone. She talks about how many notebooks she has filled and the number of unbound journals on the shelf which began to accumulate when she started her analysis. Magically she equates the three-year total with the end of her analysis, but she miscounts and sees 13 rather than 11— the difference between 2¾ years and 3¼ years of analysis. *A* told her she wanted the analysis to last 13 quarters.

S points out that *P* also wants to feel she had some part in filling the notebooks of her case history. *S* emphasizes that the ability to give up analysis needs to be rewarded by a sense of independence and growth. *S* feels that *P*'s fantasies about stopping at the end of three years is setting a premature date (only six weeks to go), that this may be a repetition of her pattern of leaving the man as soon as she is involved. *A* reports that no date was set, but that he told her it could be discussed.

P avoids any discussion of a date and talks about trying to hang onto the coat of someone who just takes off his coat and walks away. *A* realized in the supervisory session that *P* reacted to his remark as if he were trying to get rid of her. *P* now feels she is helpless and can make no decisions of any kind. She says, "Maybe I am reluctant to talk about it because I feel I would hurt you by deserting you." Anyway, there are too many problems left unsolved." At this point, *P* had a feeling it was time to go, although 5 minutes remained of the hour. *A* interpreted, "You feel it's time to go but you don't know how to go about it."

Comments: It took *P* about six weeks to be able to talk about her fantasy of ending the analysis after three years and in conjunction with a change in her job. The way this fantasy repeated an old defense was pointed out by *S* with the recommendation that the analysis should continue much longer. *A*'s inexperience in recognizing the signs of shifting defenses and the intensity of her separation anxiety is clear. Like KF in Example 19, *A* continues to make historical or genetic interpretations when the affect requires discharge in the present and when the re-solution of a developmental conflict requires some recognition of progress from *A* in order to make the structural changes more secure.

Episode 4 (Supervisory Sessions 77-82, Analytic Hours about 524-560—
2 Months)

During this period of analysis, *P* regresses and repeats all of her old conflicts and defenses on various levels. She talks about not wanting to leave, feeling helpless, afraid of success, afraid of losing everything. *A* interprets that she wants to end without finishing. *P* seems to ignore this idea and threatens *A* with getting pregnant. He responds by interpreting her anger with him and her need to get revenge for leaving her for a week. She agrees but says she also knows *A* is really acting in her best interests. She thinks if she is angry and hates him, then she can stop without a sense of loss. The anger is a protection against the pain of separation. Referring to the number of journals again, she hints at a three and one-half year analysis, but neither *A* nor *P* deal with this explicitly. She wants to make *A* fall in love with her and then leave him.

After another round of going over many of the same themes—such as curiosity about *A*'s private life followed by feeling like a helpless child, being tired of analysis and angry at *A* who takes away her protective fantasies— *A* interpreted the incongruity in this resistance to change. "You dislike the relationship here, but you make no move to terminate it." She said, "I don't think the analysis is finished." *A* replied, "It can't be if you refuse to prepare for termination." *P* had never thought of it this way and for a few hours expresses more of her anxiety at the loneliness and sense of loss. She reports that in the recent week when *A* was away, she was less shaken than at other similar times. She has been in a good mood and gets along well with people. She was able to get up in the morning when the alarm rang without depending on the landlady as she used to on her mother. She begins to think about the summer when there will be no classes and a lot of time to fill. She realizes she is thinking about when the analysis will be over and it makes her panicky.

In the next two supervisory sessions (80 and 81), *P* thinks about meeting *A* after ending. This leads to more frustration and feeling abandoned, rejected, and misused. She regresses to playful talking in nonsense riddles and continues to repeat her old patterns. Both *P* and *A* seem to be avoiding the fact that January is approaching and no date has been set.

January comes and goes and *P* feels *A* is angry at her and is really telling her analysis is over. *A* reminds her she has avoided discussing it (but so has he). *P* says that's all she has been talking about. She dreams of an inspection in the office, her inventory is off and there are two extra flight bags. Since there is a penalty if the number is not just right, she has to hide them. Her associations are to "healthy married couples with babies" and to an eligible man she met on the weekend. Then she talks of the future being empty without analysis. The next hour she talks of her approaching vacation and not knowing what to do with it. *A* becomes impatient and confronts her with her procrastination and resistance to direct expression of her feelings. *P* protests but the next day agrees she has been talking in riddles. She really wants *A* to tell her to stay and not go away.

Comments: The repetitiousness of this episode is striking, as is *A*'s continuing to confront *P* with her avoiding discussion of termination. He seems to expect something different from what she tells him. She insists she is talking about terminating. *A*'s confrontations apparently make *P* feel pushed out and disapproved of, while at the same time they also permit her to act out her rebellion in the transference. She seems to feel she is getting away with something in the dream about the two extra flight bags.

S during this period is relatively inactive and does not object to *A*'s technique, simply taking this as a manifestation of the necessary working through.

Episode 5 (Supervisory Sessions 83-85, about Six Weeks of Analysis, Hours 568-584)

P enjoyed her vacation. "I was able to live in the present." She had the feeling she had cut the cord between herself and *A*, but this feeling was followed by guilt. A few hours later she returns to this topic. "I don't know whether I should leave in three months or six or twelve, but sometime near." She says her task is to get rid of *A* and that *A* should get rid of her because her time is running out. She wants to leave with a feeling it is right. *A* asks her when she thinks that is, and she becomes frightened. She tells a dream about being unprepared for a huge bill but discovers she has the money to cover it. *P* connects ending the analysis with feeling that since her father's soul was immortal they would never have to separate. She wants to discuss this. *A* says this is different, that even with unfinished business an analysis can end and she is free to return if she has problems. *P* says, "I want to refrain from saying a final goodbye just like I refused to kiss my father when he was in his coffin." She associates she might be ready the end of March (six weeks away). *A* responded by saying that the analysis will continue as long as indicated, that the end of March is not a rigid deadline. She felt full of hope and courage. The next hour she has a dream about buying herbs in a store—parsley and thyme. *P* was aware that she wanted to "buy time." In the dream, the box containing the thyme was dusty and the herb was moldy. There was a big worm. She was horrified at first. Then she was at home and no longer a customer. The worm was a part of her which she accepted.

A reports some anxiety of his own at this point, which he associates with the termination of his own analysis and his wish to return after it was over. *S* reassures him that it was all right to tell *P* she could return and to reassure her that separation is neither death nor an amputation. *A* feels the end of March is unrealistic, to which *S* agrees and suggests working until the summer vacation.

In Session 84, *A* tells *P* he feels that judging by her dream about buying time, the end of March was felt by her as too soon. But the material slips off this topic to her fear of being alone and having pregnancy fantasies as compensation. No date is set. The next analytic hour *P* is depressed and frightened about leaving. She wants to sleep for the duration.

In Session 85 *A* reports that *P* is finally working through the separation without acting out. She has started to grieve and reports a dream of being at a cocktail party. When she went to get her coat to leave, it wasn't there. "I knew it would be gone. I had known it all along. Not that I came without it, but when I checked it I knew I would never get it back. I had a hopeless feeling and woke angry." She associated to the first dream in the analysis where she was trying to protect her coat. Now she gives it up but prefers to pretend it is stolen. Then *P* says, "I could afford to be casual because in reality I have decided to buy a new coat to console myself." She thinks the coat refers to her facade and the defenses she came to analysis with. "It is all the strategems I used to keep from seeing myself."

In the next hour, a return of resistance against being forced or prodded to set a date alternates with feelings of elation at the prospect. *P* recalls her panic at being asked to set a date some months ago. "It's a good thing you really did not ask me to commit myself." *A* asks her, "You mean you don't really intend to stop the end of March?" *P* says, "I did when I told you but I didn't know then there was a battle yet to come." She talks of wanting to avoid responsibilities but fighting against it. At the end of this hour *A* asks when she thinks she would be ready to set a date. *P* replies, "I don't want to say exactly, but before the end of June." She is scared she can't separate from *A* without "having extreme emotions," and asks, "Why am I so reluctant to leave mother? I thought I would not cry again, but I'm afraid I'm going to."

Comments: During this date-setting period of the end phase, two things stand out relevant to *A*'s behavior. In the first place, he obviously wanted this patient to terminate; in the second place, he proceeded cautiously and slowly, waiting for *P* to take as much initiative as she could in deciding on a date. The painful stress which *P* experienced in trying to bring herself to the point of giving up the analytic situation was reflected in the stress which *A* revealed from time to time as he reexperienced some of his own separation anxiety. Simultaneously, he faced the need to master his irritation over her slow pace. He understood her need to go slowly and he persistently interpreted *P*'s resistance to accepting the need for change and to recognizing the changes she had made.

The case of KF (Example 19) and the case of GB (Example 20) illustrate phenomena associated with the beginning of the end phase where the analytic task is to recognize the signs of economic and structural change and to assess the patient's readiness to undertake the work of terminating. In both of these cases, the patients tended to cling to the analytic relationship with masochistic defenses. The defenses of KF's patient were reinforced by the frequency with which KF's technique tended to perpetuate them. In the case of GB, the patient's immaturity and her successful use of the mechanism of denial in fantasy was reinforced by the subtle seduction to continued regression inherent in the analytic situation. Inexperienced as GB was, it is to his credit that he understood the dynamics of the return of old symptoms (e.g., asthma) as defenses against progression. By so interpreting his patient's retrogression, he did not permit her to settle into an endless round of repetitions as seemed to be likely with KF's patient.

After making the transition from the middle phase to the end phase, the length of the date-setting period varies, dependent on many factors. GB's case in Example 21 illustrates some of the vicissitudes for both the patient and the analyst. Most of the difficulties have to do with resistances against working through to acceptance of the necessity to give up the analytic relationship. Once this reality has been recognized a date can be set. (Freud's suggestion that the analyst fix a time limit in certain cases will be discussed later in this chapter.)

A date which has been decided on, especially when it has been done by mutual agreement and not arbitrarily determined by the analyst, confronts the patient with a reality which could be ignored until then. The reality of an impending date produces a different impact on the patient's leisurely and sometimes chronically effective defense of putting off into some vague point in the future the time when separation and progression to maturation must be accomplished. A date has the effect of activating a mourning reaction and the regressive repetitions of old defenses observed during this period possess an overtone of renunciation. This is to be contrasted with an overtone of stubborn hanging on which is often clearly felt by the analyst during the date-setting period. One might think of the last step in the process of terminating as mourning for all past object losses and in anticipation of a new one, the analyst. Such an anticipatory experience which includes sharing one's feelings about it with the object about to be given up is relatively rare in the lives of most persons outside the analytic relationship. Working through this kind of "termination work" offers an opportunity for insights not achievable in any other way.

Student-analysts often have difficulty in managing this phase. This is especially true for a beginner who has not terminated his own analysis and therefore has no experiential knowledge of working through to this point and of living through the immediate post-analytic period. Even if he has terminated his own analysis, he will not have experienced it from the position of analyst, and therefore will not have been confronted with the various counterreactions which the end phase with a patient can reactivate. When the student has terminated a patient's analysis with a good re-solution of the transference neurosis, he will have had the opportunity to learn how to differentiate progression from regression and psychological growth from resistance. This learning experience is a maturing one for him as well as the patient. For these reasons we look upon the terminating phase as crucial for a student-analyst.

These learning objectives are often difficult to accomplish. Consequently, in this area especially a supervisor's experience in analyzing equips him to give valuable assistance to a student-analyst. It is not unusual to find manifestations of serious countertransferences in the terminating phase, even if they have been absent for the most part in the initial and middle phases. The end of an analysis stimulates separation reactions in the analyst as well as the patient. Some of them are motivated by a therapeutic ambition to produce a perfect case, and consequently the analyst refuses to let the patient go. Some of them stem from "student problems," expressed in the desire to produce a completed case sooner than other students, etc. Some counterreactions have their roots in more idiosyncratic problems, depending on the life history of the analyst, the meaning of a particular patient to him, and many other factors.

Emotional involvement with the supervisor is one factor which has to be considered from several angles. Termination of the analysis means termination of the supervisory relationship too, and even if the currents of feeling are normally positive and not burdened with undue transference distortions, the supervisory experience tends to stir up affects that give its ending a coloring of loss as well as pleasure. In our experience, this situation has been more frequent when the analysis has been successful and the learning profitable. Occasionally, such an attachment to the supervisor has temporarily stood in the way of skillful analytic technique. Such instances, however, can usually be prevented by a timely interpretation from the supervisor with acknowledgement of mutual satisfaction from the supervisory collaboration.

The opposite can be seen also when a supervisor develops a countertransference to his student. Instances of this sort are especially difficult for the participants to become aware of by themselves. They are more easily identified by a third party. Occasionally, reports from supervisors reveal excessively high expectations of a student, or what looks like an unnecessarily prolonged analysis. This difficult topic will be approached from another point of view in the next chapter. Relevant to termination problems, however, is a difficulty common to analysts, supervisors, and parents who find it anxiety-producing to recognize growth in their patients or children, and as a consequence sometimes interfere with the individuation-maturation process. In the terminating phase of the supervisory process it is just as essential for the supervisor to be aware of the growing independence of his student as it is for him to teach his student to be aware of progress in the patient. Teaching tasks naturally vary with the progress of the student as well as with the different phases of an analysis, and supervisors need to be alert to the necessary adjustments in themselves.

To illustrate the final step in the process of terminating an analysis, we turn again to GB and follow the vicissitudes of the experience for the patient and the analyst. The supervisor's activity in this instance was minimal, except when an unexpected countertransference began to block *A*'s understanding and disturb his technique.

EXAMPLE 22

GB (Case II), Supervisory Sessions, 86-92, Analytic Hours 590-630

In the first episode presented here, we see the characteristic reactions to setting a date for termination. The patient responds with mixed feelings of euphoria, sadness, anxiety, anticipated loneliness, appreciation and resentment toward the analyst. All of these feelings oscillate in intensity coupled with moments of regression and outcroppings of clear-cut transference repetitions which even the patient can interpret as carry-overs from the past. In this episode, evidence for structural change in the patient becomes more apparent.

Episode 1

A—Well, nothing is terribly new; it's been pretty much of the same with, oh, kind of back and forth in her ability to mourn and then she denies the whole import of the separation for her, but she's really quite preoccupied with it all the time.

S—When she doesn't deny it, how does she feel then?

A—Some of the time she's angry and tends to displace her anger onto outside situations, but sometimes she's aware that she's angry, although more in a cerebral kind of a way than actually feeling angry, judging from her behavior or her tone of voice. Some of the time she feels sad, actually tearful on occasion. She quotes, "Parting is such sweet sorrow," and knows she will feel melancholy after she leaves. She seems to prefer to be angry rather than to experience the positive aspects of her feelings and she pretends that I'm turning her away.

She talked about—with more speculation than memory—how she must have felt being separated from her mother. She was questioning which separation from mother is being repeated now; she wonders how she was weaned, she feels that her mother rejected her, and somehow she can't differentiate between "being sent away" by me now and something that her mother did to her then. And then she says, "What am I going to do when I don't have you to come to see anymore?" She is a little agitated about this and she says, "Apparently I need you very much; I have nothing to put in place of this."

She said that during the night she had a happy dream in contrast to the sadness now. When she feels no one is close to her, it's so difficult to give up the analysis as if she were asked to sacrifice what she prizes most right now. She would be ready to offer almost anything else if she could keep this, and she's angry because she feels so helpless and that's why she resents me. She says it's always a risk to depend on people. She doesn't really feel able to go now and somehow she can't even discuss the issue directly: "I'm very frightened about not coming anymore." So I pointed out to her that she seems to be struggling against admitting that she's mourning over the separation, over her loss, and then she asks, "For whom am I mourning?"

The next hour she tells a dream in which a friend's mother died—a wonderful, beautiful woman. In her associations she mentioned several friends whose mothers died. Then she associates, "The husband of the mother in the dream is an alcoholic, a weak character; that she is married to him indicates that something is wrong with her too. I am killing off parents in the dream. I wonder why I chose this particular woman."

Suddenly she changed the subject and talked about her job. It does not give her any satisfaction. It came out what she would really like to do is the kind of work I do, but that it's not within her reach. I commented that apparently she thought that if she lost me she would like to be like me. And she said, "Perhaps I would like to help people scientifically. How can I emulate this? My job is so shallow. It almost made me cry when you said I want to do what you do. It seems so unfair; it's beyond my reach."

So I asked her why she felt that she must be exactly the same as I am —for instance, wouldn't it be enough for her to be able to do a good job with her own children? She started to cry, "Yes, that would be enough," and then she said this woman that she killed off in the dream is an extremely successful business woman. And she says with real venom, "I hate career women; they're awful." So this gave me the idea that what she is so angry with her mother about is the mother's going to work after the father's death.

Well, the next day she felt very good. It's as if this interpretation about her need to identify globally had really made sense to her. And then she said that as she entered my room today, she looked around and had the feeling that this was either the first time or the last time that she was seeing the room, as if she had never seen it before and would never see it again, and she says she became somehow conscious of my identity as a real person. She looked at my desk and there was an envelope addressed to me and she was aware (laughs) that I'm somebody in my own right. She has the feeling that everything is transient and today she doesn't hate her work; it doesn't feel so empty. Then she started to talk about carbon paper and how the carbon was missing from something and so she didn't get a duplication as she had expected to. So I commented that until now she had to be either someone's carbon copy or not at all like them, 100 per cent or zero. She says, "I don't want to be anybody's carbon copy."

Then she said that her roommate will be away this week, so she'll be all alone and it's sort of like a test of how she can manage alone, and then she says, "But having children wouldn't really help this because I don't want a substitute now. I should really take what exists in reality. Maybe I can take some of your professional skills, but if I thought you were a mother, I would not become a good mother by imitating you." So I commented that she was identifying me with the working mother who is not a good mother and so that this woman in the dream must have referred to me.

And she says, "What was horrible about the dream was not that she died, but that I wanted it. I wonder whether I want you to die or I wanted my mother to die; no, I wonder whether I want you to die *as* my mother."

Comments: This last statement expresses in very condensed form evidence of the integrative process in operation. It demonstrates *P*'s ability to differentiate between a dream and reality, between the wish and the event wished for, while at the same time she accepts the superego condemnation of her wish without the former sense of conflict, need to punish herself, or fight with an externalized conscience. Structurally we can infer that her ego has achieved a degree of independence and mastery over primitive impulses and archaic superego forces. She has introjected the analytic experience, identified with A's objectivity, and begun to observe herself in an autonomous way. Independently, she differentiates A from the transference imago and then proceeds to make a transference interpretation which implicitly refers to separation from childhood as well as from the analyst.

Describing her impressions on entering A's office, P told of new perceptions and new awareness of A as an individuated person existing "in his own right." This experience of his existence, independent of her need for him, illustrates a step taken along the developmental line of separation-individuation so well-formulated by Mahler and her co-workers.[72] It is evidence of maturation of her sense of self, associated with better discrimination in her reality perceiving function. This organization of structure, taking place unconsciously, seems to be not yet finished, however; since it is accompanied by a sad tone, "everything is transient." Nevertheless, she could experience A as an object outside of herself, understand his objectivity without feeling rejected, and demonstrate some ability to empathize with A's detached behavior in his work with her.

A was only partially aware of the significance of these analytic events, since he introduced Session 86 with the remark, "Nothing is terribly new." He was more impressed by what he saw in terms of mourning work and did not connect P's communications with the inferences that could be made regarding structural change. This level of learning would probably be too much to expect of a beginner. A did, however, respond to P with intuitive sensitivity for the evidence of her progress and maintained good system equilibrium.

S was impressed with A's empathy and, realizing that he was experiencing this phase of analyzing for the first time, she decided not to burden him with a theoretical discussion of the concept of "structural change." Recognizing this learning as an objective of the end phase of the supervisory process, she nevertheless in this situation felt that such an intellectual focus would distract A from his empathic contact with the analytic process. Consequently, she did not interrupt his reporting and focused on reinforcing his understanding of the dynamics involved. In other teaching situations, discussions of behavioral evidence of structural change can be entered into with profit.

Episode 2

In the next supervisory session, 87, both A and P retrogress. P demonstrated a typical response to this stage of termination in which leaving A

had become more real and was now only two months off. She returned to old defenses of anger and provocative spitefulness which had helped her to avoid commitments in the past or to detach herself from anxiety-provoking relationships. *A*, on his side of the situation, reacted to *P*'s retreat with a sense of frustration. He felt the terminating process was going badly and responded with impatience and interpretations which were out of tune with *P*. She resented them and became even more defensive. *A*'s countertransference came into clear focus in this supervisory session.

A—Well, we've had some very intense hours; there's been a lot of strong resistance, a lot of anger, a lot of mourning about the approaching termination. She says, "Probably I was kidding about the end of June," and she wonders whether I am aware of how much anger she feels because she knows it doesn't show outside. And she added that she felt frightened to be all alone now; when she is by herself she gets scared. She's often appeared childish but never before has she appeared to me so much like a really little child, like maybe a two-year-old. At this point I said that it is clear that she is not only afraid to be alone, but she is afraid to commit herself to anyone—as we discussed it here last time. She responded, "That's true," that even in the analysis with me she hasn't completely committed herself; she still sometimes has the feeling that her thoughts are not my business, so she withholds them. I reminded her that she feels angry when she cares for someone and becomes dependent, that she is so afraid of disappointments that she never permits a relationship to become permanent. She replied, "Yes, that is how it was—first with my mother, then with my father, my sister, and later with other people too." She talked as if she were interpreting the dynamics by which this disappointment caused her to feel disengaged from people.

The following hour, she appeared tense and somehow disturbed. She talked at first about deliberate attempts at identifying with me, then about her obsessional thoughts at the beginning of the analysis. She called them "wild thoughts" of hurting people; then she stops herself and talks about trivialities in a disconnected way, very resistive, but admits that she is very upset. Yet, as if to cover up these feelings, she talks about a cartoon in which two children are talking a sort of nonsense talk, a verbal play; she didn't know that children could do this and at the same time the flavor of it is that she is doing it with me—sort of precommunicative use of language, just expressive of emotion. She really used a regressive way to cover up; I did not know yet what.

Her resistance was expressed next day by her coming a half hour late. She said that she had been having terrible insomnia as if she were wrestling all night; she felt beaten and tortured when she got up in the morning. At this point she didn't tell me, but it came out in the next session that she had a very upsetting dream during the night. The next day she told me the dream from the previous night. She remembers that she wasn't really completely asleep. It was during that insomnia, a sort of a half-awake, half-asleep dream.

"I was somewhere; I was a prisoner, maybe a political prisoner. Someone was with me; there were two of us. We were taken into the forest; we'd been dropped there, miles away from everyone. Our captors were very cruel, but they didn't put any chains on us. They took off our shoes and stockings and cut our soles and ankles with razor blades." She had various associations to her cruelty. She says, "I was brave; I said I will crawl away on my knees, and as soon as I thought of it, they skinned my hands and knees." Whichever method of escape she thought of, they immediately mutilated that part of her body. And she talks of how sickening it was, how cruel, how ingenious—Oriental tortures; nobody has ever thought of this before, how she was apparently let free but it was impossible to get away. Her first thought when they cut her feet was, "Ha, is that all they are going to do? That's nothing; I'll get away," but they could always keep up with whatever system she thought of for getting away. And she awakened when she felt that she would not be able to drag herself away.

S—Who were "those others" so cruel to her? She feels masochistic in her suffering.

A—Well, yes. She interprets the dream as a masochistic dream; I interpreted it as a sadistic dream. We had quite a battle about this; she made this a big issue, but not immediately. At first she wondered who it was that was with her, who the second figure was. She says, "This person lent comfort and courage; I wasn't alone, but I was alone in my thoughts. This other person was going through the same thing I was; it was a test, we were on a common mission."

I commented, "In other words, this was your own idea." She added, "But only a sadist would do such a thing." I said, "Well, apparently you are willing to be sadistic in order to be sure that there won't be a separation. I mean that these two people who are cut up can never get away from each other."

S—And to what does that relate?

A—I think she feels that I am sending her away; not giving her some extra time means we have to separate.

S—Yes, she considers this cruel, and she says, "I will show you that however cruel you are, I can crawl away on my hands and knees." As always, she compensates for her anxiety: "I am not dependent on you, I can crawl away." Then she feels that she cannot crawl away, she is caught. Therefore she feels that you are cruel, but she also feels that you are on a common mission. You seem to feel that she really could hurt you.

A—Well, she could by being very resistive and helpless or with mocking baby talk. I think she is to some extent aware of what she is doing.

S—The problem is, how much you are aware of your vulnerability and how are you making her aware of it?

A—I don't know yet, because it took the whole next week to get it. I was very provoked and could not hide it. She continued this childish nonsense talk in a hostile way; she was making nonsense out of everything. So I was very irritated and told her the dream disturbed her because it implied she was sadistic. She said she knew that but she tortured herself too. I pointed out she could not take responsibility for her cruelty and blamed the others.

S—Now, here, one really does not know who is the patient and who is the analyst. (Laughing) I believe she really wanted to hurt you, but your response is so out of tune. Her statement in the dream, "We were on the same mission," had some positive implication. You have to ask yourself why this response of feeling hurt.

A—Well, at this point I still was too angry to get onto that. She continued to rebel and argue. She told me, "You shouldn't get so vehement and sarcastic. You should be above that." (Laughs) I said, "Why do you insist I be perfect?" She agreed that she can be very aggravating. She said her provoking me was her way of trying to cease being a patient. We are still struggling, both of us. (Laughing) I don't feel good about losing my temper.

Comments: These transference-countertransference exchanges could be given a great deal of comment. A and P are clearly not in tune with each other. A is responding to the manifest cruelty in the dream and feels threatened by defensive sadism. He neglects the meaning of the common mission which could be interpreted as P's hope that the coming separation will hurt A as much as it hurts her. A feels it as a sadistic frustration of his wish to terminate.

S directed her teaching toward mobilizing A's insight into his vulnerability to feeling professionally frustrated. A was clearly surprised and ashamed to become so inapprorately involved at this late stage in the analysis. The obvious provocation and the necessity to face the intensity of his affective response as he presented it to S enabled A to objectify his attitude and gain some insight into it. The details of his insight were not discussed in the supervisory situation. S saw her task as directing A's attention to facing his vulnerability and stimulating his self-analytic faculty to understand his angry reaction, and in addition S helped him to see how he could use such an incident to advance the analytic process with this patient.

Episode 3

After the reconciliation reported at the end of supervisory Session 87, P continued to make progress, albeit with some ups and downs. Her mother came to visit and they got along well together. P suddenly realized that she has at last really separated from her mother. She recalls vague memories of her mother's early indulgences and self-sacrifices during the days following her father's death. During the last six weeks of the analysis, this material was worked over repeatedly.

In the last analytic session she felt joyous, like celebrating. She said, "Although I know I will miss you intensely, I cover everything with a shield of joy. I don't admit that I don't feel as joyous as I want to feel. I guess it is normal to have a sense of accomplishment and enjoy it, but whom will I have to tell this to in the future? Even if I have someone to talk to,

I'll always think of you when I talk like this." I said, "Well, there is no need for you to forget me; I am a real person, not merely a ghost of your child-hood." She said, "I know. Maybe that is why I want to cry. I guess women cry in such situations." I said, "Well, everybody feels sad when they separate; I feel sad too."

After this interchange she spoke again of wild ideas, magic and helpless-ness. I interrupted this by saying, "Perhaps we shouldn't continue the illusion that you are the child and I am an adult. Why don't you sit up for the last few minutes?" She did, but she was embarrassed, and could not look at me. She said, "I am conscious of leaving and covering it up with hilarity. I am still afraid, but it's not so bad; I know what I'm afraid of." In leaving she said, "Why don't you say something?" I answered, "I wish you well and I have enjoyed working with you." She was crying as she walked out.

S said nothing during A's presentation. After he finished, she asked A, "What do you think?" He replied, "I have only one analysis to compare with—my own that ended similarly."

Comments: It is not possible to evaluate whether or how much A in this situation was reexperiencing the termination of his own analysis which had occurred before the analytic treatment of this case began. S enjoyed A's sensitive handling of the actual "parting." It seems he recovered his analytic posture and was able to express his own sadness in the "common mission." This knowledge P could take with her as a support for her "new beginning"[16] and for the internalization of a positive image of A, which Loewald[71] discusses as a significant factor in the continuing process of postanalytic structural modifications. Pfeffer, in a follow-up study of analyses,[79] supports this concept with data confirming that after analysis, "the patient retains an important and complicated intrapsychic representa-tion of the analyst." This observation has been made repeatedly following unsuccessful and interrupted analyses. In Pfeffer's cases, the analyses had been considered successful and well terminated. This interesting point, which is relevant to the theories of development and transference as well as to theoretical explanations of "cure," cannot be discussed further here.

During the last two weeks, new material came to the surface about her mother's sacrifices during P's early childhood. A realized there was not time to work this through sufficiently. Consequently, he did not interpret its meaning, hoping that P had achieved the ability to explore some of these areas by herself.

One might be tempted in this situation to extend the analysis, since it is obvious that problems remain for which analytic work might be helpful. However, keeping in mind this patient's tendency to remain at an imma-ture level of development and remembering the significance of separation and object-loss in her childhood experiences, the accomplishment of separation-termination as a goal-directed choice seems to be the most important therapeutic task at this time.

This problem brings up the technique for setting a date for termination, which Freud discussed in his paper, "Analysis Terminable and Interminable."[47] Freud described how he set the date himself in certain cases, thus limiting the time remaining for analytic work. This was done with patients who showed unusually strong resistance to progress and who seemed to be making the analytic relationship into a way of life in the same way that GB felt his patient was doing ten months prior to termination. The technical device of arbitrarily setting a time limit needs to be differentiated from the practice of arbitrarily keeping to the date once it has been decided upon. Experience tends to substantiate Freud's thought that a date once set should not be changed. There are cases, however, where analyst and patient can benefit from flexible handling of this matter. Moreover, since Freud's paper was published, many patients have returned to their analysts for additional analytic work—a fact which confirms Freud's concept that the analytic situation ends but that the analytic process is interminable.

The specific developmental value of accomplishing the individuation task inherent in the experience of terminating a period of analysis is a most significant topic and is given emphasis in the material of GB's patient. What she terminated was an anachronistic pattern of relating and adapting, and what we hope she gained is a new level of development more appropriate to the current reality of herself and her environment. Confirmation of this latter point is lacking since contact with the analyst has not been renewed. This fact creates a problem when an evaluation of the results of psychoanalytic treatment is attempted. It also presents an obstacle to the learning which the feedback of a post-termination contact can provide the student on the success or failure of his analytic work. This is unfortunate but is a frequent handicap for clinical learning and investigation. Pfeffer's follow-up studies[77-79] offer an ingenious solution in their use of a given number of interviews undertaken with a different analyst. This procedure, however, might be difficult to carry out in the case of patients analyzed by students. Yet, the idea offers a fertile field for investigation of many interesting questions and for an extension of a student's learning experiences in the area of evaluating the results of his work.

– VIII –

Evaluation of Progress

EVALUATION IS AN INTRINSIC PART OF TEACHING. "IT IS AT ONCE A continuous process designed to facilitate learning and an intermittent activity to determine whether an acceptable amount of learning has occurred." Thus George E. Miller, Director of Research in Medical Education at the University of Illinois College of Medicine, defines it as he differentiates evaluation which assists the student in learning from evaluation "for the certification of adequacy."[74] The continuous task is the ongoing appraisal of the student's current learning needs and simultaneously what he has already accomplished. To be of the greatest value this appraisal should be shared with the student so that he too can be fully aware of what he has learned and what is yet to be accomplished. Intermittent assessment of learning represents a summary of progress over a period of time in relation to given objectives. It also constitutes an important guide for the student and for the administrative body responsible for his advancement to the "terminal assessment" of certification.

Both continuous and intermittent evaluations are an intrinsic part of psychoanalytic supervision. However, in the days when supervision was essentially a privately arranged consultation between a beginner and an experienced analyst, evaluation was probably not as much in the foreground of attention as it is today. The student sought to learn technique and the supervisor to explain dynamics and suggest what to do to promote the analysis. The teaching aim was primarily instructional and, for the most part, knowledge of what happened in the supervisory situation was confined to the relationship between the student and his supervisor.

Today with the growth of institutes and formulated graduation requirements, a supervisor's evaluating function has expanded and has become more significant in relation to decisions about promotion, graduation, or withdrawal from training. This change in administrative responsibility reflects a change in educational philosophy which occurred around 1950. The principle was stated by the American Psychoanalytic Association that a group of educators, rather than an individual, should have the responsibility for organizing and managing an educational program. This principle of group responsibility created a different atmosphere between teacher and student. Moreover, it has served to insure the maintenance of high standards by opening the way for psychoanalytic educators to share their experiences and to discuss problems encountered in teaching psychoanalysis. Group discussion has resulted in efforts to define educational goals and examine teaching practices, both steps being essential for the development of good teaching. Group responsibility has emphasized the necessity for every supervisor to formulate what the student is expected to learn, for only then can individual progress be measured and the effectiveness of an educational program be evaluated.

In this book we have consistently emphasized that teaching and learning have reciprocal effects. Each member of the two-way system in supervision teaches and learns, just as in the therapeutic process both patient and analyst gain insight into each other as well as themselves. A large share of this achievement in the analytic situation results from a process of constant, although primarily implicit, evaluation and re-evaluation. In the supervisory situation a similar process goes on in both student and teacher. The vigilance with which a student analyst is expected to listen to his patient and himself for evidence of the effect of numerous interactions is applicable to the supervisor as well and becomes an essential component of the teaching-learning experience. This vigilance plays a significant role in maintaining a good learning alliance and it aids the supervisor in assessing his teaching skills as well as the learning progress of his student. The student, too, should participate in the evaluation of himself. It seems logical to assume that for a student to recognize his deficiencies and their causes puts him in a more advantageous position than when he remains ignorant of defects. In the process of analysis, the same assumption underlies striving to make the unconscious conscious. Evaluations should have similar purpose for a student, not as rewards or punishments, but as objective measures of the degree of success in accomplishing what one has set out to do.

Responsibility for making evaluations belongs to the supervisor as a clinical teacher and as such he uses it to promote learning. As the student develops, the supervisor makes evaluative judgments about his readiness to become independent of supervisory assistance. These judgments form the basis for changes in the frequency of supervision and for recommendations made to the administrative body responsible for such promotional decisions as new cases, graduation and certification.

Like the analytic process, supervision moves ahead in an intricate spiral of transactional events. In previous chapters, we have illustrated these events in cross section at various points along the spiral. In this chapter, we intend to present a more longitudinal view of the student's progress in learning and how the supervisor operates as an evaluator. We reviewed the transcripts for evidence that the objectives we had formulated (Chart II) were attained by our two project students. The elementary cases were studied first to find out whether initial learning difficulties were mastered as the analyses proceeded and how much improvement could be shown in basic skills. Then we looked at the advanced cases to assess evidence for increasing competence. In other words, we asked the questions: What learning was accomplished during the supervised analysis of an elementary case? What skills showed a fairly reliable degree of mastery? What problems indicated a need for further work? In addition, we asked to what extent these problems were alleviated and how learning developed through additional experience and teaching as evidenced by the performance of these students on their advanced cases. What refinements of aptitudes, skills, and cognitive learning were accomplished as the student moved toward graduation? We asked ourselves what contribution the supervisors made to the students' learning.

As we examined our material from this point of view, we discovered that "signs of learning" were difficult to spell out. What appeared to be evidence of progress in one context was neither definite nor stable, but performance vacillated during the course of analytic and supervisory experience. Progress in learning was not easily identified except as a reflection of progress in the analysis of the patient. Undoubtedly, these two lines are correlated in most cases, but what appeared to be learned in one hour sometimes disappeared later under different analytic or supervisory pressures, and a learning difficulty present with an elementary case showed up again with an advanced case.

From observations made elsewhere we know that the expectations and teaching tactics of a different supervisor may create a different set of tensions in the learning alliance and may result in an evaluation of the student which is remarkably out of line with the evaluations by others. A student may seem to be making progress in learning as measured by progress in the patient, or in terms of his supervisor's expectations, but close examination reveals that he has adapted to his supervisor's prescriptive techniques. He has done what he was told to do and the analysis moves along, but only because the student was able to follow directions and not because he understood them or could use them independently.*

We were faced with the problem of deducing change and measuring it in relation to learning objectives. This problem has confronted educators and researchers into learning and therapeutic processes in all fields. A

---

* Louis B. Shapiro made this observation from a comparison of supervisory reports on students he supervised with those of other supervisors for the same student. He found the same learning problems described independently by other supervisors on cases both before and after his. His findings were presented to the Chicago Training Analysts' Seminar, June 8, 1960 (unpublished).

related problem, equally complex, involves trying to evaluate the relative significance of the multiple variables which enter into the final outcome. In the field of psychoanalysis, these two problems are especially complex because the variables to be measured belong not only to objectively observable performance, but also to capacities and qualities of inner experience that so far have eluded definitions adequate for precise measurement. This obstacle prevents the assignment of quantitative measures to the observed results and leaves us at this stage of our knowledge about learning in supervision to descriptive statements which can be quantified only on the rough scale of good, average, or poor. The evaluation of progress in learning, like evaluation of therapeutic change, remains for practical purposes confined to a scale of improved or not improved. More precise measurement must wait for further study by psychoanalytic educators.

Consequently, in the study of our transcripts we have relied on efforts toward precision of descriptive statement of our observations of change and its assessment. To illustrate the evaluative aspect of a supervisor's work as it was observed in this phase of our study, we turn again to student G whose first recorded sessions can be found in Examples 2 and 5 and whose end phase performance has been described in Examples 20, 21, and 22. An evaluative summary of this student, in the initial phase of his learning, will be presented. A diagnostic description of his learning problems will be compared with his work in his second year of experience as an analyst. Further comparison will be made with material from the third year and from the termination phase. Then G's performance on his first case, GB, will be compared with his performance on his fourth case, GF. We will also give some material from the reports made by other supervisors of G. A similar summary will be presented for student H.

EXAMPLE 23

GB (Case I), Evaluation of Initial Level of Learning

G's first case, GB, demonstrated the common signs of inexperience which a beginner manifests. His analytic attitude—an attitude of watchful expectancy, waiting for the meanings of P's messages to become clear and the transference relationship to unfold—was not developed. His skill in associating to P's material needed exercising; his diagnostic perceptiveness was not readily available for translation into explicit interpretations. This student-analyst knew intellectually the value of listening with freely hovering attention, but he had not learned to practice it. He could describe the concept of transference and he knew that premature interpretations or affectful responses by the analyst would distort development of the transference. Yet he failed to recognize transference meanings of P's behavior in the early hours. The cause of his mistakes was not lack of knowledge but inexperience in applying it. This psychologically well-endowed student, however, had difficulty in functioning to his full capacity even on the level expected in a first case. As the transcripts of the early phase of supervision reveal (Examples 2 and 5), a personality problem interfered. His sensitivity to criticism stirred up defenses against P's expression of feelings; his impulsive anger required energy for its control and blocked effective empathy. G recognized his mistakes, but did not like to admit them, and he had not yet learned how to examine them to understand their cause. If we allow for inexperience, his learning problem at this stage of his development seemed to be in the field of self-knowledge and self-control rather than in more cognitive areas. With this problem of self-knowledge and self-control, supervisory teaching can be most helpful, since a student-analyst is often not aware of his behavior along this line. Becoming aware is the first step, and a supervisor's objective observations can assist the student's self-observation to operate more effectively against his internal resistance.

With G's first case, however, there were additional problems for the supervisor. He was overly sensitive in respect to what he considered to be criticism from her. His justifiably high opinion of his ability and artistic intuition contributed to a problem about learning which created frequent tensions in the $S \leftrightarrows A$ relationship and compelled him to create distance from his supervisor as well as from his patient. This behavior presented a special teaching problem for the supervisor who had to maintain a balance in the learning alliance which would insure therapeutic progress for the patient and permit learning at the same time.

The following material from the forty-first supervisory session of GB demonstrates the progress which this student made in a little more than a year of analyzing his first case. The analysis of his patient progressed, due to the student's increasingly sensitive empathy and use of interpretations. His own progress in learning had its ups and downs, and it became clear that something seemingly well learned appeared to slip away under various stresses in the supervisory situation, the student's life experience, or the regressive transference in the patient. The skill demonstrated in this next example was shaken in the end phase of this analysis (see Example 22), again in Case IV (see Example 15), and in the summary of this student's complete supervisory experience as revealed in his supervisors' reports. A continuing line of improvement can be seen through it all, however.

EXAMPLE 24
GB (Case I), Supervisory Session 41, Analytic Hours 190-193

Exchange 1

A—She opened the hour with, "Suddenly yesterday I had the feeling that I was in mourning. I almost cried, 'My father is dead.'" She says this with the utmost surprise in her voice. I just cannot reproduce it here—the feeling that literally this is the first time she realized it. She wonders whether very soon everything will shift back to "normal," meaning a belief that he is not dead.

So I said I thought that could not happen anymore because it was harder to deny reality at 28 than it had been at 6 [when her father died]. And she said, "What do I do now that my father is dead? It sounds so stupid after 22 years." She wonders if she cried at her father's funeral and talks about her inability to cry since then. Now, for the first time in analysis, she feels like crying. So I said she couldn't cry because if she started, it would bring back to her the thing she most wanted to cry about, that the father was dead.

Then she remembers that when she graduated from high school, she cried interruptedly for a day and a half with the thought, "I will never see them again," meaning her classmates. Her mother did not come because of a quarrel, but even though everyone else was there, she felt alone. So I said, "Perhaps you felt the most important person was missing, your father." And she began to cry again. So I said, "This feeling at graduation applies to your father too. It's really not the same and not enough to love a doll" [referring to her pregnancies]. She cries again and says, "What comes after mourning? It is a withdrawal from reality to contemplate the future." I said, "It seems to me it is more to tear oneself away from the past."

S—Both of you are right. In mourning one tears oneself away from the past and contemplates the future without the incorporated person. What she did was a massive incorporation without mourning. The heart pain, asthma, and all her physical symptoms represent her incorporation of her father, but not an emotional intrapsychic working through of the real separation.

A—She wonders which part of the past she has to tear herself away from —the time when she had her father in reality or when she had him only in fantasy, or both.

S—So she never really gave up her father.

A—She thinks if she had been 16 instead of 6 when her father died, she would have reacted by missing a menstrual period. I asked her what she meant and she didn't really know. Then she said, "I wonder why I take it out on my uterus." So I said I thought she was taking something in like with the heart pain, that she was trying to make father part of herself.

Comments: The pattern of G's reporting of the therapeutic material is freer than in Session 13 (Example 2) and more adequate for assisting S to understand the trends in the analytic process. His tendency to withdraw from the intensity of P's transference expectations is remarkably different than his earlier sarcastic, depreciating defense against the patient's hostile attack, and he is able to empathize with her reliving the sense of loss of her father and to mobilize long-repressed affect by well-phrased interpretations. G's increased interpretive skill is a natural sequence of his improved understanding of P and his tolerance of her regressive fantasies.

Exchange 2

A—On Monday she reported a dream about having the weekend off and going to Italy with some extra leave. She awoke with the feeling that this would be her last weekend. To me she said, "In other words, I was going to commit suicide." I think she means that I should not leave her on the weekends.

S—She wants to hold on to the father, the fantasy.

A—She was terribly upset on the weekend—felt alone and worried about being pregnant. But when the idea came to her, "I am pregnant after all," she felt better.

S—She feels alive when she is pregnant.

A—She says, "When I feel alone and lost, it's a relief to be pregnant." She knows she is not pregnant but she said, "I felt empty; I had no father. I tried to find replacements for years, like with Peter. I had fantasies of aborting myself, but you are right—I do want to make myself sterile but I cannot kill myself. I had a terrible struggle."

S—It is also a danger not to get rid of the father. Now she knows that pregnancy is having father inside of her; the conflict is so conscious, she feels that she has to do something destructive to get the father away.

A—She says, "I never did have a father—not much, really—so why can't I keep him the way I always have? If I can't keep him I have to do something violent." Then she returns to the dream. She wonders why Italy and associates to the Pope. So I said, "Like having contact with your father in Heaven." She agreed. Then I asked her about the extra days in the dream and the suicide, and she said it was very curious that although she was going to go to Italy, she would still be keeping her appointment with me.

After some other remarks she said, "I know why I said I dislike you [referring to a previous hour]. You can't substitute for my father." So then I interpreted that in the dream I did substitute for her father, that going to Italy means coming to her analysis. She said, "That's true. On Saturday it seemed so far from the last hour on Thursday and so far to the next on Monday; I felt I was so far away from my father." So I said, "It seems you wished there would be no more weekends separated from me." She says, "From you or from my father?" So I said, "Do you see a difference in this now?" And then she said, "No, you're not him. You just listen to me talk about him."

In the next hour she ruminated about several things—writing a girlfriend to stay in her house and how having her first baby made her stop school. She realized I am a substitute for her father and how, "If I'm dependent on my father's memory, I can use you as a reincarnation of him and then separate from you. That way it will be easier."

S—She will menstruate now because she says, "I don't need to hold on to the pregnancy when I accept the transference." The transfer relieves the painfulness of the mourning and permits gratification in fantasy. So in that sense the transference is resistance against the painful working-through of the mourning.

Comments: The analysis of this "parent-loss case" was progressing due primarily to G's more sensitive empathy, especially as he used it in interpreting. Here we see the step-by-step work of G to develop P's awareness of her transference identification of him with her father, her recognition of the unreality involved, and some insight into how her imagined pregnancy fulfills in an almost concrete, tangible way her fantasy of clinging to him. We see how G moved at a gradual pace, facilitating P's expression of affect but keeping her to the analytic task. His interpretations demonstrate his good system-sensitivity in tune with P's level of resistance, empathizing with both her pain and her ego's wish for another solution to the conflict. This wish underlies the therapeutic alliance and permits the transference. Interpretation of the fantasy produced conscious conflict that, in turn, created anxiety, resistance and regression in subsequent hours.

Here we can see definite signs of the student's progress. Not only are his interpretations sensitive and at the same time direct, avoiding cliches or technical terminology, but his consistent focus on P's conflict indicates that he estimated correctly the patient's resistance and anxiety, that he judged timing and dosing correctly and thus was able to keep the analytic process in a productive equilibrium. (Chart II, 3', 4') This example by itself demonstrates his freer use of empathic responses to the patient, his growing self-confidence and consequently decreased vulnerability to negative reactions from the patient.

In Chapter VII material from the seventy-second supervisory session with data from Session 71 in Example 20 was used to demonstrate the signs that indicate the beginning of the end phase of analysis. Now, we will use material from the seventy-second supervisory session as we concentrate on the signs of learning.

EXAMPLE 25

GB (Case I), Supervisory Session 72, Analytic Hours about 465

This supervisory session took place five weeks after the previous session, since the analyst was absent for a three-week vacation. He had only two weeks of analytic material to report: one week before he left and one after he returned. A mainly summarized P's interpretation of the meaning of his vacation for her—that is, separation is equated with death.

Exchange 1

A—And then the idea struck her that I might die while I was away and she was quite frightened by it. It occurs to her that I had said that she had been angry with her father even before he died—it wasn't just that he left —and then the thought comes to her, "It's because he made noise." She means during the night. And then she realizes that somehow she must have become disillusioned with her father during his lifetime, that he wasn't the idealized person that she wanted him to be, and she must have realized this. She wonders whether it had to do with arguments between the parents, with the father being drunk, and she sort of recreates a fantasy of what it must have been like, of how as a little girl she would have refused to believe that this drunken, violent man is really her father, but then it was repeated and repeated until she had to admit it. And then she said, "My father was a good man, and if a good man is capable of being so violent and cruel, then what about the average man? He must be even worse."

And she talked with some insight about how she attempts to idealize people and it's not the real person that she makes a relationship with, but the idea in her mind. I pointed out to her that she has been acting this fantasy with her boyfriend now and that she is confusing violence with sex and that I thought probably it was love making and not fighting that she had overheard during her childhood. She immediately denied this and then came an association like a command, "You're not supposed to talk that way about your parents." Now, I pointed out to her that not only had she denied the father's sexuality but currently she is trying to deny mine by making me into a Christ-like figure in a dream.

That night she had a series of nightmares and she could not remember the content of her dreams. In the hour she was worried how it would be for her while I was away. She starts to ruminate about what it was she could have heard in the parents' room, because she was not allowed to go in there; even during the day she wasn't supposed to go in there.

She was very tangential during this hour and I wondered whether she was defending herself against expressing any curiosity about my vacation, and she became very frightened and she said she couldn't possibly ask about it—it's too frightening. It reminds her of her parents' bed. She says she refuses to be curious because if she were so nosy, I would rebuff her and it's a terribly frightening idea.

S—Why?

A—The very idea of being curious is a terrible threat to her. And then she talked again about not understanding death, and when somebody leaves, it's as if the person dies, or as if she died, and she sees that this is an entirely self-centered view, where the other person's interests are completely disregarded. And she knows that she feels this way only when the other person leaves. If she is the one who leaves, then it doesn't bother her. This was the last hour before I left.

S—She is clinging like a child.

A—Yes. And she wasn't talking to me at all; it's as if she had been talking to a third person in the room and sort of studiously disregarding me. I pointed this out to her and she said she felt lonely and sad, as if I were punishing her for having been so difficult a patient—that's why I'm leaving. And then she recalls that as a child she used to be punished by isolation, being sent to her room, and this is what it feels like. Then she repeats that she feels she has no *right* to be curious, that if she were a nosy brat, then I would punish her even more. It's a trap for me to invite her to express her curiosity. I would get angry, and I would devise some further punishment for her.

Three weeks later when I returned she was genuinely glad and in the first session she told—not chronologically but in a free associative manner —what had happened in the three weeks. She realized that she really missed me and that she depends on me; she thinks that she experienced all the feelings she must have had as a child after her father died. She felt as if she had incurred my anger and I were punishing her. Then she reported that the first two nights she became enuretic. Her childhood symptom recurred. It persisted for two years after father's death. After she realized that somehow this must be connected with father's death—my going away— it stopped. She summed up her feelings in the idea: "Please come back. I'll be a good girl. I do love you, please forgive me." She added, "It was like a magic incantation."

But then she came to the realization that she was really in love with her image of what I am like, not with me as a real person, and knowing this was reassuring to her.

Comments: It is clear that G's impending vacation activated P's separation anxiety. Comparing the material of these exchanges with that of Example 24 (Supervisory Session 41), one can recognize that in Session 72, P was not in an acute state of revived mourning but rather in the process of working through her transference neurosis. The interesting economics and dynamics of this movement in the analysis are not pertinent to our discussion here, since our objective is to focus on G's progress in learning.

His reporting in the seventy-second supervisory session demonstrated his increasing understanding of the analytic process and the importance of communicating his own associations to S. Here he presented not only what P had said but his diagnostic thinking about it. His interpretive technique led P through the steps of the transference manifestation to the memory of significant childhood experiences. She could begin to modify the introjected image of her father. G's work in this area gives evidence of progress in interpretive skill. Fifteen months before, in the forty-first supervisory session, it was G's empathy with the sudden outburst of P's grief that kept his interpretations in pace with P's emotions; in supervisory Sessions 71 and 72 his interpretive technique was directed by his understanding of the transference dynamics. His system sensitivity influenced him to hold his awareness in check until P appeared ready to accept and synthesize the multiple motivations of her emotional reactions. G was using his perceptive and associative functions intuitively and cognitively at the same time.

Exchange 2

A—(to *S*): Why is she unable to separate an actual man from her idealized introject?

S—Because she does not accept herself as a real person, but a conglomeration of introjected objects and introjected fantasies. The two extremes are expressed in her magic omnipotence and her sense of worthlessness. The interesting thing is that both extremes can destroy father. "He is dead; he left me because I am bad—enuretic." In either case she is guilty. What are you thinking about?

A—Well, I was thinking—how can this be analyzed? (*S* responded by orienting about general theory and technique of interpretation and added:)

S—But she was also teasing you: "I am not in love with you but with my image of you." At the same time she is in love with her image of herself. She sees that image clearly but she feels intensely that she herself cannot approach it so she complains about her lack of identity.

A—Yes, it's very interesting. She talks about herself exactly as if she were really the little girl who either feels totally helpless or omnipotent.

S—Some time she will have to be able to change and become more realistic toward the various aspects of her own self as well as toward other people.

A—Well, but can I help her to view it more realistically through interpretation?

S—Yes, by confrontation of her perception of current external objects with the images of introjected objects of the past.

A—It is interesting; this is exactly what she went on to talk about at this point.

S—Really? Patients always seem to talk about what the analyst is able to perceive. (Laughs)

A—Yes. What she said was that she is afraid of being close to me because she feels I am going to scold her, laugh at her. Then she said, sort of wonderingly, how is this possible? She must have experienced loving attachment as a child, yet now she feels she cannot give; she has nothing to offer. . . .

Comments: This exchange is different from the previous one in the same supervisory session. G, taking distance from the immediate need of the therapeutic situation, raised questions which reached beyond the problem of the *re*-solution of the oedipal transference neurosis. They involved *P*'s self-concept and identity problems. They brought into focus a level of psychoanalytic therapy which he had not yet experienced as a therapist. Although for several reasons it was contraindicated to continue the analysis for an unforseeable period to deal with this aspect of *P*'s pathology, posing the question was a valid index of G's maturation, of his growing independence in the supervisory situation. He was able to see possible limitations of psychoanalytic technique as applied so far and was groping for theoretical concepts to be applied in the therapeutic situation in order to help the patient achieve healthier integration of her self-concept.

To summarize a longitudinal view of how G changed in the course of his first case, it seems clear that he developed his capacity to listen and to hear the multiple levels of meaning in his patient's communications (Chart II, 1', 2'). His natural perceptiveness and intuition developed with experi-

ence and supervisory help in freeing his empathy for the therapeutic benefit of his patient. As the analysis proceeded, G's skill in estimating resistance and in understanding the regressive state of his patient was better
correlated with interpretive activity (Chart II, 3', 4'). He became more
sensitive to transference and countertransference phenomena and gave evidence of understanding the shifting movements of the analytic process.
He conducted this analysis to a successful termination (Chart II, 5', 6', 7').
In the beginning, G showed a problem about learning which reflected a
self-esteem conflict. Defensiveness stemming from this conflict produced
tensions in the learning alliance with his first supervisor which were worked
out without too much difficulty. This character problem remained, however, as we shall see from a study of G's progress with other cases and
other supervisors. His self-esteem needs also made it difficult for him to
recognize some of the patient's idealization of her father as transference.
His initial tendency was to accept the positive feelings exposed by the
patient as appropriately referable to himself. This is a common learning
problem for beginners. It was exaggerated in this instance but was gradually mastered by G as this case progressed.

It seems pertinent at this point to take up the aspect of a supervisor's
evaluative responsibility that involves making recommendations for promotion. At the Chicago Institute, each successive supervisor makes a recommendation to the Education Committee before a student is assigned a
new case with a new supervisor. This evaluation is part of his administrative work. Procedures such as this one vary among institutes, but since
we studied Chicago students and since such evaluative recommendations
contribute significant information to the picture of a student's career
through the supervisory phase of his training, we will follow the operation
of the Chicago procedure and turn to the supervisory reports on student
G before summarizing the evidence for progress as seen with his fourth
case, GF.

Chart IV diagrams G's progression from one case to another in relation
to the length of time spent on each case before beginning another with
a new supervisor. $S1$, the supervisor who supervised case GB, recommended that he be approved for his second case ten months after beginning his first. There was a delay in starting, probably due to difficulties
in finding a suitable case or to a short supply of available supervisors.
$S2$ made a recommendation for a new case after nine months on the second. After nine months with the third case, $S3$ decided that persisting
troubles in the learning alliance indicated a transfer of supervisors. $S3b$
took over for six months supervision of the case which interrupted because
of the patient's pregnancy. Since $S3b$ did not meet the same difficulties
in teaching G as $S3a$ had found, a fourth case was recommended at the

Chart IV.—Student G's Progression in Supervision

Year	1957				1958				1959				1960				1961				1962			
Quarter	J	A	J	O	J	A	J	O	J	A	J	O	J	A	J	O	J	A	J	O	J	A	J	O

Case I S1(B) weekly   Biweekly   Terminated

Case II   Appr.   S2 began—weekly   biweekly-Terminated

Case III   Weekly S3a   S3b*   interrupted *new supervisor

Case IV   S4(F)—bi-weekly   Monthly until Term.—June '63

Graduated

time of interruption. Case IV, GF, began eighteen months before graduation and supervision was continued until termination of the analysis in June, 1963. Three of G's cases had good terminations, two of them prior to graduation.

Before discussing general points to be considered in making promotional decisions, we will present some excerpts from the reports which G's four supervisors made to the Education Committee.

EXAMPLE 26

Supervisory Reports on Student G

Case I, GB, Female Patient, Female Supervisor

The supervision of GB began three years before we even planned our project to investigate the supervisory process. It was finished six months before we started to study the transcripts in August, 1960 (see Chart IV). Recording had begun in Session 13 with a different research goal in mind. The first two reports, therefore, are based on notes made after supervisory session.

Report 1

The first quarterly report read: "G is a perceptive and intelligent student. The patient is an unmarried white woman, a complicated 'fate neurosis.' G is able to keep distance from the patient and be warm and consistently interested. He is eager to learn, uses supervision to great advantage. My impression is that he will be able to analyze this case which generally would be considered too difficult for a first supervised case."

Report 2

Three months later: "My good impression of G's ability as a psycho-analyst has not been disappointed, although it must be stated that as the analysis progresses from its initial phase to a more complex situation in which the beginning of the transference is becoming noticeable, he is less sure in responding to the material. This leads to some schematic responses. Since the patient presents a very interesting research problem, it was agreed that the supervisory sessions should be recorded."

Comments: These first two reports made to the administrative body clearly minimize the problems revealed in transcripts of supervisory Sessions 13 and 14 (Examples 2 and 5). The evaluative opinions expressed in these reports are stated in very general and relatively favorable terms, representing the supervisor's strong primary impression that G's aptitude and potential for learning outweigh the indications of character problems seen later in the transcripts. Retrospectively, this supervisor was concerned lest more specific statements about G's learning difficulties would prejudice the members of the Education Committee and prevent their objective evaluation of a good student who at this stage in his development showed serious problems which the supervisor felt he could overcome.

This interesting discrepancy between transcript and official report reflects the supervisor's doubts about the reliability of evaluative statements made about a student's performance, since they are frequently taken out of the context of the evolving learning experience. Moreover, opinons in administrative reports are necessarily short and represent a distillation of many factors before a supervisor comes to a conclusion. The supervisor in this instance also lacked confidence in the evaluative skill of the Education Committee, an opinion held by many supervisors. "How can a committee appreciate the whole story?" is a very legitimate question. It points up some of the difficulties inherent in group responsibility and highlights the necessity for more intensive study of the task of evaluating in relation to defining learning objectives in general before the learning needs in a given student can be adequately understood and his progress toward certification be assessed. Our study of the supervisory reports on the four cases of our two students clearly emphasize the difficulties. More will be said about this subject later in this chapter.

Report 3

Between the last report and this one a summer vacation intervened and G carried on the analysis without supervision for several weeks. S1 had the impression that he had advanced enough to begin a second case and made this recommendation in an interim statement without spelling out the evidence for progress in learning.

The third supervisory report followed the second by a half year: "The analysis is progressing satisfactorily. G is gaining more confidence in dealing with the transference material and separating himself from the idealized father image."

Comments: The Education Committee agreed to the recommendation without asking for more information. In this discussion, various members of the committee emphasized the talent observed in this student at selection and matriculation interviews. This action calls attention to the administrative body's reliance on the supervisor's evaluation without expecting documentation of the basis for her opinion. Although the confidence of the committee in the supervisor's judgment was substantiated later, their action logically raises questions as to the significant determinants of their decision. It suggests that it would be valuable for both supervisors and administrators to attempt to determine what kind of information is most useful in making promotional decisions.

Reports 4 and 5

Three months later *S1* reported: During this quarter the patient made analytic progress; she became aware of the meaning of her father's death as motivation for her illegitimate pregnancies. The patient went through a brief period of imaginary pregnancy with delay of menstruation. G handled the patient's impulse to become pregnant on the realistic level and on the analytic material of the fantasied pregnancy very well."

Next report: "This quarter was difficult. Patient's relationship to her sister and to her mother came into the transference. Such shifts are difficult for G to see and respond to immediately. He accepts the transference position of being the father and lover and can handle it with the necessary level of uninvolvement. This made it more difficult for him to empathize with the patient's struggle against her identification with her sister and her mother, or to conclude from this ambivalence in her feminine role the motivation for her depreciation of men."

Comments: In each of these reports, the information focuses on the patient's progress and the vicissitudes in the analysis. The student is referred to as handling the analytic material well or as finding it difficult "to see and respond" or to "empathize" and understand specific conflicts and transferences. This information describes the movement in the analysis and indicates areas where G met difficulties and also where he demonstrated competence. Such statements are helpful to an education committee since they specify problem areas which can be compared with statements by other supervisors for making an overall evaluation of progress or lack of it.

Reports 6-12

These reports covered the last two years of this supervised analysis. Their brevity is notable.

(6) "The analysis of this case is in a phase of working through the father transference. The negative aspects of her relationship to men does not come into the analysis since the positive transference seems to be gratifying to both analyst and patient."

(7) "During this quarter G handled the transference neurosis (of the patient) in a more detached manner and this brought about a change in the patient's genetic material. Patient became more aware of her narcissism and depreciation of men. G shows growing independence in dealing with psychoanalytic material; his presentation reveals more clearly his understanding of the dynamics of the patient's production."

(8) "Nothing new or special to report."

(9) "The analysis has progressed and during the fall quarter it seemed indicated that a termination date be set that would allow enough time for working-through of the termination phase (end of the academic year). The material indicates that a more basic working-through might occur during that period."

(10) "The analysis progresses toward termination."

(11) "The last quarter dealt with the separation that appears to be a significant experience, not only for the patient, but also for the analyst. This and the countertransference mobilized by the termination have been discussed. The regression and the increased dependency of the patient brought about a shift in the introjected mother image that became manifest in the patient's changing relationship with her mother. G was deeply impressed not only by the genetic material, but also by the dynamic movement of the separation process that brought it to the surface."

(12) In her terminal report S1 stated: "The patient seemed to terminate the analysis with a conviction of the necessity to control her impulsive behavior and with a sense of her integrated self, since she felt able to differentiate reality from fantasy and to take full responsibility for her actions. At the end she had the feeling that termination is final and that one has to learn to live without a fantasied father."

Comments: The emphasis in all of these reports is on progress by the patient. G's progress is correlated with P's therapeutic movement in terms of his ability to facilitate the analytic work. In the sixth report there is a hint of slowing down in working through the transference conflicts as a result of mutual gratification experienced by patient and analyst. In the next report, a statement is made about G's growing independence, but there is little information regarding development of analytic skills or the attainment of specific learning objectives. Only one reference is made to countertransference as such, explaining that it was mobilized by the events of termination.

This series of reports taken as a whole is representative of the majority of evaluative statements made to our Education Committee during the period when these reports were written (1957-1960). This was especially true when the student's work was considered satisfactory by the supervisor. Unfortunately, the reader of these reports must, for the most part, make a judgment of competence on the basis of the absence of information regarding serious blocks to learning. The positive achievements of G in development of himself as a sensitive analytic instrument are not made explicit.

Later in this chapter we intend to discuss what might be considered a good supervisory report and to give examples. Here, however, we will continue our study of the supervisory reports on G's subsequent cases.

Case II, GK, Male Patient, Male Supervisor

The second case was fortunate for the student's development since it differed in every respect from the first case. Although the patient was a chronic compulsive neurotic whom the student at first did not consider a promising risk for psychoanalytic treatment, the supervisor, S2, saw learning opportunities that the analysis of such a case would offer.

Report 1

In his first report S2 commented: "After initial hesitation, G has changed into a comparatively self-confident approach to his analysand. He seems to have convinced himself that it is worthwhile to analyze an over-conscientious, chronic compulsive neurotic. The patient is an excellent object for studying transitions from over-conscientiousness to self-consciousness with some ideas of reference." [We omit a description of the patient's pathology reported by S2.] "After his initial hesitation G has become able to endure the transferred ambivalence to both parents who indoctrinated P with massive goodness, faith and obedience. G became aware that his countertransference was influenced by a threatening identification with analysand and, to judge by the progress of his work, he has done some successful working through."

Comments: Reports on the first quarter of work with the student point up (1) his ambition to succeed and therefore hesitation about taking a case which was not promising, (2) his tendency to identify with the patient and his defense against it. This is a learning problem similar to the one diagnosed in the beginning of the first case. This time G became aware of his countertransferences. S2 made reference to the successful self-analysis (working-through) by G that indicated his growing ability to become the instrument of the analytic process. Possibly one can say that there is evidence of the student's learning from the experience with his first case.

Report 2

In the next quarter S2 reported: "G has made further progress in analyzing his patient; he learned to gain and to convey relevant insight into his patient's severe superego. So much of what seemed to be untouch-

able at the beginning has turned out to be touchable without bad consequences and accessible to understanding. G seems to be steadily moving
forward from the initial level of a good student to the level of a more independently thinking prospective psychoanalyst."

Comments: On the basis of such impressions S2 recommended that
the student be assigned a third case. However, he continued with weekly
supervision on the second case for two years. Whether this was because
of the difficulty of the case or because of the supervisor's special interest
in the case is not stated in the report. One can infer from the supervisor's
initial **report** that he found many interesting aspects to the patient's psychology, and that G was an eager learner.

Reports 3-6

(3). Six months later the supervisor, reporting about the summer and
fall quarter, stated: "G presents systematic reviews of data gathered while
working with his patient. However, his formerly rather dry presentation
is more and more animated by his own thoughts and observation of details
which have to be kept in mind for further interpretations. G is interested
in his work; his intuitive grasp of his analysand's unconscious is definitely improving. He is tactfully cautious in interpreting the strict superego
of his patient. . . ."

(4). "G is always ready to discuss practical and theoretical problems. His
careful approach to his patient's defenses is justified. If he errs by being
too cautious, he errs on the safe side. . . . His intuition for his patient's
unconscious is markedly improved."

(5). "G's slightly pedantic reports continued to prove his very good empathy for his patient's obsessive compulsive over-conscientiousness and
moral masochism. In dealing with repetitions and critical aggravations G
displayed patience, tact and intuition."

(6). And at the end of the second year: "G has the knowledge and
patience which are required for well-timed, careful and tactful interpretations of potentially explosive issues."

Comments: After two years of supervision, the supervisor explicitly
commented on what he had often indirectly suggested before: the well-
timed and tactful (well-dosed) interpretations of the student. The frequency of supervisory sessions was reduced to one every two weeks.

In this series of reports, the second supervisor makes specific reference
to G's presentation of the analytic material with the implied evaluation that
it is quite adequate to enable him to follow the analysis. Statements about
improvement in understanding, empathy, patience, tact, intuition, and
interpretive skill make the reader feel that G is making progress in learning. But more than that, they reveal to the administrator that S2 has paid
particular attention to these points as learning objectives—objectives he
considers important enough to comment on. Such comments indicate what

*S*2 expects G to learn and they are helpful in an education committee's overall evaluation. *S*2 has spelled out the areas in which he is assessing G's progress.

Reports 7-9

(7). The next supervisory report, three months later: "G's patience seems to be temporarily exhausted when the resistances of his chronic compulsive patient are recurring too frequently. The problem of 'flight into health' has shown up. In spite of all difficulties, some loosening up has taken place. G regains time and time again his patience in slowly guiding a fundamentally intelligent patient out of the blind alley of compulsive goodness."

(8). This entry covers the summer and fall quarters: "G's presentations continue to prove that he understands the unconscious dynamics of his patient's compulsive personality, i.e., not only the 'logical sequence' of manifestations but also their latent depth. G is well aware of the necessity of carefully working through every apparent therapeutic success which occurs in the magic of 'positive transference.' He understands even short hints which redirects his attention to condensations and multiple representations in dreams and in analogous creations in mythology. G's presentation reveals that he is in touch with the unconscious."

(9). The next entry is the final report. "The analysis conducted by G has been terminated according to plan. As described in previous reports, G was able to deal successfully with this patient's complicated, predominantly compulsive ego defenses. During the last months his patient was increasingly able to use his analytically acquired knowledge of himself to know how to get himself out of social and sexual isolation. My final impression of this supervision is that this student is a well-trained, conscientious and intuitive young analyst."

Comments: In these reports *S*2 described in various ways the student's progress. He seemed to grasp multiple unconscious meanings with increasing facility after having learned to deal with and to take apart cautiously and gradually the ego defenses of his patient without taking apart the total personality structure. *S*2 indicated the good communication in the $S \leftrightarrows A$ system as well as $A \leftrightarrows P$ system, and pointed out what he considered significant for learning. He described G's lapses as temporary and made a final evaluation of excellent progress.

Case III, GL, Female Patient, Male Supervisor

The third case began with weekly supervision after the second case had been in analysis seven to eight months. It became necessary to change supervisors after about nine months because of problems in the learning alliance.

Comments: Unfortunately, for discretionary reasons, the signs of learning difficulties on G's Case III cannot be reviewed in detail. The initial vulnerability to criticism, observed by *S*1 in the beginning of G's analytic work, seems to have been stirred up again and to have produced defensive reactions which neither G nor *S*3a could overcome.

*S*3a noted in his final report: "The evaluation of his work with me is not reliable as a criterion because of the domination of displaced transference which has colored his relationship both with the patient and with me."

Such situations develop and are always difficult to explain and to know what to do about them. In this instance a new supervisor, *S*3b, was assigned. His first report was made after six months, during which time the frequency of supervision was made biweekly.

Report 1 by S3b

(1). "The student does an excellent job in presenting the material. He is intelligent, intuitive and talented. He accepted correction and supervision with appreciation and there has never been any serious controversy over the technical or clinical aspects of the case. During the past six months the analyst was able to help the patient see the important aspects of her basic conflicts.

"This patient has been pregnant during this six months and the conflicts surrounding her feminine identification became focal. At first G entered into the masculine protest defense of the patient in the form of competition and in this way gave it credence not as a defense but as reality. When this was pointed out to him, he was able to handle it quite well. From this point on he concentrated on her difficulty in her feminine identification. The patient seemed to make excellent progress. The analysis will be interrupted with plans for resuming after delivery. I recommend G be given a fourth case."

Case IV, GF, Male Patient, Female Supervisor

The begininng of G's fourth case coincided with the last quarter of the analysis of his third case. The first and second cases were still in psychoanalysis, the first approaching the termination phase. Supervision of Case IV was conducted on the basis of biweekly supervisory sessions until graduation and monthly after that until termination.

Reports 1 and 2

(1). "This patient presents many interesting and difficult problems. He had resistance against committing himself to the analysis expressed in his wish to accept an opportunity for changing his job that required leaving the city. Analyst handled this problem gently and firmly, refusing to become involved in the decision about the job.

"There are signs of countertransference in that G tends to compete with the patient in making clever literary allusion and prematurely deep interpretations of resistance against homosexual conflict which the patient responds to by feeling dominated. This technical mistake has been pointed out. We shall see what happens."

(2). "The patient is definitely involved and is clearly repeating with G the ambivalent homosexual conflict with his father. It takes the form of subtle provocative competition with guilt about success, followed by swings to mother transference with projection of responsibility for his sense of frustration to the analyst as the mother figure. G still enters into the transference too much. It is difficult to stay out because the patient uses any intervention to fit his own defensive need. But the countertransference remains and G's need for his own dominance makes it difficult for him to perceive how the patient is responding by using G for his own defensive goals. G is somewhat more relaxed with me, less in need to prove his adequacy. Therefore, he can accept better my differences of interpretation and observe the analysis with more objectivity. Working through the supervisory transference should help him work through the same problem with his patient."

Comments: These two reports imply, but do not explicitly state, that G's presentation of material is good and that he has learned how to maintain the uninvolved stance of an analyst when confronted by a patient's anxiety about committing himself to analysis. The same character problem seen in Case I seems to be in evidence, although not as intense. In these reports, written prior to studying the transcripts, S4 like S1 was aware of tensions in the learning alliance, but by this time they seem under better control.

Reports 3-5

(3). S4's next report covered the summer and fall quarters. "The patient is definitely committed to the analysis; he has more insight into his superego lacunae and how he uses it to provoke his analyst. During the last month, the patient is approaching a more intense mother transference and expresses openly a need for control and limitation from the analyst. The analyst focuses on minor points of patient's behavior rather than on interpretations of underlying conflict or the defensive purpose of behavior. This mistake reveals insensitivity to the material caused by blind spots. In supervisory sessions I handled the student's resistances against the patient's material and against my interpretations. Occasionally he makes a good intuitive interpretation which comes close to the target, but he does not follow through either with his understanding or with further interpretation of the patient's responses."

(4). The fourth report stated: "In the last three months G achieved insight into the workings of the patient's defenses and he is working more as an analyst with the patient. With this greater detachment and better technique, the movement in the analysis is obvious. With his countertransference at least partially worked through, G's potential for intuitive and skillful analysis comes through also."

(5). Three months later: "Much improved; the patient is working within a transference neurosis that is interpretable. G is doing well. He was graduated, but since this is a research case, the supervision will continue once a month."

Comments: The third report shows retrogression from the positive, optimistic tone of the second. It indicates that this patient's personality and problems caused G to inhibit his ability to use his empathic understanding. $S4$ mentions blind spots without any specific definition of them. She vaguely refers to "handling" the student's resistances against learning. Such information is too meager to be of much value to an administrative reader of these reports. The statement would be more helpful if it indicated what the supervisor did and whether G was aware of his resistances as a learning problem. Supervisors so often report on errors and problems but do not say anything to the student, so that he remains in ignorance of his mistakes. The report would also have been more helpful if it had stated that the student had been confronted with the criticism and what his response was. Otherwise, the administrator is in doubt about how much to expect the student to be aware of the problem.

The last reports contain a positive evaluation, but expressed as a rough overall impression rather than in terms of objectives achieved.

After reviewing the reports from G's four cases, it must be concluded that in general the supervisors found it easier to describe in a meaningful way the therapeutic progress by the patient than learning by the student. From a scrutiny of these data, there seems to be wide latitude for improvement in a supervisor's learning how to evaluate progress and even more room for cultivating the habit of making clear-cut statements of what a student has learned and what is left for him to learn. This is not easily accomplished, as we discovered repeatedly in examining our transcript data. We recognized again and again that following the evaluation of the analytic events was an ingrained, automatized activity compared to following the learning process. It also occupied a larger share of the $S \leftrightarrows A$ interaction. Occasionally, when all seemed to be going well, the supervisor might say very little to a student during a supervisory session. Yet, in order to know that all was well he has to listen intently to the $A \leftrightarrows P$ interactions. We observed that tuning in to errors and technical difficulties was clearly more compatible with the mainstream of our supervisory experience than was estimating the seriousness of those errors and assessing the level of competence in a form which could be used to promote learning.

At this point we will leave the data on the evaluation of G as seen in the periodic statements made for administrative purposes, and return to our transcript data on patient GF, his fourth case. To give explicit and full evidence for his development would necessitate presenting several additional examples drawn from the transcripts at the beginning and at various stages throughout the supervision. This would place an unwarranted burden on the reader who has already been expected to assimilate a large mass of primary data. We have chosen to depend on a summary of notes from the study of the first five transcripts of GF and to refer to Example 15 which covers three supervisory sessions over a period of eight months and 100 analytic hours. We will attempt to correlate this material with the description of G's level of learning and initial learning problems given earlier in this chapter as they were observed in the material of GB, his first case.

EXAMPLE 27

GF (Case IV), Summary of Progress in Learning

When G began the analysis of his fourth supervised case, he was assigned to a supervisor who had had supervisory contact with him during his residency. The beginning of that contact was burdened by G's intense resistance to being supervised. He was reluctant to admit he needed help in treating his patients or that he might learn something by discussing them even if he needed no assistance. S recognized his defensiveness, felt he was protecting his self-esteem, and did not force the issue, leaving the responsibility for continuing the contact entirely up to him. G relaxed, brought interesting case material, and found he could learn without feeling threatened. This preamble is important because it colored the attitudes of both G and the supervisor as they found themselves in another supervisory relationship. Both of them appeared overly cautious in the early sessions and there was evidence that the old problem persisted although it had been substantially modified. Gradually a good learning alliance was established. Interference from his character difficulty was remarkably diminished for the analyst and thus for the supervisor, compared to the problem it presented on his first case (Examples 2 and 5).

It is interesting to note that the patient in Case IV manifested reluctance to commit himself to the "threatening" analytic situation in much the same way as G had resisted supervision in his residency. With his patient, however, G held a steady analytic position, remained uninvolved, and interpreted the anxiety in its defensive context. He had learned to put this fundamental attitude into practice since starting his first case.

G was also perceptive of transference reactions and understood how P's provocative competition was a repetition of the past when both his father and mother had expected great things of him long before he could realistically accomplish them. At the onset of his fourth case, G was able to recognize his mistakes, thus giving evidence of development of his self-observing function.

There were two areas, however, where S4 felt that G should have progressed further by the time he was considered ready to begin the last case required before certification. The first had to do with his lack of awareness of the analytic process (Chart II, 6). This learning defect was evidenced by his pattern of reporting. At first, G tended to present material without including his own thinking and seemed to wait for the supervisor to respond with her own diagnostic associations. However, with a few suggestions and explanations, his presentations improved. Perhaps what appeared to be a problem was due more to the tension in the learning alliance since he had been able in the later phases of his first case to present a clear picture of the analysis as a process (Examples 20 and 21). In other words, he had acquired the ability but it could be shaken by anxiety.

The second area that was repeatedly diagnosed as a learning problem was G's technique of interpretation. His interventions were often made in more descriptive than dynamic terms. They simply restated what the patient had said without opening up a new way of looking at the patient's struggles. In the beginning of the analysis, G's interpretations tended to be premature and too much for the patient to assimilate. If the dose was smaller, there was a lack of follow-through in response to the patient's response. The step-by-step process of interpreting back and forth from one level of meaning to another was not carried on assiduously.

These learning difficulties have been documented in Example 15, which also gives evidence of G's progress with this skill. The development of interpretive technique itself has its phases that can be well demonstrated in this intuitive student. What at first is rooted in the basic processes of intuition and empathic understanding is then subjected to cognitive scrutiny in order that the synthesizing step in diagnostic interpretation could be more clearly understood before becoming again more preconscious and useful as the "trained intuition" of the experienced psychoanalyst. One significant sign of G's development is found in Example 15. He learned to "accept" the projected feminine role of P's transference without the defensiveness observed in many students. He interpreted that P seemed sexually interested in the analyst as if A were a woman. This matter-of-fact statement stimulated sexual excitement in P to which G did not have any obvious counterreactions. The analysis of this fourth case developed a good analyzable transference neurosis and proceeded to a good termination with insight and maturation for P. G's development is also observable.

Since we have offered a number of examples from the elementary case analyzed by student H and two from his fourth case, we will not add to the amount of his transcript data in this chapter. Instead we will present a chart of his case assignments and their course through his five academic years before graduation and a brief summary of progress.

The time schedule of promotions for student H can be readily observed in Chart V. He matriculated for theoretical courses in the fall of 1954, began his first case in April of 1955, and was approved for his second case six months later. Case I continued to a good termination in January 1959. Case II (HB) began in November 1955 and was interrupted by the patient's being transferred to another city in June 1959. Case III, which

Chart V.—Student H's Progression in Supervision

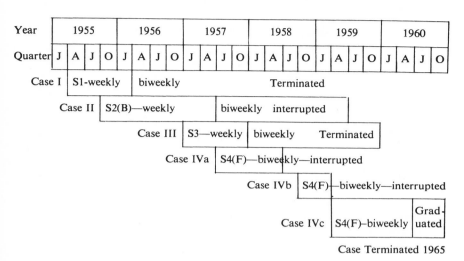

Year	1955	1956	1957	1958	1959	1960

Quarter | J | A | J | O | J | A | J | O | J | A | J | O | J | A | J | O | J | A | J | O | J | A | J | O

Case I S1-weekly   biweekly   Terminated

Case II S2(B)—weekly   biweekly   interrupted

Case III S3—weekly biweekly   Terminated

Case IVa S4(F)—biweekly—interrupted

Case IVb S4(F)—biweekly—interrupted

Case IVc S4(F)–biweekly Grad-uated

Case Terminated 1965

was not approved by the second supervisor for about twelve months, began in March 1957 and continued to a good termination in January 1960. Case IV was approved by the third supervisor in the fall of 1957. Two fourth cases were started but were interrupted after less than a year of analysis. Case IVa moved out of town with her husband's change of job; Case IVb took flight in a state of resistance; but Case IVc (HF) remained for a long and successful analysis, terminating after six and one-half years. H was graduated in June 1960 but continued supervision biweekly for five more years.

EXAMPLE 28

Summary of Progress by Student H

Study of the supervisors' reports to the Education Committee on Student H does not add to our understanding of the evaluative function of a supervisor. Consequently, we will not present them in detail. The reports on H follow the pattern already exemplified for Student G in Example 26. They focus largely on the patient's progress, adding rather general approval of H. Statements about learning problems are few and recommendations for promotion are phrased as an impression that he is doing well and should have another case. Frequent comments were on his excellent presentations of analytic material, his sensitive perceptiveness of unconscious meanings, his good understanding of the psychoanalytic process. These comments appear in evaluations on each of the cases H analyzed, so that we must assume that he demonstrated not only talent but also a high level of learning even on his first case.

It was from the intensive study of the transcripts of HB and HF, however, that his talents and his problems could be documented more significantly for understanding the learning process and evaluating what H learned. His quick grasp of psychodynamic constellations and his sensitive, all too quick response to them expressed not only his talent but also his tenacious learning problem. This could be diagnosed as a problem in controlling his empathy. His "need to be needed," his wish to be recognized as the ever-understanding human being as well as the helpful doctor was a disturbing influence. Keen as his system-sensitivity was, he responded too quickly on the level of accepted standards of social relations, thus impeding the analytic process. Related to his undisciplined empathy was his tendency to identify with his patient, revealed conspicuously in Example 9 taken from Session 23. There it was spontaneously recognized as a countertransference by H, who then reported on his attempt at self-analysis.

Another manifestation of the same problem can be seen in Examples 4, 10, and 14, which show his impulsive responsiveness, clearly not caused primarily by inexperience but by some persisting intrapsychic conflict for which more personal analysis seemed indicated. H struggled with the problem by himself, then sought more analysis and made progress. The same difficulty showed itself again in HF, as illustrated in Examples 17 and 18.

This problem was interesting from a diagnostic point of view, since the behavior which interfered with good analysis was undoubtedly an ego-syntonic solution to an earlier conflict. It had become a gratifying part of a socially well-adapted character structure and it reinforced his excellent perceptiveness and empathy. The pedagogic dilemma was how to preserve this valuable character trait and at the same time change it from a professional handicap to a useful part of his analytic equipment. His earnest self-scrutiny and increasingly skillful self-analysis came to his aid so that H's development as an analyst proceeded to a high level of professional effectiveness.

Throughout this book, we have emphasized the constantly operating evaluative function of a supervisor. In Chapter IV we attempted to describe it in detail as it was focused on making an educational diagnosis of learning difficulties—a diagnosis which would give the supervisor a reference frame for deciding on his teaching tactics. In this chapter, we have been concerned with the long-range assessment of what was learned. Now we turn to the question of making a prognosis for professional development.

An educational prognosis involves two kinds of evaluations: (1) the severity of the learning difficulties observed, and (2) an estimation of the student's basic aptitudes. Both evaluative tasks require the supervisor to weigh and balance the factors which contribute to a talent for analyzing and which are responsible for various learning difficulties. The first seems to be easier to do, since mistakes are more conspicuous and since a supervisor's training has taught him to focus more sharply on pathology than on assessing resources for healthy adaptations. The second kind of evaluation approaches teaching from the more positive view of the student's potential for development. It looks on education itself as a developmental process moving toward mature professional competence.

In evaluating the severity of a learning difficulty, the four broad categories of causal factors are employed which have been mentioned in Chapter IV concerning an educational diagnosis (lack of aptitude, lack of knowledge, inexperience, and interfering character problems). However, since a learning difficulty is rarely due to one cause alone, a supervisor needs to determine the proportionate combination of causes and the degree of handicap for future progress before he can estimate how a student will respond to teaching efforts. For instance, inexperience (e.g., a first case) plus lack of aptitude obviously has a poorer prognosis than inexperience combined with good aptitude, or than inexperience plus lack of knowledge. In the latter instance, one would expect instructional methods to suffice. But even a character difficulty, when coupled with a capacity for self-analysis, will respond to good supervisory teaching, as we have seen in student H (Example 28).

The formulation of this balance of factors usually takes shape early in an analysis but is held in suspended judgment pending the results of time and teaching effects (see GB, Example 2, and MF, Example 6). In other words, a supervisor observes a learning difficulty over a number of supervisory sessions, and before he arrives at a seriously negative conclusion, he decides how well it responds to his attempts to assist the student to overcome it (see DF, Example 8).

For the second, more positive type of prognosis, we find the same diagnostic categories useful, but the evaluation begins with an assessment of basic aptitude for analyzing. Here the focus on how much talent the student possesses, where his strengths and weaknesses lie, are questions whose answers give a more creative direction to a supervisor's educative work. The correctional emphasis of the first evaluative approach is essential, but there is more to supervision than correction of mistakes. Attention must also be given to assessing the student's capacities for professional growth, his system sensitivity, system responsiveness, and self-analysis. How to detect their presence and to determine whether or not there is adequate talent for undertaking psychoanalytic training is a matter for decisions at the time of admission to training. But it also becomes the responsibility of the first case supervisor to evaluate the level of their potential and to make a prognosis for their development. In addition, it is the responsibility of subsequent supervisors to make similar assessments based on higher expectations of performance for advanced cases.

This positive approach to the task of evaluation is intimately correlated with a clear understanding of learning objectives. Once a supervisor knows what he expects a student to learn from the supervisory experience, he can provide better goal-directed teaching and can help a student become aware of his learning needs. With this evaluative work accomplished, a supervisor can make reports to the administrative body which are more useful for its own evaluative task. In this way he cooperates with the principle of group responsibility for the professional education of psychoanalysts.

The administrative function of a supervisor becomes increasingly important as the psychoanalytic student body enlarges and the need for faculty members expands accordingly. Ekstein and Wallerstein[29, p. 11] very pertinently added an administrative angle to the clinical teaching-learning situation, more commonly seen as a triangular structure composed of analyst, patient, and supervisor. With their four-sided "clinical rhombus" they represented the complicated relationships between the differently functioning members of a clinical teaching-learning team. We agree with them wholeheartedly, although our study has concentrated on the analytic supervisory process and we have placed more emphasis on conceptualizing the events in this process and the objectives toward which supervision aims. Nevertheless, comparison of transcript data with the administrative reports on our two students and our experience in making administrative decisions highlighted the importance of adequate information on which the administrator can base promotional decisions—decisions of great significance for a student's professional career.

A study of administrative supervisory reports was not part of our investigation until the last phase of working on the material. At that time our impression of the importance of evaluation in the day-to-day supervisory work was renewed, and in trying to formulate overall summaries of progress we decided to look at the evaluative reports of other supervisors on the same students. The reports made by us, as given in Example 26 on student G, were independent of our investigation since they were not yet influenced by our study of the transcript data. The other supervisors were not involved in the research at all and were informed about some of our findings only after their supervisory work with these students had terminated.

We found that reports to an Education Committee (the pertinent administrative body in most instances) were in general impressionistic summaries of segments of the analysis. The primary orientation seemed to be toward the therapeutic process, and the learning of the student appeared to be secondary, except if the "learning problem" were a countertransference which interfered with the analysis of the patient. The evidence for either therapeutic progress or countertransference was usually not given in any detail. If a learning problem was indicated, there were few attempts to explain its cause, to describe what had been done to correct it, or to prognosticate its outcome. There seemed to be a common assumption that if the patient improves, the student is learning. In many instances, the opposite is true: the patient improves but the student does not learn.

We asked ourselves what information an Education Committee would find most useful and we offer the following suggestions. In its broadest definition a supervisory report is one which reflects the student-analyst's functioning with his patient and with the supervisor in such a way that it makes the student's progress or lack of it (his assets and his liabilities) understandable to the members of the Education Committee. (1) A good report gives more than the dynamics of the patient and the state of the transference or the presence of countertransference. (2) It should evaluate the therapeutic alliance and the learning alliance by describing the skill of the student in communicating with the patient and with the supervisor. The student's capacity for communication is revealed in his pattern of reporting, as discussed in Chapter V. (3) The supervisor's report should also include the persisting areas of learning needs with a diagnosis of probable causes, an estimation of the student's awareness of these needs, and what the supervisor has tried to do about them. (4) In subsequent reports, there should be a follow-up statement of outcome. (5) The *most valuable* supervisory report will include evidence of critical incidents that correlate learning difficulties with learning objectives. Description of a single episode may be very meaningful in identifying a particular problem but a series of such anecdotal statements is even more helpful, especially if they include appraisals of the degree of success or failure in overcoming difficulties and in developing specific therapeutic skills. (6) An evaluation of a student's self-analytic functioning is a most important point, especially when accompanied by a comment about indications for more personal analysis. (7) Any information concerning a student's ability to apply theoretical concepts is very useful for certification decisions. Such ability represents a measure of the student as a psychoanalytic clinician who aims to be a scholar and a scientist also.

Much more could be said on the subject of what constitutes a valuable supervisory report. Our primary interest, however, is in the study of the supervisory process. Consequently, without going further into the content of administrative evaluations, we wish to point out two ways in which periodic evaluations can be used to promote learning: first, the learning of the student; and second, the learning of the teacher. We think that the advantages of employing evaluations for both of these purposes have been for the most part overlooked by psychoanalytic educators.

This importance of making the student aware of his errors and deficiencies has already been mentioned, but he should also be informed of his strong points and his progress should be recognized. Students often feel that only mistakes are noted by the supervisor. The problem to a large extent is due to a shortage of time for this kind of exchange, but we feel that the recommendation of Ekstein and Wallerstein deserves serious consideration. They advocate that a supervisor's evaluation be shared with the student in a conference set aside for that special purpose.[29, p. 282] Such a conference provides the setting for an essential phase of a two-way feedback on the accomplishments of each of the parties involved. In such a setting the teacher's learning can be promoted as well as the student's. In this kind of evaluation conference, Ekstein and Wallerstein recommend that the student be expected to evaluate himself and to tell his supervisor what he thinks he has learned during a period of supervision. The supervisor discusses this, adding his own comments on advances and remaining shortcomings, thus drawing the student into the process of evaluation and making a learning experience out of it. From such a discussion, moreover, the supervisor can hear an evaluation of himself, even if it is only implicit or inferential (see Example 3). If he listens from this point of view, he can assess his own achievements as a teacher, can learn about how to use evaluation as an educational tool, and where to sharpen his own teaching skills.

We realize the many objections to instituting such procedures, yet we offer the idea as a pertinent suggestion to be considered. It has an increasingly prominent place in today's theory of teaching. We feel the chief reservations concerning evaluation conferences for analytic supervision seem to lie more in the reactions of supervisors than in the reactions of students. Supervisors often take the attitude that evaluation means "grading," a term which is burdened with traditional prejudice against "judging" and "being judged." Especially is this true for analysts and other clinicians whose professional work demands freedom from making "value judgments" of their patients. Here again we meet the conflict between the supervisor's identity as a therapist and as a teacher. In the latter role, evaluation as we have described it is an essential part of the teaching-learning process. A solution to the problem might be found in a more systematic attempt to understand the function of evaluation in education in order to differentiate its constructive use for promoting learning from its destructive use so often unconsciously motivated. Procedures, such as faculty conferences, need to be developed that will provide for frank discussion of supervisory learning objectives and the goals and methods of evaluation. A quotation from Robert Oppenheimer seems relevant to the concluding thought of this chapter. "We told each other what we did not know and learned much in the telling."

– IX –

Conclusion

As we come to the final chapter in this report of our investigation, we will briefly recapitulate our general findings and then present a point of view regarding an educational philosophy for psychoanalysis.

Our study has examined the phenomena of psychoanalytic supervision as they illustrate the problems of clinical learning and teaching. We feel that pedagogic events in the psychoanalytic supervisory process have general application to all clinical fields in that learning from experience as well as by experience becomes the principal objective. How one learns from experience is a most intriguing question and one we can only partially answer. What one learns from experience, however, has to do with the difference between experiencing and integrating an experience, between doing and knowing the what, the how, and the why of the doing, between art and science. So much of what is experienced in psychoanalysis, whether by patient or analyst or supervisor, remains on an intuitive, implicit level of awareness; the art or the craft of doing predominates over observing the doing; it supercedes discovering and learning or teaching the science—the how and the why.

Nevertheless, we have attempted to tease out events in supervision so that they could be observed in isolation and thus help us to identify components of the total experience that facilitate the process of learning. This resulted in our being able to construct a sequence of learning objectives (Chart II) that could be correlated with the content of theory and technique which a student of analysis needs to know. This formulation of objectives can aid the student in his understanding of the process of psychoanalytic treatment and the teacher in orienting himself to what has been learned and what needs to be learned.

Learning objectives viewed in this way lead to a reinforcement of the concept of the analyst as an instrument in the evolving analytic process, a concept implicitly accepted by psychoanalysts for many years but not explicitly examined. The term "instrument" was used by Freud in his 1912 paper on recommendations on treatment. In this paper, he compares the analyst's unconscious to the receiver of a telephone.[41, p. 115] Freud goes on to talk about the necessity for the analyst to free himself

233

from resistances which would select and distort what his unconscious perceives and "to submit to a psycho-analytic purification," a personal analysis, to avoid "blind spots in his capacity for analytic perception." This concept of the analyst's unconscious as instrumental in the conduct of his professional work has become more meaningful as the study of ego functions has progressed. A correlation has been established between the therapeutic process and the operation of ego functions associated with introspection, empathy, and the perception of reality. An impetus has been added to this concept from sociological studies on the dynamics of interpersonal interactions in small groups and from child development research where the responsiveness of the object has assumed increasing significance.

Our investigation of the supervisory process documents the importance of this instrumental activity of the analyst, and our observations in this area stress the significance of self-knowledge and capacity for self-analysis as parts of the instrument to be developed further in supervision. The intimate correlation between freedom in self-communication and effective communication with the patient which was revealed in such clear-cut ways in the transcript data provides confirmation for Isakower's thesis that "clarification of the instrument" is an essential task of supervisory teaching.[56] It is this goal that makes supervision different from more familiar teaching methods.

We have attempted to separate these aims from traditional instruction and have tried to represent these relationships in a diagram of supervisory activity (Chart I). The diagram emphasizes the supervisor's pedagogic approach to his task. As he enters the supervisory situation with all the tools with which his own analytic training has equipped him, he is sensitively attuned to both the therapeutic and the teaching-learning relationships, assesses the state of rapport in each, evaluates the student's understanding and technique, and diagnoses the blocks to therapy and learning. His teaching tactics are guided by these pedagogical diagnoses and are aimed at supplying more than information and more than a model for imitation. A supervisor's teaching exercises the student's self-observing and integrative functions and so develops those aspects of himself which will serve as a creatively effective analytic instrument.

At this point we wish to discuss a point of view about theories of supervision. To make such formulations is a complicated task because it involves the mutually dependent processes of learning and teaching. This mutuality influences statements about supervision which frequently do not distinguish between supervision from the position of the student and supervision from the position of the teacher. Granted, the two are intimately connected and what one teaches is supposed to be learned, yet the fact something is "taught" does not guarantee it will be learned. Only the learner can accomplish that. Ekstein[26, p. 260] refers to this confusion when he quotes Bernfield concerning the analytic teacher who, like some gardeners, thinks he makes the flowers grow. Instead, he only cultivates, fertilizes, and waters the soil. In other words, his activity creates only the conditions which facilitate growth, not growth itself.

Applying this concept of teaching to the study of supervision, we can appreciate better the necessity to separate the supervisory situation from the supervisory process. The teaching situation provides the setting in which learning can occur. The teaching activity provides the conditions which facilitate it. The supervisory process can be looked upon as the reciprocating interaction of the nurturing, catalyzing gardener-supervisor with the growing student-analyst through the early stages of his development.

We have tried to examine supervisory data from this point of view. We have attempted to focus on the phenomena of supervision from the position of the teacher in interaction with his student, emphasizing the importance of the teacher's awareness of what he wants the student to become, as well as the various vicissitudes of that development. To carry the gardener analogy further: the gardener (analytic educator) should be aware of what kind of plant he is cultivating (an analyst, not a surgeon) and should know what difficulties may appear in the course of development (resistances and regressions). From our point of view, a theory of supervision should be primarily a theory of teaching rather than a theory of learning.

Traditional theories of learning which emphasize the factors of motivation, readiness, and reinforcement and the processes of conditioning, identification, and cognition are fundamental and contributory to any theory of teaching, but knowing the psychology of learning does not ensure good teaching any more than knowing the theory of psychoanalysis makes a good analyst. It can also be said that an analyst who knows the theory of unconscious motivation does not on that account make a good teacher of analysis. At this stage in the development of our knowledge of both learning and teaching, we believe that further study of the teaching process will provide fruitful leads to concepts contributing to a theory of learning based on psychoanalytic premises. Beginnings have been made in this direction,[55, 73, 80] but more investigation needs to be done.

Several authors have recently made formulations of a theory of supervision which we would like to examine and compare with our own. The first assumes that the clinical teaching of psychoanalysis is largely a matter of demonstrating techniques.[27] According to such a theory of teaching, the supervisor would show the student-analyst how he (the supervisor) would have conducted the analysis, what interpretations he would have made, how he would have behaved. Such a theory would assume that if the supervisor were a good analyst, he would be a good teacher. We would call this formulation primarily a patient-centered rather than a student-centered pedagogic approach, demonstrational in its teaching tactics and based on a theory that learning occurs primarily by imitation. E. R. Collins[18] illustrates this kind of teaching with a story about a man who was looking at a skittish, seemingly undisciplined harness horse. The man asked the owner if the horse had been broken to harness. The owner replied, "Oh, sure, he's been broke all right, he's watched the old horses work."

Learning does result from imitation but it does not make the student independently creative. As can be seen from many of our illustrations, this kind of teaching behavior did occur in our supervision; but it was not and should not be the main activity of a supervisor. If it does happen, it should be used because of a specific learning need and should be only a step in the total learning process. It should be preceded by an exploration not only of what the student did with his patient, but also of what he understands about why he did it; and if a demonstration is given by the supervisor, it should be followed by an explanation of why he would have done it that way.

A second theory of supervision is largely based upon the instructional and demonstrational tactics of the first, making the supervisor responsible for formulating the dynamics of the patient and prescribing what should be interpreted. This theory extends the first, however, by being more student-centered since the supervisor also points out the student's mistakes. Occasionally, he explains why he considers the student's behavior wrong; more often, this explanation is omitted and, strangely enough, the student may not ask for it. We would call this pedagogic approach correctional, since it takes into account the student's learning difficulties and attempts to make him aware of them. With this approach the supervisor recognizes the "flaws" in the analytic instrument and the need to deal with them in some way, but he has not developed a teaching philosophy to handle the supervisor's dilemma over his double role as therapist and teacher.[91] After pointing out countertransferences, such a supervisor leaves the student to his own devices for handling his neurotic limitations; and if he is not in personal analysis, both teacher and student are thus forced to rely on what capacity for self-analysis has already been developed.[2] This approach may work very effectively or it may avoid giving important assistance to the student and alleviate a handicap of which he is not aware.

We feel that these two theories of supervision are incomplete and pay more attention to the content and directive aspects of the teacher's behavior than to the experiential and developmental nature of the supervisory process. Learning psychoanalysis requires involvement with unconscious-preconscious processes and experiences which permit integration into new structures as learning occurs. The teacher must not only be aware of these processes, but also must be able to enter into the experience of learning on an empathically communicating level himself, using himself as an instrument in the service not of "analyzing" his student but of the development of ego functions essential for analyzing.

Arlow,[2] in his important paper on the supervisory situation, refers to Freud's recommendations concerning the analyst's attitude of receptivity to observations from the patient and to his own inner mental processes. Arlow feels that other aspects of empathic functioning are to be encouraged in the learner and employed by the teacher in his supervisory work. He says, "The supervisory session is an experience of confrontation with reality; it serves to dispel certain unrealistic, neurotically distorted notions concerning the nature of analysis as well as the nature of the psychoanalytic situation. In this respect the supervisory situation may be compared to a kind of working-through experience in which neurotic reactions to the role of therapist and to the process of empathy may be observed and studied phenomenologically."[2, p. 590] With this statement we entirely agree and have given evidence to support it in the illustrations published here. Arlow differentiates the "true working-through of these conflicts" possible in the analytic situation from a lesser degree of working-through achievable in the supervisory situation. With this we also agree, but we place more emphasis on the activity of the supervisor in catalyzing the functions of self-analysis where this is indicated. On this point also, we have presented a number of examples which probed resistances to various depths always pertinent to the conduct of the analysis and compatible with the student's insight. We agree with Arlow that the supervisory situation should not be equated with the analytic situation and its methods of achieving self-knowledge. But, with Freud[47] and Kramer[61] we believe that "the processes of ego transformation" set in motion in the training analysis, which "go on of their own accord" and which qualify "the learner who has been analyzed to become an analyst," can be assisted by the confrontations and working-through experiences possible and often necessary in supervision.

Ekstein and Wallerstein[29, p. 262] specifically formulate the supervisory process as a "new experience of growth" which may be limited by irrational attitudes and resistances in either student or teacher, but which "is analogous to the psychotherapeutic process in which we hope to help our patients" to a point of independence and new insights. It is with their stress on the concept of supervision as an experience which involves the whole personality of both student and teacher that we would like to align ourselves—an experience where the teacher who is also an analyst can use his system-sensitivity and system-responsiveness, and his self-analytic functions as flexibly for teaching as for analyzing, recognizing the different goals in each experience.

We would base our theory of supervision and our philosophy of psychoanalytic education on three broad assumptions derived from the nature of the work an analyst is called upon to do and from our study of recorded supervision: (1) An analyst's education is necessarily more experiential than cognitive; (2) the basic objective of his educative experiences is the development of himself as an analytic instrument; (3) each phase of his training contributes in different ways to this basic objective. We feel that this statement of our philosophy takes into account the special structure of an analyst's "work-ego," described by Fleiss in 1942.[32] It brings learning and teaching into relation with the mutually creative experience which each should be. The educational process can be seen in its totality as an integrated experiential process of teaching and learning, where learning-by-experience in the training analysis is coupled with learning-about-experience in studying theory and becomes learning-from-experience in supervision.

Supervision is "post facto" teaching, a retrospective scrutiny of interactions and their reciprocal effects. What the student learns in one supervisory session about his patient and/or about himself, he can apply only in the future to situations which are similar but never identical with the one on which the supervisor's intervention was based. The "experience" itself cannot be repeated. Yet, it is this quality of freshness in each new encounter which arouses and sustains the emotional interest so important for learning. According to John Dewey,[22] it is under such conditions that the best learning can take place, since the freshness of emotional interplay encourages the activity of intuitive as well as cognitive processes and permits new perceptions to take shape. This kind of experience is generated by analytic material and sustains the empathic understanding of the analyst for the repetitious working through of the analytic process. It becomes an essential element in sustaining the emotional investment of the learner and the teacher in the supervisory process, and it supplies a most vital force for developing the equipment of both student-analyst and supervisor in their efforts to reach beyond the boundaries of the known to achieve new correlations, leading to the creation of new knowledge from experience.

So it was in our experience in studying the material. No matter how many times we read the transcripts and faced our teaching, we were intrigued by the freshness of our encounter with the material. Each rereading became *an* experience in Dewey's sense of the word. As we look back upon the six years of this investigation, we recognize that our research provided us with an opportunity for experiential learning as intensive and vital as the experiences we hoped to facilitate for our students. As we worked through again and again the transcripts of recorded supervisory sessions, not only the student's psychic processes, but also our own, became the subject of investigation. Preconscious intuitive responses to the student, to his patient, and to the interaction between them became the object of cognitive scrutiny free from the pressures of the immediacy of the supervisory situation. Repeated experiences of this sort permitted "working-through" to a level of conceptualization that was retrospectively examined, and it included the immediate impact of the investigative process as well. In other words, we created as we learned and learned as we created.

A third level of "working-through" involved the task of writing up our investigation for a report to others. This task confronted us with the challenge of translating our experiences of inquiry into describable terms that would permit a more widespread sharing of ideas on the supervisory process. We make no claim to completeness or to perfection of formulation. What is in a book cannot substitute for the experiences of inquiry. It can, however, serve as a stimulus for inquiry and a framework for conceptualizing the experiences of other teachers of psychoanalysis. We expect that the body of psychoanalytic theory itself will deepen and broaden with social-cultural changes, and in reciprocal exchange with other disciplines. As this happens, the teaching of psychoanalysis will also change. But it is our hope that the aim of each psychoanalytic teacher will be to make teaching and learning a creatively productive experience for his students and himself and to make inquiry a constant element of each experience.

Bibliography

1. Alexander, F.: Two forms of regression and their therapeutic implications. Psychoanal. Quart. 25:178-196, 1956.

2. Arlow, J. A.: The supervisory situation. J. Amer. Psychoanal. Ass. 11:576-594, 1963.

3. Bales, R. F.: Interaction Process Analysis. Cambridge, Mass., Addison-Wesley Press, Inc., 1951.

4. Balint, A.: The part played by the analyst's personality in the handling of the transference: Report of the first Four Countries Conference. Int. J. Psychoanal. 18:60-61, 1937.

5. Balint, M.: On the psychoanalytic training system. Int. J. Psychoanal. 29:163-173, 1948.

6. —: New beginning and the paranoid and the depressive syndromes. Int. J. Psychoanal. 33:214-224, 1952.

7. Bateson, G.: Social planning and the concept of "deutero learning." Conference on Science, Philosophy, and Religion. Second Symposium, 1942.

8. Beiser, Helen R.: Self-listening during supervision of psychotherapy. (To be published.)

9. Benedek, T.: Countertransference in the training analyst. Bull. Menninger Clin. 18:12-16, 1954.

10. Beres, D.: Communication in psychoanalysis and in the creative process. J. Amer. Psychoanal. Ass. 5:408-423, 1957.

11. —: Structure and function in psychoanalysis. Int. J. Psychoanal. 46:53-63, 1965.

12. Bibring, E.: Methods and techniques of control analysis: Report of second Four Countries Conference. Int. J. Psychoanal. 18:369-371, 1937.

13. —: Psychoanalysis and the dynamics of psychotherapy. J. Amer. Psychoanal. Ass. 2:745-770, 1954.

14. Blitzsten, N. L., and Fleming, Joan: What is a supervisory analysis? Bull. Menninger Clin. 17:117-129, 1953.

15. Breuer, J., and Freud, S. (1895): Studies in Hysteria. New York, Nervous and Mental Disease Pub. Co., 1936.

16. Bruner, J. S.: Going beyond the information given. In Contemporary Approaches to Cognition. Cambridge, Mass., Harvard University Press. 1957.

17. Buxbaum, E.: Freud's dream interpretation in the light of his letters to Fliess. Bull. Menninger Clin. 15:197-212, 1951.

18. Collins, E. R.: Teaching and learning in medical education. J. Med. Ed. 37:671-686, 1962.

19. DeBell, D.: A critical digest of the literature on psychoanalytic supervision. J. Amer. Psychoanal. Ass. 11:546-575, 1963.

20. Deutsch, Helene: On supervised analysis. (To be published.)

21. Devereaux, G.: Some criteria for the timing of confrontations and interpretations. Int. J. Psychoanal. 32:19-24, 1951.

22. Dewey, J.: Art as Experience. New York, Minton Balch & Co., 1934.

23. Eitingon, M.: An address to the International Training Commission. Int. J. Psychoanal. 7:130-134, 1926.

24. —: Report to the Int. Training Commission. Int. J. Psychoanal. 9:136-140, 1928.

25. —: Report of general meeting of the Int. Training Commission. Int. J. Psychoanal. 18:346-348, 1937.

26. Ekstein, R.: On current trends in psychoanalytic training. In Explorations in Psychoanalysis (R. Lindner, Ed.). New York, Julian Press, Inc. 1953, pp. 230-265.

27. —: Report of the panel on the teaching of psychoanalytic technique. J. Amer. Psychoanal. Ass. 8:167-174, 1960.

28. —: Working through and termination. J. Amer. Psychoanal. 13:57-78, 1965.

29. Ekstein, R., and Wallerstein, R.: The Teaching and Learning of Psychotherapy. New York, Basic Books, 1958.

30. Ferenczi, S., and Rank, O.: Die Entwicklunsziele Der Psychoanalyse. Vienna, Leipzig, Zurich, Int. P. V., 1924.

31. — and —: The Development of Psychoanalysis (NMD Mono. Series #40). New York, Nervous and Mental Disease Publishing Co., 1927.

32. Fleiss, R.: Metapsychology of an analyst. Psychoanal. Quart. 11:211-227, 1942.

33. Fleming, J.: What analytic work requires of an analyst; a job analysis. J. Amer. Psychoanal. Ass. 9:719-729, 1961.

34. —: Evolution of a research project in psychoanalysis. In Counterpoint (H. S. Gaskill, Ed.). New York, International Universities Press, 1963.

35. Four Countries Conference, 1st.: E. Glover, Ed. Bull. Int. Psychoanal. Ass. Int. J. Psychoanal. 16:505-509, 1935.

36. Freud, A.: The widening scope of indications for psychoanalysis: Discussion. J. Amer. Psychoanal. Ass. 2:607-620, 1954.

37. Freud, S. (1891): On Aphasia; a Critical Study. New York, International Universities Press, 1953.

38. —(1887-1902): The Origins of Psychoanalysis: Letters to W. Fliess, Drafts and Notes, 1887-1902 (Marie Bonaparte, Anna Freud, and Ernst Kris, Eds.). New York, Basic Books, 1954.

39. —(1895): Project for a scientific psychology. In Origins of Psychoanalysis (Marie Bonaparte, Anna Freud, and Ernst Kris, Eds.). New York, Basic Books, 1954, pp. 347-445.

40. —(1910): The future prospects of psychoanalytic therapy. S. E. 11:141-151. London, Hogarth, 1957.

41. —(1912): Recommendations to physicians practicing psychoanalysis. S. E. 12:111-120. London, Hogarth, 1958.

42. —(1913): Further recommendations in the technique of psychoanalysis: on beginning the treatment. S. E. 12:121-144. London, Hogarth, 1958.

42a. —(1914): Remembering, repeating, and working through. S. E. 12:145-156. London, Hogarth, 1958.

43. —(1914): On the history of the psychoanalytic movement. S. E. 14:7-66. London, Hogarth, 1957.

44. —(1916): Fixation to trauma—the unconscious. Lecture 18. *In* Introductory Lectures. S. E. 16:273-285, London, Hogarth, 1963.

45. —(1923): Two encyclopedia articles. S. E. 18:235-259. London, Hogarth, 1955.

46. —(1932): New Introductory Lectures. S. E. 22:5-182. London, Hogarth, 1964.

47. —(1937): Analysis terminable and interminable. S. E. 23:210-253. London, Hogarth, 1964.

48. Gitelson, M.: Problems of psychoanalytic training. Psychoanal. Quart. 17:198-211, 1948.

49. —: Concerning the problem of the countertransference. Discussion of papers by T. F. Benedek and E. Weiss at Chicago Psychoanalytic Society, March 22, 1949. (Unpublished.)

50. Glover, E.: Research methods in psychoanalysis. Int. J. Psychoanal. 33:403-409, 1952.

51. —: Counter-resistance and counter-transference. *In* The Technique of Psychoanalysis. New York, International Universities Press, 1955.

52. Greenson, R.: The working alliance and the transference neurosis. Psychoanal. Quart. 34:155-181, 1965.

53. —: Empathy and its vicissitudes. Int. J. Psychoanal. 41:418-424, 1960.

54. Grotjohn, M.: The role of identification in psychiatric and psychoanalytic training. Psychiatry 12:141-151, 1949.

55. Hilgard, E. R.: Theories of Learning. New York, Appleton-Century-Crofts, 1948.

56. Isakower, O.: Problems of supervision. Report to the Curriculum Committee of The New York Psychoanalytic Institute. November, 1957. (Unpublished.)

57. Jones, R. M.: The role of self-knowledge in the educative process. Harvard Ed. Rev. 32:200-209, 1962.

58. Keiser, Sylvan: Report of the panel on the technique of supervised analysis. J. Amer. Psychoanal. 4:539-549, 1956.

59. Kohut, H.: Introspection, empathy, and psychoanalysis; an examination of the relationship between mode of observation and theory. J. Amer. Psychoanal. Ass. 7:459-483, 1959.

60. Kovacs, Vilma: Training and control-analysis. Int. J. Psychoanal. 17:346-354, 1936.

61. Kramer, Maria: On the continuation of the analytic process after psychoanalysis (a self-observation). Int. J. Psychoanal. 40:17-25, 1959.

62. Kris, E.: Psychoanalytic Explorations in Art. New York, International Universities Press, 1952.

63. —: On the vicissitudes of insight. Int. J. Psychoanal. 37:445-455, 1956.

64. Kubie, L.: Neurotic Distortion of the Creative Process. Lawrence, Kansas, University of Kansas Press, 1958.

65. —: Research into the process of supervision in psychoanalysis. Psychoanal. Quart. 27:226-236, 1958.

66. Landauer, K.: Difficulties in controlling an analysis: Report of second Four Countries Conference. Int. J. Psychoanal. 18:371, 1937.

67. Langer, Marie, Puget, J., and Teper, E.: A methodological approach to the teaching of psychoanalysis. Int. J. Psychoanal. 45:567-574, 1964.

68. Lennard, H. L., and Bernstein, A.: The Anatomy of Psychotherapy. New York, Columbia University Press, 1960.

69. Lewin, B. D., and Ross, Helen: Psychoanalytic Education in the United States. New York, W. W. Norton, 1960.

70. Loewald, H. W.: On the therapeutic action of psychoanalysis. Int. J. Psychoanal. 41:16-33, 1960.

71. —: Internalization, separation, mourning, and the superego. Psychoanal. Quart. 31:483-504, 1962.

72. Mahler, M.: Certain aspects of the separation-individuation phase. Psychoanal. Quart. 32:1-14, 1963.

73. Marmor, J.: Psychoanalytic therapy as an education process: common denominators in the therapeutic approaches of different psychoanalytic "schools." *In* Science and Psychonanalysis, Vol. 5. New York, Grune & Stratton, 1962, pp. 286-299.

74. Miller, G. E.: Evaluation in medical education: a new look. J. Med. Ed. 39:289-297, 1964.

75. Minimal standards for the training of physicians in psychoanalysis. Bull Amer. Psychoanal. Ass. 6:2, 1-5, 1950.

76. Minimal standards for the training of physicians in psychoanalysis. J. Amer. Psychoanal. Ass. 4:714-721, 1956.

77. Pfeffer, A. Z.: A procedure for evaluating the results of psychoanalysis; a preliminary report. J. Amer. Psychoanal. Ass. 7:418-444, 1959.

78. —: Follow-up study of a satisfactory analysis. J. Amer. Psychoanal. Ass. 9:698-719, 1961.

79. —: The meaning of the analyst after analysis. J. Amer. Psychoanal. Ass. 11:229-244, 1963.

80. Piers, G., and Piers, M. W.: Modes of learning and the analytic process. *In* 6th Int. Congress of Psychotherapy, London, 1964; Selected Lectures. Basel, S. Karger, 1965, pp. 104-110.

81. Pollock, H.: Historical perspectives in the selection of candidates for psychoanalytic training. Psychoanal. Quart. 30:481-499, 1961.

82. Reik, T.: Surprise and the Psychoanalyst. New York, E. P. Dutton & Co., 1937.

83. Sachs, H.: The Creative Unconscious. Cambridge, Mass., Sci-Art Publishers, 1942.

84. Schlesinger, H. J.: Developmental and regressive aspects of the making of promises. (Unpublished.)

85. Sloane, P.: Report of the second panel on the technique of supervised analysis. J. Amer. Psychoanal. Ass. 5:539-545, 1957.

86. Spitz, R. A.: Minutes of Chicago Geographic Analyst Seminar—June, 1962. (Unpublished.)

87. Stekel, W.: Psychoanalysis and Suggestion Therapy (Trans. by James S. Van Teslaar). London, Kegan, Paul, Trench, Trubner & Co., Ltd., 1923.

88. Stewart, W.: An inquiry into the concept of working through. J. Amer. Psychoanal. Ass. 11:474-499, 1963.

89. Stone, L.: The Psychoanalytic Situation. New York, International Universities Press, 1962.

90. Szasz, T. S.: Psychoanalytic training: a socio-psychological analysis of its history and present status. Int. J. Psychoanal. 39:1-16, 1958.

91. Tarachow, S.: An Introduction to Psychotherapy. New York, International Universities Press, 1963.

92. Towle, Charlotte: The Learner in Education for the Professions. Chicago, University of Chicago Press, 1954.

93. Weigert, E.: Contribution to the problem of terminating psychoanalysis. Psychoanal. Quart. 21:465-480, 1952.

94. Whyte, L.: The Unconscious Before Freud. New York, Basic Books, 1960.

95. Zelditch, M. Jr.: A note on the analysis of equilibrium systems. Family: Socialization and Interaction Process (T. Parsons and R. F. Bales, Eds.). Glencoe, Ill., Free Press, 1955, pp. 401-408.

96. Zetzel, E.: The theory of therapy in relation to a developmental model of the psychic apparatus. Int. J. Psychoanal. 46:39-52, 1965.

Index